R-2883-CF

The Cleveland Metropolitan Economy

Aaron S. Gurwitz, G. Thomas Kingsley

March 1982

Prepared for The Cleveland Foundation

Rand

SANTA MONICA, CA. 90406

PREFACE AND ACKNOWLEDGMENTS

The Cleveland Foundation has embarked on a process aimed at improving the analysis of, and information about, the economy of metropolitan Cleveland. This report was prepared by The Rand Corporation, at the Foundation's request, as one of the first steps in that process. It offers an assessment of economic trends in the Cleveland area. The research sought a better understanding of how the metropolitan Cleveland economy works, what its special role has been in the U.S. economy, and how it has been responding to its environment.

Aaron S. Gurwitz and G. Thomas Kingsley planned and edited this report using contributions from a number of Rand staff members. Gurwitz was the principal author of Chapters III, IV, VII (with the assistance of Susan J. Bodilly), and X. Kingsley, assisted by Priscilla M. Schlegel, wrote Chapters I, II, V, and VI. Chapter VIII was written by Deborah R. Both and Ellen L. Marks, and Chapter IX, by Kathleen N. Lohr and M. Susan Marquis.

The authors are indebted to Stanley M. Besen and John Pincus, who reviewed earlier drafts of the report, and to David W. Lyon, Rand Vice President in charge of Rand's Domestic Research Division, who gave active support to the project throughout.

The authors are also indebted to the many persons in the Cleveland area who so willingly gave information, advice, and other assistance to support this research. Space prevents mentioning all of them here, but the authors must single out the guidance and support provided by Susan N. Lajoie, The Cleveland Foundation's project officer for the study, and the Foundation's Director, Homer C. Wadsworth. They also wish to give special thanks to Richard W. Pogue, who served as Chairman of the Advisory Committee established by The Cleveland Foundation for the project and to the members of that committee (listed in Appendix A).

SUMMARY

The past decade has indeed been troubling for many of America's large industrial centers. After a century of economic growth that seemed almost automatic, they experienced a slowing of growth in some sectors and absolute losses in others. As world markets for key industries—notably steel and automotive products—became more competitive, their absolute share of those markets decreased. Volatile changes in the national economy created an environment of increasing uncertainty.

In these circumstances, metropolitan areas have begun to compete with each other more aggressively to attract and retain investment. Cleveland's leaders in the public and private sectors are well aware of this new competitiveness. In the past few years, they have jointly launched several new initiatives to prepare for the economic battles ahead. The goal of one of these initiatives is to enhance the level of "economic intelligence" in the community; to build information and understanding that will help the community respond more rapidly and effectively to the new economic realities.

This report is the first step in a process aimed at achieving that goal. In late 1980, The Cleveland Foundation asked The Rand Corporation to (1) prepare this baseline study of the metropolitan economy; (2) prepare a detailed computer data base on local economic conditions that could be expanded and used by others in the future; and (3) design a plan by which Cleveland area leaders could most effectively obtain and use information on changing economic conditions to guide decisions over the years ahead.

The plan that has evolved envisions the development of a permanent economic monitoring capability in metropolitan Cleveland—a new staff unit probably affiliated with a university or other local institution. By systematically assembling economic data as soon as they become available, the unit would serve as an efficient information clearinghouse. In the future, other local agencies and firms would only have to go to one place to secure reliable and up-to-date information about the local economy. More important, the unit would apply the techniques of economic analysis to examine the implications of changing conditions. Regular dialogue about research findings between technical experts and community leaders would improve the reliability of the analysis and its usefulness in practical decisionmaking. Better economic intelligence will not enable Cleveland's leaders to overturn the local impacts of major forces operating in the world economy, but in a highly competitive environment it could prove to be an important edge.

While the objective of our work is a long-term process rather than a short-term product, that process could not be well-designed without a comprehensive baseline review of the available facts about metropolitan Cleveland's economy. The purpose of this study has been to understand how the Cleveland economy works, what its special role has been in the larger U.S. economy, and how it has been responding to its environment. The conception we have developed is more complex and in many ways less pessimistic than some commonly held views of the local economy based on surface appearances.

MAJOR TRENDS IN THE CLEVELAND ECONOMY

Three broad trends characterize economic conditions in the Cleveland area over the past two decades and especially during the 1970s. The total population of the metropolitan area has been declining. Total employment has increased annually but at a much slower rate than the nationwide average. Employment in manufacturing industries has decreased, and employment in nonmanufacturing industries has increased.

The City of Cleveland began losing population in the mid-1950s. Until 1970, the suburbs grew more than enough to make up for the city's loss, but between 1970 and 1980, the entire Standard Metropolitan Statistical Area (SMSA)[1] began to lose population.

Even though total population declined, total employment has continued to grow in the Cleveland area at slightly less than one percent per year between 1967 and 1977. Cleveland's total growth rate in employment, however, is slower than that of the earlier postwar period (1.2 percent) and slower still than the increase in employment nationwide (2.1 percent) during the last decade.

Most new jobs created by the Cleveland metropolitan economy over the 1967-77 period were in the nonmanufacturing sectors.[2]

---

[1]Most statistics used in this report are for the Cleveland SMSA, which includes the Counties of Cuyahoga, Lake, Geauga, and Medina.

[2]In most of our analysis, we examine change from 1967 to 1977—two years at approximately the same position on the business cycle. Some economic data are available through 1980, but they are much less detailed. Also, because of the 1980 recession, using that year as our endpoint would have led to a distorted characterization of the forces at work over most of the 1970s. As expected, the more recent figures show that economic conditions have worsened locally as well as nationally since 1977. The 1980 data do not alter any of our basic findings about relative differences between major sectors, however.

Manufacturing employment actually declined during the period, but the creation of new jobs, especially in the service sectors, more than made up for the losses in Cleveland's traditional economic base.

These, then, are the familiar trends as they appear on the surface. Taken together, they seem to suggest a deeply troubled region with a basically stagnant economy. If these surface trends suggest a hope, it is that the service industries will assume the role of the disappearing manufacturing sector in keeping the local economy on, at best, an even keel. When we take our first look just beneath the surface, however, a different picture emerges.

Beneath the Surface: Interpreting Regional Change

Metropolitan Cleveland's population is decreasing, but that fact does not reflect any unique problems in the area's environment. In losing population, the Cleveland area is simply sharing the fate of most of the largest metropolitan areas in the northeastern quadrant of the United States. The general movement of population to the sunbelt responds to fundamental social and economic changes in the United States and not to specific conditions in particular metropolitan areas.

So marked are differences in population and economic growth rates between the northeast and the sunbelt that it might seem as if the Great Lakes industrial belt is being decimated. This is not the case. The northeast quadrant of the United States still remains the nation's population and economic heartland. In 1978, more than half the population of the United States lived within 500 miles of Cleveland, and more than 60 percent of U.S. metropolitan durable goods manufacturing fell within the same circle. What is more, by the same measure, Cleveland remains much more centrally located with respect to economic activity in the United States than any similarly sized city except Pittsburgh.

What is more surprising is that, in spite of the sizable percentage increases in economic activity in the sunbelt during the 1970s, Cleveland's comparative locational advantage has changed very little. For example, the percentage of total U.S. metropolitan employment in several industry groups located within 250 miles of Cleveland actually increased slightly between 1970 and 1976.

In other words, economic activity in the United States is still heavily concentrated in the industrial northeastern quadrant. The shift to the sunbelt regions has not yet been large enough to alter this basic fact.

Beneath the Surface: A Slowly Growing But Dynamic Economy

Compared with the nation as a whole, especially its most rapidly growing regions, employment growth in the Cleveland area has indeed been slow. However, a fairly constant total number of jobs in a region does not necessarily signify a stagnant economy, and in fact, the Cleveland metropolitan economy has been undergoing substantial changes over the past decade. One important aspect of the essential dynamism of the metropolitan economy during the 1970s is revealed by employment, productivity, and investment trends in a number of narrowly defined manufacturing industries.

If we look only at broadly defined manufacturing groups, we do see what looks like a fairly dismal picture. Between 1967 and 1977, about one out of seven manufacturing jobs was lost to the metropolitan Cleveland economy. In the primary metals industry (mostly steel production), about one out of five jobs was lost; in transportation equipment manufacturing (mostly the automotive industry), one out of three jobs was lost. In fact employment declined to some extent in almost all of the area's major manufacturing groups over this period.

However, a different picture emerged when we looked at the trends for 84 narrowly defined components of the major groups. A significant number of these industries had gained jobs in the Cleveland area. While the automotive industry was losing jobs rapidly, the number of jobs in the stampings and other fabricated metals industry increased by more than 50 percent. Employment in the rubber and plastic products industry increased by more than 40 percent and employment by firms manufacturing measurement and control devices grew by more than 75 percent.

Nor were all of these rapid growth industries insignificant to begin with. Thirty-six percent of Cleveland's employees in 1977 were working in industries that had grown in employment by five percent or more between 1967 and 1977.

Other measures of the recent performance of the Cleveland area's manufacturing sector tell us more about its recent past but do not change the general conclusion that manufacturing industries employing a substantial proportion of the region's work force have been performing relatively well over the last decade. Average value added per production worker hour was higher on average in Cleveland than in the United States as a whole throughout the 1967-77 period. Almost 40 percent of Cleveland's manufacturing employees worked in industries in which value added per production worker hour was increasing at a faster rate than the national average.

A final measure of industrial performance is investment. Capital expenditures per production worker hour in Cleveland manufacturing were about equal to the U.S. average of that measure from 1967 through 1972, but dropped to only 83 percent of the U.S. average over the 1973-77 period. Still, there were a number of industries (e.g., electrical industrial apparatus, general industrial machinery) in which Cleveland investment per production worker hour remained well above the national average for the industry.

The different implications of the surface view and the detailed view can be illustrated very simply. Total manufacturing employment in the Cleveland area decreased by 13.5 percent between 1967 and 1977. This summary figure suggests a dismal prospect for this broad sector. However, if each of the 84 manufacturing industries for which data are available continues to grow or decline at the same rate it did between 1967 and 1977, total manufacturing employment would decrease by only two percent between 1977 and 1987. Neither of these figures—13.5 percent or two percent—is, in any sense, a prediction of what is likely to happen over the next decade. They do, however, illustrate that Cleveland's slow rate of total employment growth does not necessarily suggest a stagnant regional economy.

Beneath the Surface: Is Cleveland Becoming a Service Center?

Between 1967 and 1977, Cleveland's nonmanufacturing industries created jobs even faster than the manufacturing industries lost them. After contemplating the summary figures, some analysts have concluded that nonmanufacturing industries, especially the service sectors, bid fair to replace manufacturing as Cleveland's economic *raison d'être*. A look beneath the surface indicates that conditions of some of the service industries are indeed becoming more important to Cleveland's economic health, but the relative importance of the manufacturing industries remains huge.

Four of our study's findings illustrate that point. First, we found that even though the nonmanufacturing industries did increase in employment substantially in Cleveland during this period, they were growing even faster nationwide.

Second, several of Cleveland's fastest growing nonmanufacturing industries that compare most favorably with national growth rates are those most closely linked with manufacturing industries: trucking and warehousing and administrative and auxiliary activities (including headquarters offices) of manufacturing firms.

Third, analyzing the composition of Cleveland's exports to the rest of the United States and the world indicates that as important as

some nonmanufacturing industries may be in terms of total employment, the bulk of Cleveland's exports still consists of durable manufactured goods. Our analysis indicates that the trend toward increased
exports of business and health services would have to continue at a
rapid pace for a long time before these sectors rivaled the importance
of the key manufacturing industries.

Finally, even though the total number of jobs in manufacturing industries decreased during the last decade, about 40 percent of manufacturing employees worked in industries that were growing at least
as fast in Cleveland as nationwide. Less than 20 percent of Cleveland's nonmanufacturing employees held jobs in local industries that
kept pace with the U.S. market. In other words, the general shift in
employment to the nonmanufacturing sectors obscures the fact that
more industries in which Cleveland has an apparent competitive edge
are found within the manufacturing sector.

It would be a mistake to overstate the conclusions of this section.
We are not saying that the Cleveland area has no strong potential
advantages in such fields as business-related services and health and
medical services or that Cleveland's function as a corporate headquarters location is not one of its great assets. Nor are we suggesting that
Cleveland's leaders pay exclusive attention to the manufacturing industries. We do say, however, that the shift in regional employment to
the nonmanufacturing sectors does not reflect a fundamental shift in
Cleveland's basic role in the U.S. economy.

DURABLE GOODS MANUFACTURING:
CLEVELAND'S TRADITIONAL MAINSTAY

A surface view of durable goods manufacturing immediately identifies five large industries that have traditionally been thought of as
the region's "anchor industries": primary metals, fabricated metals,
nonelectrical machinery, electrical machinery, and transportation
equipment. Changes in employment levels indicate that these industries all encountered serious problems in the 1970s.

Explanations abound as to the main forces that influence change in
these industries, but three stand out in most discussions. In one view,
Cleveland is regarded as dominated by the automotive industry, since
many other local industries sell a large share of their output directly
or indirectly to the automotive sector. The implication of this view is
that Cleveland's economic future depends almost exclusively on the
future of automobile production in the United States.

A second view sees Cleveland as a more diverse economy and

stresses local production of machinery and related products used to equip or supply new factories here and elsewhere. Local problems are laid to the United States' becoming a consumption-oriented society. Local prospects are dim because too few of our national resources are being invested in new plants and equipment.

A third view emphasizes that Cleveland's manufacturing wages are out of line with wages paid elsewhere in the United States and the world. The average manufacturing wage in metropolitan Cleveland is 20 percent higher than the U.S. average. With this differential, many find it hard to believe that Cleveland will be able to attract any new manufacturing investment in the future.

Although there are facts to support each of these views, all are too simplified. None tells the whole story. Taken together, they could create misleading expectations about the Cleveland area economy in the years ahead.

Beneath the Surface: The Role of the Automotive Industry

Automobile production is the single most important manufacturing industry to the U.S. economy as a whole. To Cleveland, that industry is even more important than to most other U.S. cities. On the surface, it might appear, then, that Cleveland is almost as dependent on the automotive industry as Detroit, albeit somewhat more indirectly.

Our analysis, however, indicates that this is not the case. We studied the relation between month-to-month fluctuations in U.S. automobile and truck production from 1975 to 1981, and local unemployment rates in a number of major metropolitan areas. In Detroit, the two variables were highly correlated: declines in production were consistently and closely followed by increases in unemployment. In Cleveland, a correlation existed but it was not nearly as strong. By implication, Cleveland production serving other markets cushioned the shocks of swings in demand from the automotive sector. In fact, our analysis suggested that Cleveland is somewhat less sensitive to that industry than either Pittsburgh or Indianapolis—metropolitan areas not ordinarily thought of as auto towns. If U.S. automobile production does not recover from its current slump, Cleveland will undoubtedly face hard times, but the regional economy has better potential for weathering that slump than some other northeastern industrial cities.

Beneath the Surface: Shifts Among the Anchor Industries

Analysis of industry employment data suggests that the Cleveland area's economic specialty is not well characterized by the simple list of five industries noted earlier. Since so much steel and automotive production takes place in Cleveland, one would expect fabricated metals production (the manufacture of parts and other semi-finished goods) and machinery production to be heavily represented in the regional economy. Even with that expectation, the concentration of these latter activities in metropolitan Cleveland is unusually high.

Since fabricated metals and nonelectrical machinery are more heavily concentrated in Cleveland than expected, given the heavy industrial character of the economy, we conclude that those two types of products, more than steel and automotive products, define Cleveland's particular role in the U.S. economy. Two other industries that are playing large or increasing roles in the region's export economy are electrical industrial equipment and instruments. Both sell most of their output to other manufacturers.

Because it specializes in semi-finished goods and investment goods, Cleveland's role in U.S. manufacturing is not as a *general* supplier of durable goods, but more as a factory town that sells things to other factory towns. Cleveland's prosperity, therefore, is very closely linked to the general condition of the U.S. manufacturing sector. Not only is a large part of U.S. manufacturing activity located in the Cleveland area, but Cleveland depends on other U.S. manufacturing centers for most of its "export" earnings.

That finding indicates that the continuation of a consumption-oriented national economy (rather than one that is manufacturing-investment-oriented) would not bode well for Cleveland. It is possible to take heart, however, in the growing recognition that this orientation also would not bode well for the United States as a whole. Stimulating investment in manufacturing is now a primary goal of both major political parties. Indeed an investment boom would provide much more stimulus for the Cleveland economy than anything else that might happen to the national economy over the next few years. In simulating the effects of different combinations of new export business on Cleveland, we found that demand generated by business investment nationwide helped the local economy much more than consumption-oriented demand.

Although Cleveland would profit from a business investment boom, there are risks involved. For example, as the machinery and fabricated metal industries become more important as a source of income for the metropolis, diversity in export earnings decreases, and the Cleveland area becomes more vulnerable to problems faced by either of those industries.

One of those industries is, in fact, increasingly threatened by foreign competition. Three years ago, for the first time since statistics have been kept, the United States became a net importer of machine tools. If this trend continues and the U.S. machine tool industry follows the pattern of the automotive industry, an increasingly important element of the local economy could be threatened. Trends in the U.S. and world markets for machine tools should be closely watched by Cleveland regional economists, and any well-considered programs that could help maintain the area's competitiveness in this industry deserve priority.

Also, it should not be assumed that a general investment boom would benefit all segments of the metropolitan community equally. In 1970, the investment and semi-finished goods industries employed relatively small proportions of blacks, for example. Unless Cleveland's key industries have become more integrated over the last decade, Cleveland's black community would not receive a proportionate share of the benefits generated by an investment boom. This does not counter our view that the investment scenario is best for Cleveland, but it does suggest a concern for policymakers. High unemployment in the black community is one of Cleveland's major problems.

Beneath the Surface: Composition of Change in More Detail

As noted earlier, although total manufacturing employment declined substantially in Cleveland between 1967 and 1977, a number of industries grew rapidly during that period and even increased their share of the U.S. market. This told us that, while decreasing, Cleveland's manufacturing sector was not necessarily in a state of precipitous decline.

Some of the industries that did exceptionally well in Cleveland also did well nationwide. Cleveland increased its share of production in the seventh (rubber and miscellaneous plastics products), ninth (blowers and fans), eleventh (other fabricated metal products), and twelfth (other instruments and related products) fastest growing industries in the United States. In other words, Cleveland was doing well in some high-growth industries. At the same time, some industries that were not performing well nationwide were more than holding their own locally. Iron and steel foundries and nonelectrical plumbing and heating equipment are good examples.

The composition of this list indicates that Cleveland's role in the

U.S. manufacturing economy may be evolving in two directions. First, Cleveland is enjoying more than its share of the growth of a number of fast-growing industries. Second, Cleveland is finding or preserving a number of what might be called "market niches." Many names for industry groups that are doing best in the Cleveland area include the words "miscellaneous" or "other." Those terms indicate that Cleveland area firms are succeeding in producing products that do not fit neatly into traditional categories. Although more analysis would be needed to determine exactly why Cleveland has been succeeding in these areas, the combination of national winners and "market niches" amounts to a sound industrial strategy for any city.

Beneath the Surface: Cleveland's Wages

The average manufacturing wage in metropolitan Cleveland ($7.06 per production worker hour in 1977) exceeded the national average by 20 percent. This comparison, however, is not a very useful one. The gap is distorted because a very large portion of metropolitan Cleveland employees work in the durable goods sectors where wages typically exceed those in other industries. It is more appropriate to look at the wage gap industry by industry. Doing so, we discovered many variations, but wages in Cleveland area industries are in most cases higher than those of their national counterparts. For all industries, they are on average six percent higher; for the durable goods producers, they are on average 12 percent higher.

Still, these comparisons do not tell us much about Cleveland's position in relation to today's "competition." Average wages for the nation as a whole are heavily weighted by other older manufacturing centers in the northern states where wages are also high. An entrepreneur seeking to establish a new plant today is more likely to compare Cleveland area labor costs against those in low wage areas like the rural south than against those in other northern cities.

Wage data for rural areas were not available in sufficient detail for our analysis, but we have assembled the information for a group of nine low wage southern states as a whole, i.e., including both metropolitan and rural areas. Even so, the contrasts are much more striking. Cleveland area wages averaging across all industries are 25 percent higher than their southern counterparts; for the durable goods industries, they are on average 38 percent higher. Fringe benefit payments are also typically much higher in northern metropolises than they are in rural areas in the sunbelt.

In these circumstances, it might seem surprising to some that the Cleveland area has attracted any new investment at all in recent years, but as noted earlier, investments have been made, and quite a number of the 84 subcomponents of major manufacturing groups grew significantly in the area in the 1970s. Some, as might be expected, were among the comparatively few Cleveland area industries where wage levels were lower than or similar to those of their counterpart industries nationally, but others grew in spite of wages higher than those of their national counterparts. In fact, statistical analysis of data for the 84 component industries showed no correlation between wage gaps and employment growth rates or changes in local shares of national employment.

What does this finding mean? It certainly does not mean that high wages are never an impediment to regional growth, but it does imply that they are not the sole determinant. The community should look into a wide range of possible causes of slow economic growth, including labor availability, the entrepreneurial environment, capital infrastructure, and technological competitiveness, to name a few, as well as wage relationships.

Our analysis suggests that the role of wage differences in economic development is more complicated than it may have appeared on the surface, but the data we assembled are too crude to tell us much about comparative effects in different kinds of industries and firms. Certainly, further research is warranted.

That research should recognize the causes of high wages as well as their effects. It should be remembered that, as high as local wages may be, U.S. workers are not flocking to the Cleveland area to take jobs at those wages. During the last decade, Cleveland wages across industries and occupations were higher than the national average and the Cleveland area's unemployment rate was lower than the national average, but the population of the Cleveland metropolitan area still declined. This means that some former Clevelanders were willing to leave the area to wait in lines for jobs that were likely to pay less than in Cleveland. There must, therefore, be some disadvantages to living in Cleveland that outweigh the wage premiums Cleveland's workers command.

One is the cost of living. Although living costs in Cleveland are lower than those of many metropolitan areas, compared to other regions now competing for manufacturing investment, the annual cost of maintaining an intermediate standard of living for a family of four in metropolitan Cleveland exceeded the national urban average by about two percent in 1974 and the equivalent figure for southern nonmetropolitan areas by close to 20 percent.

A second set of wage determinants are the specific amenities and disamenities associated with life in Cleveland. There are several of both. For example, among similarly sized metropolitan areas, Cleveland had by far the best set of cultural institutions. By contrast, Cleveland's climate was poor by most commonly accepted measures and its violent crime rate was high.

A final factor that can raise local wages is the quality of local industrial labor relations. It is difficult to measure this factor, but we know that Cleveland, even given the industrial composition of its economy, has a highly unionized work force and that the percentage of work time lost as a result of work stoppages tends to be high in Ohio.

Although direct attention to labor relations in some industries may very well be in order, the attention of the community as a whole should focus on the underlying causes of high wages by enhancing Cleveland's advantages as a place for workers to live.

The Context in Which Policy Is Made

A metropolitan area as large as Cleveland generates ideas for economic development policies, programs, and projects at a high rate. Some of those ideas are accepted by enough of the community's leaders to be implemented. Of those that are, some meet their objectives and others do not. The function of economic analysis in this process is to increase over time the proportion of implemented projects that are successful. By producing and disseminating a more realistic view of how the local economy works and what its strengths and weaknesses are, analysts can decrease the likelihood that the community will be sold on misguided projects.

On the basis of our work to date in Cleveland, we are able to suggest a number of principles and points of fact that regional leaders should keep in mind when they consider specific action proposals for development. In this section, we highlight several of the most important.

Most basic of all is the understanding that community actions alone cannot determine an area's prosperity. The condition of the local economy depends more on how well Cleveland's entrepreneurs and plant managers respond to the changes they perceive in the U.S. and world economies.

Our analysis demonstrates that much of the change in the Cleveland area economy during the 1970s was strongly influenced by national forces. This implies that actions to promote economic development will be most effective if they explicitly recognize—not run counter to—changing conditions nationally. Given the recent volatility of events at that level, it also implies that metropolitan leaders need to keep close watch over national and international trends so that opportunities and threats can be recognized expeditiously.

The Importance of Manufacturing

This report reemphasizes the importance of the durable goods manufacturing sectors to the Cleveland economy. We have noted that the Cleveland area's specialty within this sector is as a producer of semi-finished metal goods and producers' durables—machine tools, electrical industrial equipment, and, more and more, instruments.

Efforts to expand the export activities of some of the service sectors may pay off, but it is unlikely that these industries will sell enough outside the metropolitan area to replace manufacturing as the core of the Cleveland area's economic base. So, in a sense, the region is still wedded to its traditional strengths. Additional threats to this strength should be viewed very seriously. Community leaders should always be ready to give local manufacturers and their trade associations a sympathetic hearing when problems call for public attention. Proposals for community action to enhance Cleveland's competitiveness as a producer of manufactured durables should always be welcomed and carefully reviewed.

We found that these industries were indeed threatened by a number of trends, some of which might be altered by community action. For instance, representatives of the machine tool and fabricated metal industries reported the absence of highly skilled manpower. Labor requirements most often mentioned were for younger journeyman machinists and electronics technicians. We did not conduct an analysis of the supply and demand for manpower with specific skills; that task should await the release of the 1980 Census. However, we can recommend that possible shortages of technical manpower be given attention. That analysis should focus on whether or not there is a shortage of given types of labor and then on why the shortage has arisen. Proposed solutions should not be adopted unless they are based on sound diagnoses of real problems. Otherwise, skilled workers, trained at Cleveland's expense, may remain unemployed or take jobs in other regions.

A second set of problems of the semi-finished and investment goods industries has to do with their small average firm size. Small firms with aging owners may find it difficult to respond to changes in markets, products, and production technology. Because small durable goods manufacturing firms are such an important part of Cleveland's economy, their potential problems deserve considerable attention. Community programs to market products or develop and disseminate "appropriate" technical assistance might help, as might short-term management training programs for owners of small firms. A more careful analysis of the operations and problems of firms of various sizes and the attitudes of their owners, however, should precede formal action. It is not necessarily the case, for example, that all firms can benefit from innovations in "high technology"; some might make better use of consulting assistance on inventory control, production timing, and workspace utilization.

HOW DO SERVICES FIT IN?

Several nonmanufacturing industries show promise of playing an important role in Cleveland's future. One of these, the medical and health services industry, is in a sense free-standing. The University Hospitals and the Cleveland Clinic may make the city a medical center for a region larger than the metropolitan area. Also, health services has been the most rapidly growing industry nationwide. However, major changes in federal health policy make the future of this industry highly uncertain. If Cleveland wishes to retain or enhance its position as a regional leader in advanced health care, concerted community action will have to replace much of the support the federal government has provided over the last decade.

Other nonmanufacturing industries that appeared to be doing well in Cleveland are closely linked to the manufacturing sectors. This suggests that part of Cleveland's service sector strategy should focus on exploiting interactions between the two broad sectors. One obvious example of potential synergy is the medical technology industry. Cleveland already has substantial resources in this field. Proposals to encourage development of those resources should be given serious consideration.

Cleveland might also enhance its role as a center for distribution and marketing of producers' durables. Business services aimed at durable goods manufacturers—engineering and design consultants, trade associations, trade journal publishers, private technical educators, and so on—could expect significant local demand on which to base potential export growth.

Finally, the Cleveland area's role as a headquarters location for large firms is of great importance to its economic base. In 1978, the Cleveland area was the home of 38 of *Fortune*'s top 1,000 industrial firms, placing it third among all U.S. metropolitan areas. Employment in headquarters' offices grew rapidly in metropolitan Cleveland in the 1970s. Although national employment in that category increased more rapidly, the gap was narrower here than in most other components of the local service sector. In addition to its employment base per se, the fact that so many of America's industrial leaders are Cleveland area residents is a substantial strength. Attention to the quality of regional life, to local, national, and international passenger transportation, and to the availability of high-quality clerical and information processing personnel can help ensure that corporate headquarters will find what they need in metropolitan Cleveland.

MINORITY CONCERNS

As we have seen, if 1970 data are a reliable indicator, an emphasis on Cleveland's key manufacturing industries along with a service sector strategy that emphasizes linkages with manufacturing, in and of itself, may not work well enough to solve the problems of the black community. A development strategy with potential for eliciting minority support might have three elements: immediate job creation, affirmative action, and training.

Immediate job creation for blacks might involve growth of some of the sectors that employ large proportions of minority workers: hotels, personal services, food processing, public employment, and so on. However, a strategy that relied only on that approach would confine minorities to low-paying, low-status occupations. Integrating blacks into Cleveland's economic mainstream requires affirmative action, but training may be more important in the long term. Programs aimed at training minorities for jobs available in the durable goods industries and emerging technical fields should be emphasized.

CONTINUED ECONOMIC MONITORING

Our analysis demonstrates that surface trends offer poor guidance to those who would further economic development in the Cleveland area. The metropolitan economy is surprisingly complex. Policies that are not based on a more complete understanding might well result in missed opportunities and resources focused on the wrong problems.

This underscores our view that an ongoing economic monitoring capability is much needed in the Cleveland area. A well-trained staff of economists and policy analysts who devote their attention to the metropolitan economy could become an invaluable resource to community leaders who find themselves confronted with varied proposals for economic development.

Our work suggests two efforts that deserve high priority in future economic monitoring. The first is to develop methods for translating observed or predicted changes in the U.S. and world economies into their effects on the Cleveland area economy. These methods should take into account the pattern of interactions that exists among economic sectors. Also, as part of this effort, the monitoring group should draw on local specialists to build and maintain an expert understanding of national and worldwide markets for each of the Cleveland area's export products.

These capabilities would be valuable not only in guiding local policy. If authoritative information on the local effects of changing state and federal policies was rapidly made available to Cleveland area officials, they should be able to exert stronger influence on those policies in Columbus and Washington.

The second effort entails more detailed analysis of problems and opportunities in narrowly defined industries. Our findings show that data on broad industry groupings alone can offer a misleading picture of the local economy, averaging out much of the diversity that must be understood for sound policy development. It is important for Cleveland to track the progress of its key industries, especially by involving managers and workers with useful insights into their industry's economic future. Conducting in-depth case studies of the machine tools or metal stampings industries, for example, an economic monitoring group could facilitate communication between industry leaders and the community as a whole.

Our analysis does not suggest that the Cleveland metropolitan economy has a secure future, but it has pointed out a number of ways in which local industries are coming to grips with their new environment. Through recent public and private sector initiatives, Cleveland's leadership has demonstrated that it is laying a foundation for a more solid future—for example, by stabilizing the city's fiscal situation and improving its management, and by establishing new institutions to bring diverse groups together to deal with local problems. We believe that continued economic monitoring can contribute much to the effectiveness of such initiatives as they address economic development issues.

CONTENTS

PART C—TRENDS IN THE PERFORMANCE OF METROPOLITAN CLEVELAND INDUSTRIES

PART D—PROSPECTS AND PROBLEMS OF THREE CLEVELAND INDUSTRIES

FIGURES

TABLES

PART A

PURPOSE AND CONTEXT

I. INTRODUCTION

Cleveland's history has been one of the great success stories in the industrialization of America. In the mid-1800s, its strategic location conferred important benefits: proximity to emerging markets as the nation's population moved west and easy access to vast mineral resources through an extensive system of waterways. Clevelanders took advantage of these benefits to build a manufacturing center of incredible strength and diversity. In 1978, more than a century after its industrial life began, metropolitan Cleveland (with 2.9 million inhabitants) ranked tenth in population among large U.S. metropolises but sixth in industrial shipments ($32.9 million) and third as a headquarters location for *Fortune*'s top 1,000 manufacturing corporations (38 firms).

Its strengths did not exempt it, however, from disturbing trends that have affected most older northern industrial areas over the past two decades: sluggish growth or decline in important economic sectors, growing concentrations of the disadvantaged, as well as physical and fiscal erosion in central cities. A heightened awareness of these trends, divisiveness, and other factors shook Cleveland's morale in the late 1970s. Frustrations peaked with the city's financial default in 1978. Pessimism about the future of the metropolis was dominant.

Today, in some important ways, Cleveland seems a very different place. A popular view locally is that the near debacle of the late 1970s brought Clevelanders to their senses and got them to work together in the community's interest. There is a good deal of evidence to support this view. The management reforms of a new administration have resulted in a restoration of the city's bond ratings. Three actions, often proposed as vital to sound governance but never before politically salable, have been approved by Cleveland's voters: a reduction in the size of the city council, an extension of mayoral and council terms from two to four years, and an increase in the city's payroll tax. The first four-year mayor in a city known for political fragmentation has been elected with overwhelming bipartisan support.

In 1980, many of the community's leaders recognized that while political and institutional reforms were needed first steps in a program of community betterment, the success of any such program would ultimately depend on the strength of the local economy.

Economic development, however, was by no means a straightforward assignment. Fundamental shifts had been occurring in individual industries and the economy as a whole, both nationally and

2

locally. The nature and implications of these changes had to be better understood. Accordingly, The Cleveland Foundation asked The Rand Corporation to help initiate a process of continued economic monitoring that would offer a basis for more informed decisions about what can and should be done. This report—a baseline assessment of metropolitan Cleveland's economy—is a first step in that process.

THE PROCESS OF ECONOMIC MONITORING

Other metropolitan areas with similar interests have sponsored large-scale one-time studies of their economies. Some made notable contributions to our understanding of the way local economies work and, thereby, to more realistic thinking about public development programs, particularly the studies of the Pittsburgh region (see Pittsburgh Regional Planning Association, 1963a, b, and c) and the New York City region (Vernon, 1963). Nonetheless, The Cleveland Foundation and Rand agreed that this was not the most promising approach for the Cleveland area in the early 1980s.

The reason was that the risks of this approach are higher now. The initial investment required would have been substantial and given the volatility of the American economy of late and the profound structural changes now under way, any single study based on current and past data might well be an inadequate guide for policy choices even three to four years ahead. The alternative was to devote fewer resources to the initial assessment and more to building toward a permanent institutional capability for effective economic monitoring in the Cleveland area in the future. As we see it, the staff of an ongoing economic monitoring capability would do three things:

- Maintain an up-to-date central *data base* on changing local economic conditions.
- Conduct *analysis* and issue reports: (1) summarizing recent trends in the economy overall and (2) examining special issues of interest to community leaders.
- Participate in a continuing *dialogue* with community leaders and other local economists both gaining information from them on important economic changes not apparent in the statistics and helping them to use the results of analysis in devising actions to enhance prospects for economic growth.

Were such a capability available, staffs of other local institutions (e.g., public agencies, the Growth Association, local utilities, banks, and other private firms) would only have to go to one place to secure reliable information about the local economy needed for their own purposes. The series of regular summary reports on economic trends would offer a context to help them interpret the specific data they obtain.

Cleveland's mayor and other leaders in the public and private sectors would have somewhere to go to get reasonable answers to important questions in their policy deliberations. (For example, what will be the impact of a particular state tax bill, or a trend in imports from Japan, or a shift in federal procurement policies on the Cleveland economy? What would such changes imply for local economic development policies?) When such questions arise today, there is seldom enough time to collect the data and do the research needed for a solid response. The existence of an economic monitoring capability would mean that the data would be readily available as would analytic tools enabling analysts to sort out patterns of effects through a complex web of economic interrelationships. It should be possible to obtain more reliable answers more rapidly.

Our emphasis on continuing dialogue between the analysts and the community sets this process apart from many activities of this kind in other cities. Our view is that the analysts, working on their own, could easily become too far removed from real forces operating in the economy and the issues of concern to policymakers. The requirement for dialogue, built into the fabric of the institution, should promote both realism and relevance.

With these ends in view, Rand's work program has been designed in two phases. In phase one (October 1980-September 1981) we had three tasks:

- Assembling available statistics on local economic trends and compiling a detailed computer data base that can be updated by others as new information becomes available in the future.
- Preparing the first drafts of a baseline study of the metropolitan economy, drawing on the data base and other information sources (this report).
- Designing an approach for the longer-term development of an economic monitoring capability.

Based on The Cleveland Foundation's approval of progress, phase two was initiated (October 1981-September 1982). This phase began with a series of reviews of earlier drafts of this report in the community. The main purpose of the work program, however, is to further test the monitoring concept and help to implement it if community support for the approach is obtained. Specifically:

- The Cleveland Foundation (with Rand's help) has set up an economic advisory committee composed of local economists and other technical specialists to participate in the process.
- Rand is carrying out the monitoring function as it would be operated on a permanent basis: collecting additional data, developing new tools for analysis, preparing and disseminating reports on regional trends and special issue analyses, and meeting regularly to discuss findings with the economic advisory committee and others in the community.
- The Foundation is evaluating the process and considering options for permanent implementation in a local institution.

There is a great interest in economic development in the Cleveland area at present. Many different organizations (in the private sector as well as the public sector) are making plans and initiating projects aimed at strengthening the local economic base. That they should all be brought together under one coordinated organizational umbrella seems not only infeasible, but also undesirable. The creativity that emerges from many independent entities seeking similar general objectives but approaching them out of different backgrounds and capabilities could not be matched in any monolithic structure.

Still, there is a need for coherence, and several mechanisms might be employed to achieve it. As we see it, an ongoing economic monitoring activity should be one of them. If a separate entity existed to provide all parties with a common data base, to analyze new problems and opportunities as they emerge, and to provide a forum where their representatives could gather to discuss and debate the facts and their implications, coordination should be facilitated and the quality of resulting policies should be improved.

THE PURPOSE AND STRUCTURE OF OUR INITIAL ASSESSMENT

The ultimate objective of our work, then, is a long-term process rather than a short-term product. Even so, the process could not be well designed or properly focused without an initial baseline review of the available facts about metropolitan Cleveland's economy. Some reasonable synthesis of this evidence is needed to provide guidance not only about general barriers to and opportunities for economic development, but also about the kinds of additional analysis and monitoring that deserve priority in the future.

Fortunately, we found that considerable data on the Cleveland economy were available that had never been analyzed before. Coupling the examination of these data with what we learned from the many interviews conducted during the course of our study, we do have a new story to tell. It is a complicated story—one that defies many of the simple generalizations about Cleveland's economic trends that have been debated locally in recent years. Nonetheless, it does present a coherent framework for understanding the forces that have been operating in the economy and what they mean for the future.

Our intention in Part A of the report has been to provide background information needed to understand the analysis to follow. In this chapter, in addition to discussing our longer-term objectives and the structure of the report, we discuss basic concepts and definitions we use in the remaining chapters (geographic areas and industries) and note our major data sources. Chapter II tells the story of metropolitan Cleveland's recent past "on the surface," reviewing summary statistics on population trends, changing employment levels in major economic sectors, and other characteristics. We compare the Cleveland trends with those in several other areas over the same period—the nation as a whole, major regions, and selected other metropolitan areas. Much of the story at this level has been told in the past, but the parts are scattered in various articles and publications. It is helpful to look at it all in one place before seeing how well implications that have been drawn from it hold up when we examine the facts in more detail.

The purpose of Part B is to explain how the metropolitan economy works and how it is similar to and different from other parts of the U.S. economy: Chapter III reviews the economy's structure and Chapter IV reviews characteristics of the Cleveland environment that affect economic change. In these chapters we initiate themes that are dominant in the rest of the report. We see the Cleveland area economy operating in an intensively competitive world. Its future will be determined by the nature of its particular strengths and weaknesses in relation to those of its competitors. We need to identify the competition and isolate the strengths and weaknesses to gain a sense of future prospects. Is metropolitan Cleveland simply a creature of the U.S. economy, such that independent local action cannot make a difference? If not, what are the areas in which the metropolis can most effectively compete?

Chapter III begins with a discussion of the way regional economies operate that aids our understanding of what economic strength really means. It continues using an input-output framework to identify the roles played by different local industries. A review of the interactions between those industries clarifies the extent to which any one among them dominates the potential for all the rest. Finally, the way different industries affect important "urban outcomes" is examined. Further growth in some of them provides more jobs for blacks and young people and has a larger impact on the central city, for example, than the equivalent amount of expansion in others.

In Chapter IV, we look at Cleveland's environment through the eyes of an entrepreneur seeking to establish new productive capacity or expand existing capacity. The introductory framework draws from national studies to show what factors entrepreneurs care about in deciding where to invest. We then examine how metropolitan Cleveland stacks up against its competitors along a number of these dimensions: access to markets and raw materials, wage rates and the characteristics of the labor force, taxes and the quality of public services, and other factors that determine the "business climate." Available data are much too fragmentary to allow us to pinpoint Cleveland's comparative rank as a place to do different kinds of business, but a clear portrait emerges as to its major advantages and disadvantages.

Whereas Part B looked at the Cleveland area economy in a static framework, Part C reviews how economic conditions have been changing. It examines the performance of local industries since 1967, showing how their size and market shares have changed compared to each other and to their counterpart industries in other parts of the country. Chapter V reviews the data for the various components of the manufacturing sector and Chapter VI covers all nonmanufacturing industries.

Several other papers and reports prepared in recent years have also reviewed employment trends for Cleveland industries. Our analysis does two things that are different. First, it examines industries in much greater detail presenting data for 84 manufacturing industries and 47 nonmanufacturing industries rather than the handful of aggregate categories typically analyzed in the past. Second, it reviews other measures of performance in addition to change in employment levels. These include variables based on employment and establishment counts and, in manufacturing, new capital expenditures (investment) and value added per production worker hour. The inclusion of richer detail and more measures does make an important difference. The conclusions we draw are quite different from those suggested by studies of summary trends alone.

One of those conclusions motivates the work presented in Part D. We found that there was no simple set of factors that accounts for variations in the performance of Cleveland industries in the 1970s. Characteristics particular to their own product lines, technologies, and markets often have a great deal to do with their success locally. For this reason, we felt it was important to study some individual industries on their own terms, using information from interviews as well as statistics to understand more the nature of their current problems and prospects.

We picked three important local industries that are quite different from each other for these case studies: machine tools (Chapter VII), hotels (Chapter VIII), and health services (Chapter IX).

Part E (Chapter X) presents our conclusions. We first explore the range of generally stated futures possible for metropolitan Cleveland's economy, given the constraints that may be set by the national economy and local structural factors. We next review the types of industries our analysis suggests are the most promising areas of opportunity for development in the Cleveland area in the next decade. Then we suggest directions for policy (public and private) that seem most appropriate, consistent with what we have learned. Finally, we consider what remains to be learned to help shape local economic development efforts more effectively, reviewing key information gaps uncovered in the process of our study and suggesting how future activities of the monitoring capability might be designed to fill them.

DEFINING THE METROPOLIS

Why should we be concerned about the metropolitan economy at all? Simple observation tells us that most of Cleveland's suburbs are reasonably well off—some are very well off. Serious problems are clearly focused in the City of Cleveland itself—poverty, unemployment, crime, physical deterioration, racial tensions, problems with public services, and incredible pressures on government financial resources. Why not just focus on the city's economy?

We recognize that the city's problems deserve the highest priority attention in public policy, but we doubt they can be "fixed" without a full understanding of the directions for change in the metropolis as a whole. In an economic sense, the metropolis is one entity and the city's boundaries artificial. The health of industries in the suburbs dramatically affects job prospects for the city's residents. It is impossible to imagine a thriving central business district consistent with economic disarray in the rest of the metropolis.

Future work in economic monitoring should indeed study city-suburban differences in detail, but this report is a starting point, and as such it must examine trends and prospects for the whole rather than any of its parts in isolation.

Having said this much, how is the metropolis to be defined? The choice is not automatic since there are several commonly used boundary definitions for metropolitan Cleveland. The two most important are standard units designed and used by the Bureau of the Census for data collection purposes. (See Figs. 1.1 and 1.2.)

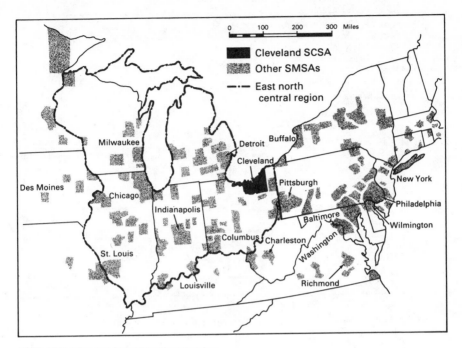

NOTE: SCSA = Standard Consolidated Statistical Area.

Fig. 1.1—Metropolitan Cleveland in the industrial north

The first is the Cleveland Standard Metropolitan Statistical Area (SMSA), which includes four northeast Ohio counties: Cuyahoga, Lake, Geauga, and Medina. SMSAs in the United States are typically defined as a single county or contiguous group of counties that contains a large city and its suburbs. The boundaries of the actual metropolitan entity (lines at the fringe where densities of population, auto travel, and other economic flows drop off sharply) usually fall within the county lines that demarcate the SMSA. Over the years, however, some metropolitan entities have grown beyond original SMSA borders and in a few cases have joined other metropolises.

This is essentially what has happened in greater Cleveland. Economic and other ties between the Cleveland SMSA, the Lorain-Elyria SMSA (Lorain County), and the Akron SMSA (Summit and Portage Counties) have grown strong enough that all three can be considered

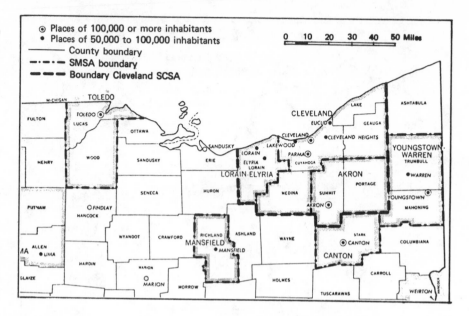

Fig. 1.2—Metropolitan Cleveland in northeast Ohio

as one metropolitan entity. Levels of interaction between these two other SMSAs and Cleveland have been significant at least since 1970. This is evidenced, for example, by commuting patterns in that year. A high percentage of all trips to work by Lorain-Elyria and Akron SMSA residents had destinations outside their own boundaries: 19 and 17 percent, respectively, in contrast to only three percent in the Cleveland SMSA. Most of these outward bound trips (89 percent in Lorain-Elyria and 82 percent in Akron) had destinations in the Cleveland SMSA. Linkages between these areas and neighboring counties and metropolitan areas (e.g., Youngstown-Warren, Canton) exist but are comparatively much weaker.

Recognizing these circumstances, the Bureau of the Census defined the Cleveland-Lorain-Akron SCSA to include the three SMSAs (seven counties). The SCSA runs about 75 miles along the southern shore of Lake Erie and stretches inland to the south from 25 to 60 miles at different locations. Altogether it covers 2,917 square miles: 1,519 (52 percent) are in the Cleveland SMSA, 456 (16 percent) in Cuyahoga County, and 76 (three percent) in the City of Cleveland.

Others have suggested that the SCSA is the appropriate unit for study and policy development in metropolitan Cleveland (see, for example, Norton, 1979). We agree with this view but have been unable to recognize it in this study. Comparable economic data in rich enough detail to enable us to move significantly beyond the conclusions of previous studies in our analysis are available only for the Cleveland SMSA at present. Thus, even though we present summary data for the SCSA in Chapter II, the rest of this report analyzes the economy of the Cleveland SMSA.

Leaving out the Akron and Lorain-Elyria SMSAs means that we have less to say about some industries (particularly rubber and chemicals) but it gives us more than an offsetting benefit in the depth with which we can analyze the rest of the economy. We believe that virtually all of our important findings are applicable to the SCSA as well as the SMSA. Expanding the data and the analysis to cover the SCSA as a whole, however, should be a priority task in future economic monitoring.

INDUSTRIES AND DATA SOURCES

Economic data for local areas almost always follow the classification scheme of the *Standard Industrial Classification (SIC) Manual* (Office of Management and Budget, 1972). We follow this system in our definitions of industries throughout this report. Within it, industries are divided into groups according to the nature of the goods or services they produce. Each establishment is assigned a multi-digit SIC code; in this report we use information from the system at four levels of detail.

The first digit designates the broad economic sector: agriculture (0); mining and construction (1); manufacturing (2, 3); transportation, communication, and utilities (4); wholesale and retail trade (5); finance, insurance, and real estate (6); and services (7, 8). Each sector is then divided into so-called two-digit categories and these are further subdivided into three- and four-digit categories. For example, blueprinting and photocopying services (SIC 7332) is a part of mailing, reproduction, commercial arts, and photography (SIC 733), which in turn is a part of the business service group (SIC 73) in the service sector. The production of aluminum sheet, plate, and foil (SIC 3353) is a component of rolling, drawing, and extruding of nonferrous metals (SIC 335), which is in turn a part of the primary metals group (SIC 33) in the manufacturing sector. The contents of the system will become more fully apparent as our analysis carries us down through its various levels in the chapters to follow.

In our analysis, we have relied on three sources of information. The first is a broad array of literature on aspects of economic development, some focusing on the Cleveland area and some discussing economic forces operating nationally and in other regions. (Our complete list of references is given at the end of the report.) Second, we benefitted substantially from over 40 interviews conducted as a part of the study. Most were with Cleveland-based individuals with special knowledge of the local economy (businessmen, government officials, university professors, and representatives of local utilities and other associations). Those interviewed, however, also included economists and others with expertise in development trends in other areas and in the nation as a whole.

Third, and most important, we have examined detailed statistical data on the metropolitan Cleveland economy drawn from several sources—for the most part, large-scale surveys conducted by state and federal government agencies. It is necessary to use data from several of these sources because each of them has different advantages and disadvantages for different parts of the analysis. One may contain highly detailed data, but only for one economic sector for a limited number of years. Others may have broader coverage over a long history but lack detail.

Where they do overlap, the numbers seldom match precisely. In some cases there can be sizable differences between sector employment totals, for example, in a given year. This does not mean that any of them are "wrong," however. Differences in account definitions, survey techniques, or the timing of the survey during the year can easily explain gaps in the numbers. In regional analysis, using data from several sources together usually creates a more reliable sense of economic change than using data from one alone.

In most cases, our use of the data entailed abstracting information for the Cleveland area and certain comparison areas from larger state or national data files. The files we created have been entered into the computer data base which, as we noted earlier, has been built as a starting point for ongoing monitoring. These files and their contents are noted in Appendix B.

II. AN OVERVIEW OF METROPOLITAN TRENDS

There is little doubt that metropolitan Cleveland entered a new era in the 1970s. Economic patterns that had been taken for granted for decades were no longer a sure thing. Disturbing shifts that had emerged quietly a number of years before were then no longer small enough to be ignored. In this chapter we summarize the measures of these changes, turning first to the size and characteristics of the population and then to trends in major sectors of the economy.

DEMOGRAPHY

In the century from 1870 to 1970, the population of the seven county Cleveland SCSA increased more than tenfold (from 270,000 to 3.0 million) (Fig. 2.1). The SCSA growth rate had been substantial from 1870 to 1900 (3.0 percent per year) but jumped even higher over the first three decades of this century (averaging 3.4 percent). After stability in the depression years, growth took off again, averaging 2.0 percent from 1940 to 1960, only to moderate during the 1960s (1.0 percent). As shown on the chart, the same general pattern was followed by the SMSA.

As late as 1920, 79 percent of the population in the SMSA lived in the City of Cleveland. Suburbanization began in earnest then, first in the remainder of Cuyahoga County and then in Lake, Geauga, and Medina Counties. By 1950 only 59 percent of the SMSA population lived in the city, whose population peaked in that year at 915,000. Ever since, the city's population has declined consistently.

The 1970s, however, was the first decade that saw the entire area lose population. The SCSA total dropped from 3.0 million in 1970 to 2.8 million in 1980 and the SMSA from 2.1 to 1.9 million. The city's population declined to 574,000 in 1980—less than two-thirds of its 1950 peak and only 30 percent of the 1980 SMSA population.

Comparison Areas

To understand the implications of Cleveland area population changes in the 1970s we must compare them to trends experienced in other areas. We have defined a consistent set of comparison units for

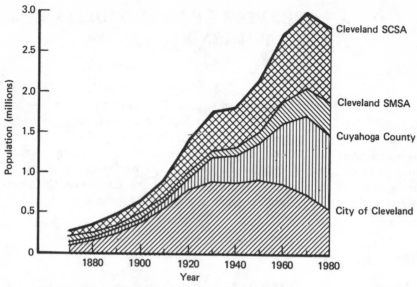

SOURCE: U.S. Department of Commerce, Bureau of the Census,
         Census of Population, various years.

Fig. 2.1—Metropolitan population, 1870-1980

use in this chapter, and as appropriate, the rest of this report. We compare Cleveland trends to those in the United States as a whole, to those in two contrasting regions, and to those in eight other metropolitan areas (SMSAs).

The two regions are the east north central region (defined by the Bureau of the Census to include the states of Illinois, Indiana, Michigan, Ohio, and Wisconsin) and a grouping of nine southern states (defined by us for the purposes of this study to include Alabama, Arkansas, Florida, Georgia, Mississippi, North Carolina, South Carolina, Tennessee, and Virginia). In the first comparison we wanted to see the extent to which trends in metropolitan Cleveland were simply representative of the region of which it is a part. In the second, we were particularly interested in comparing changes in Cleveland with those of areas known to be growing rapidly in manufacturing.

Actually, we did not set out to choose southern states. We selected all states that: (1) had an average manufacturing wage of $5 or less per production worker hour in 1977 and (2) experienced increases of 50,000 manufacturing employees or more from 1967 to 1977. The states listed above were the only ones that met both of these criteria.

The eight metropolitan areas include: Atlanta, Baltimore, Denver, Minneapolis, Pittsburgh, St. Louis, San Diego, and Seattle. They were selected as those nearest to the Cleveland SMSA in total population size (just above or below). As such, they represent Cleveland's natural competitors more than would, say, New York or, alternatively, a very small metropolis. Nonetheless, they exhibit a broad range of diversity with respect to regional location, economic structure, and recent economic trends.

Change in Total Population

Changes in total population for the Cleveland SMSA and the comparison areas in the 1960s and 1970s are given in Table 2.1. From 1970 to 1980 the United States population increased by 11.4 percent— a slower rate than the 13.4 percent recorded from 1960 to 1970. The well publicized shift to the sunbelt is highlighted by comparing the data for the two regions. The east north central region population grew at a rate just slightly below the U.S. rate in the 1960s but much more slowly than the nation in the 1970s. The southern states in contrast grew more rapidly than the nation in both periods; that area's 15.1 percent increase in the 1960s was only modestly higher than the national growth rate, but its 21.6 percent increase in the 1970s was almost twice the national rate.

Metropolitan area growth rates generally reflect these regional differences. Sunbelt SMSAs have generally grown much more rapidly than the United States as a whole and those in the northeast and north central regions have either grown slowly or declined. In the 1960s there were only a handful of SMSAs that experienced an absolute loss in population (Cleveland was not among them); over the 1970s, 28 of the nation's 282 SMSAs lost population (Cleveland was among them). All but one of the latter were in a northeasterly quadrant of the nation bounded by Duluth to the west and St. Louis to the south.

The Cleveland SMSA's 8.0 percent decline was the largest among the selected metropolitan areas shown on the table. Among the 56 SMSAs with 650,000 people or more in 1980, Cleveland's decline was equalled only by those of Buffalo (−8.0 percent) and New York City (−8.9 percent). It is difficult to make the case, however, that the population loss rates in the greater Cleveland area were really out of line with those of other major SMSAs in the north. We noted in Chapter I that the county boundaries that define the SMSA are not broad enough to encompass the entire interdependent urban area. In fact, the Cleveland SMSA (1,519 square miles) is comparatively small; the

Table 2.1

CHANGE IN TOTAL POPULATION, CLEVELAND SMSA
AND COMPARISON AREAS, 1960-80

Area	Total Pop. 1980 (000s)	Percent Change in Population	
		1960–70	1970–80
Central City			
Cleveland	574	-14.3	-23.8
Atlanta	425	1.6	-14.1
Baltimore	787	-3.5	-13.1
Denver	491	4.2	-4.5
Minneapolis	371	-10.0	-14.6
Pittsburgh	424	-13.4	-18.5
St. Louis	453	-17.0	-27.2
San Diego	876	21.7	25.5
Seattle	494	-4.7	-7.0
Standard Metropolitan Statistical Area (SMSA)			
Cleveland	1,899	8.1	-8.0
Atlanta	2,030	36.2	27.2
Baltimore	2,174	16.6	5.0
Denver	1,620	33.3	30.7
Minneapolis	2,114	32.6	7.6
Pittsburgh	2,264	-0.2	-5.7
St. Louis	2,355	14.5	-2.3
San Diego	1,862	31.4	37.1
Seattle	1,607	28.7	12.8
Other Comparison Areas			
United States Total	226,505	13.4	11.4
East North Central Region	41,670	11.1	3.4
Southern States	42,831	15.1	21.6

SOURCE: U.S. Department of Commerce, Bureau
of the Census (1978 and 1982).

Dallas SMSA, for example, covers 8,360 square miles and the Los Angeles-Long Beach SMSA, 4,069 square miles.

The question, then, is what happened to population in counties surrounding the Cleveland SMSA during the 1970s. If we look at the three other counties in the Cleveland SCSA we find that their population in total remained stable. The population of the SCSA as a whole dropped from 3.0 million in 1970 to 2.83 million in 1980, a decline of 5.5 percent. If we look at the ring of counties surrounding the SCSA we find modest population increases.[1] The full 18 county area (the SCSA plus 11 adjacent counties with a total area of 8,382 square miles) decreased in population from 4.52 million to 4.40 million, a decline of 2.8 percent.

While sunbelt SMSAs typically grew and northern ones declined, this pattern was not so consistent for central cities. They were much more likely to decline in all regions. Of the 56 large SMSAs noted above, 1970-80 central city population losses were experienced in 33; suburban population losses in only five. Thus suburbanization was far from dead in the past decade. The City of Cleveland's decline over the decade (23.8 percent) was more precipitous than that of any of our other comparison cities except St. Louis. Among the central cities of the 56 large SMSAs, Detroit and Buffalo were the only others whose loss rates exceeded 20 percent.

Population Characteristics

Because only a small portion of the information collected in the 1980 U.S. Census is yet available, a full and up-to-date comparison of changing population characteristics cannot be made at this point. The purposes of this summary, however, can be met using just three indicators: nonwhite population as a percentage of total, the elderly (age 65 and over) as a percentage of total, and the percentage whose incomes classify them as impoverished. The data are given in Table 2.2.

The percentage nonwhite increased in the nation as a whole from 12.6 in 1970 to 16.8 in 1980. In general, the geographic distribution of the nonwhite population did not change markedly in the 1970s; concentrations are still much higher in the south than the north. Nonwhite proportions increased in all of our comparison SMSAs and in all of their central cities. In almost all cases central city proportions remain significantly higher than those for the SMSAs. The numbers for the Cleveland area (SMSA and central city) do not stand out as

---

[1]Includes Erie, Huron, Ashland, Wayne, Columbiana, Ashtabula, Carrol, Stark, Richland, Mahoning, and Trumbull Counties.

Table 2.2

POPULATION CHARACTERISTICS, CLEVELAND SMSA
AND COMPARISON AREAS
(Percent of total population)

Area	Percent Nonwhite		Percent over 65 Years of Age		Percent in Poverty, 1979
	1970	1980	1970	1980	
Central City					
Cleveland	39.0	46.5	10.6	13.0	(*a*)
Atlanta	51.6	67.5	9.2	11.5	(*a*)
Baltimore	47.0	56.1	10.6	12.8	(*a*)
Denver	10.0	25.2	11.5	12.6	(*a*)
Minneapolis	5.7	12.7	15.0	15.4	(*a*)
Pittsburgh	20.7	25.3	13.5	16.0	(*a*)
St. Louis	41.3	46.5	14.7	17.6	(*a*)
San Diego	10.7	23.8	8.8	9.7	(*a*)
Seattle	11.7	20.5	13.1	15.4	(*a*)
Standard Metropolitan Statistical Area (SMSA)					
Cleveland	16.6	19.8	9.2	11.7	10.5
Atlanta	22.0	25.7	6.8	7.6	11.9
Baltimore	24.2	27.2	8.4	10.1	12.1
Denver	5.4	12.3	7.8	7.8	8.8
Minneapolis	2.6	5.0	8.9	9.5	6.3
Pittsburgh	7.3	8.5	10.7	13.3	8.0
St. Louis	16.1	18.3	9.9	11.7	10.3
San Diego	7.8	18.7	8.8	10.3	11.0
Seattle	6.0	10.1	8.5	9.9	7.6
Other Comparison Areas					
United States Total	12.6	16.8	9.9	11.3	12.5
East North Central Region	10.2	13.3	9.5	10.8	10.6
Southern States	22.3	22.6	10.0	12.0	15.5

SOURCE: U.S. Department of Commerce, Bureau of the Census (1973, 1980c and 1982).

*a*Data not available.

atypical either in relation to the proportionate size of the nonwhite population or its rate of change.

The same general conclusion can be reached about the age structure in the Cleveland area—its experience is not atypical. Like most of the other SMSAs (and the United States as a whole) the proportion of population that is elderly increased during the 1970s. The difference between central city and total SMSA proportions is much less marked than it was for the nonwhite population.

Data from the 1980 Census on poverty in central cities are not yet available, but poverty comparisons for the other areas remain of interest. The Cleveland SMSA indeed had a significant proportion of its population (10.5 percent) in poverty in 1979. That percentage was in the middle range of scores for our comparison SMSAs, substantially below that in the southern states, and only slightly smaller than the percentages in the total east north central region and the nation as a whole.

Migration

Migration patterns explain a great deal about a region's character. Again, with 1980 Census data not yet available, we are unable to explore recent trends. The topic is too important, however, to be avoided. We can at least note conclusions based on 1965-70 data for the Cleveland SMSA (data derived from U.S. Department of Commerce, Bureau of the Census, 1973).

The most relevant is that even though more people moved out of the Cleveland SMSA than moved in, the metropolis did not have an unusually high rate of outmigration (11.2 percent of 1970 total population five years of age or older). Comparable outmigration rates were, for example, 9.5 percent in Pittsburgh, 13.0 percent in Atlanta, and an average of 12.7 percent for all SMSAs nationally. Some of the fastest growing SMSAs, in fact, had higher rates of outmigration; Anaheim, California (18.6 percent), is a good example.

The reason for Cleveland's comparative net decline was a dearth of new people moving in rather than an excess of outmigrants. Cleveland's inmigration rate was 8.5 percent in contrast to 30.4 percent in Anaheim, 17.7 percent in Atlanta, and 14.8 percent in the typical U.S. SMSA (Pittsburgh's rate was 6.2 percent).

The data for that period show that the composition of both in- and outmigration in the Cleveland SMSA was also quite similar to that of other U.S. metropolitan areas, i.e., Cleveland was not losing or gaining younger and better educated residents any differently. Persons from 20 to 29 years of age accounted for 29.4 percent of all outmigrants in the Cleveland SMSA, 34.2 percent in the Pittsburgh SMSA, 29.8 percent in the Atlanta SMSA, and 28.0 percent in the average SMSA nationally. Males 16 years of age or older who qualified as professionals, managers, and craftsmen accounted for 13.7 percent of all outmigrants in Cleveland, 14.6 percent in Pittsburgh, 18.9 percent in Atlanta, and 14.0 percent in the typical SMSA.

ECONOMIC CHANGE

Growth has characterized change in the metropolitan economy throughout the post-World War II era. The size of an economy is most often measured by employment—the number of jobs it supports. In 1945, Cleveland SCSA private nonagricultural employment totaled 657,600. By 1980, it had grown by 59 percent to just over one million (1,044,500). The SMSA accounted for 756,600 jobs, 72 percent of this total. Many national media references to the Cleveland area's recent history have made heavy use of the term "decline"—appropriate enough when referring to population but not when referring to the metropolitan employment.[2]

Composition by County

All counties in the SCSA shared in this growth (see Fig. 2.2) but there were important differences in rates between the components. Over the 35-year period shown on the graph, Akron SMSA employment grew by only 0.9 percent per year and Cuyahoga County by 1.1 percent per year. Employment in the other counties (Lake, Geauga, Medina, and Lorain) expanded much more rapidly as suburbanization of both population and economic activity occurred. The total number of jobs in those counties in 1980 was almost four times what it had been in 1945 (an annual growth rate of 3.7 percent).

In 1980, Cuyahoga County still dominated the metropolitan economy but the extent of its dominance had diminished. It accounted for 63 percent of all SCSA employment then, compared to 69 percent in 1945. Over the period the Akron SMSA share of the total decreased

---

[2]In this and the next two paragraphs, we cite data from the Ohio Bureau of Employment Security (OBES), the only source that includes separate accounts for each Cleveland SCSA county over the 1945-80 period. Employment totals from this source are somewhat lower than those given in other sources because they include only those employees covered under the state unemployment compensation law. For example, total 1977 private nonagricultural employment for the Cleveland SMSA was reported as 737,000 by OBES, but 762,000 by the U.S. Department of Commerce, Bureau of Labor Statistics.

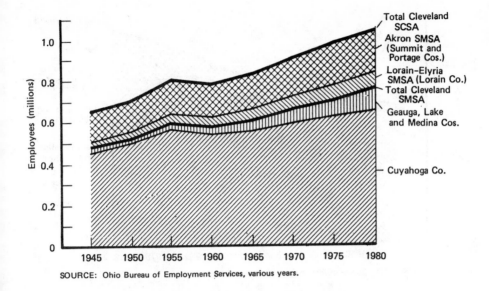

SOURCE: Ohio Bureau of Employment Services, various years.

Fig. 2.2—Metropolitan Cleveland private nonagricultural
employment by county, 1945-1980

from 24 to 20 percent and the share of the other counties increased
from seven to 17 percent.

Composition by Sector

More dramatic shifts appear when we examine changes in metropolitan employment by sector (Fig. 2.3). Employment in manufacturing, the historic mainstay of Cleveland's economy, remained
comparatively level through most of the postwar era, but then declined in the 1970s. The 1970 total, 428,200 employees, was just
slightly below the 1945 total. The number then declined to 380,800 in
1975, a recession year. The chart masks the fact that manufacturing
employment had rebounded to reach 401,300 in 1979, but the subse-
quent recession caused it to drop significantly again over the next
year alone. The 1980 total was 368,800, three percent below what it
had been at the low point of the 1975 recession. Over the decade, the
sector had suffered a net loss of 59,400 jobs (14 percent). The annual
rate of change in manufacturing employment from 1945 to 1980 was
−0.4 percent.

This loss was more than compensated for, however, by growth in

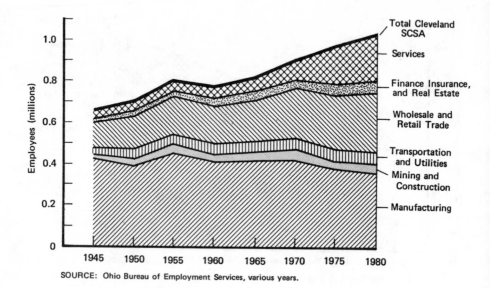

Fig. 2.3—Metropolitan Cleveland private nonagricultural
employment by sector, 1945-1980

nonmanufacturing activity. All of the other sectors shown on the
graph increased employment significantly over the 1945-80 period.
The slowest average annual growth rate was 1.7 percent for transportation and utilities. Three sectors had average rates in the two to
three percent range: mining (2.3 percent), wholesale and retail trade
(2.5 percent), and construction (2.8 percent). Finance, insurance, and
real estate activity grew by an average of 3.5 percent per year over
the period, but the highest growth rate was recorded by the service
sector, which grew on average by 4.0 percent annually.[3]

The effects of these changes on the structure of the metropolitan
economy have been substantial. In 1945, manufacturing accounted for
65 percent of all SCSA jobs but by 1980 it accounted for only 35
percent.

---

[3]Because of an important change in OBES coverage requirements in the early 1970s
that particularly affected the service sector, the 4.0 percent rate may be an overstate-
ment for that sector over the full 1945-80 period. From 1975-80, however, without any
such changes in data coverage, the SCSA service sector grew at an annual rate of 4.25
percent.

Comparisons with Other Areas

While in the aggregate there has been no cessation of employment growth in metropolitan Cleveland, its pace has been slower than that in the total national economy. In Fig. 2.4 we express Cleveland SCSA and total U.S. employment each year from 1945 through 1980 as index numbers (1945 = 100) to make the comparison directly at different points in time. Through the mid-1950s, there was little difference between the curves; both economies expanded and contracted with the business cycle at about the same pace. Thereafter, the gap began to widen. By 1980 the Cleveland index reached 159; i.e., SCSA employment had increased by 59 percent over its 1945 value. The national employment index was 215 in 1980; the U.S. economy had more than doubled in size in the same 35 years.

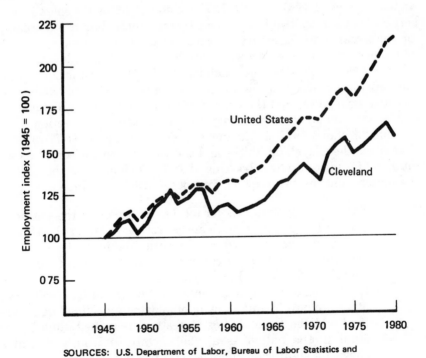

SOURCES: U.S. Department of Labor, Bureau of Labor Statistics and Ohio Bureau of Employment Services, various years.

Fig. 2.4—Index of total private nonagricultural employment, United States and Cleveland SCSA, 1945-1980

The contrast in the curves around the times of national recession (1958, 1961, 1971, and 1975) is noteworthy. Typically for Cleveland, the slope of the decline was steeper and the upturn was comparatively sluggish. This pattern has been common for America's large manufacturing centers in the postwar era (Vernez et al., 1977, and Victor and Vernez, 1981).

Changes by Sector

How do the employment changes in Cleveland's major economic sectors that we noted earlier compare with trends elsewhere? To answer this question, we focus on only the recent past and present data for the comparison areas defined earlier in addition to the United States as a whole.

The selection of points in time over which change is measured makes a difference. Here, and frequently in other parts of this report, we use data as of 1967 and 1977. These points define the most recent periods that satisfy two key criteria. First, ample data are available for each year (only summary information on a few measures of economic performance are now available for metropolitan Cleveland for the years since 1977). Second, each point falls at about the same position (during upturns) on the business cycle (see Fig. 2.4). Obviously, measuring changes from the peak of the cycle to the trough of a later one (or vice versa) could seriously distort our sense of direction.

Table 2.3 shows 1977 employment levels as well as 1967-77 rates of change for the Cleveland SMSA and the various comparison units, in total and for major sectors. Looking at 1967-77 change, for the SMSA, the nation, and the two regions, four observations are relevant:

- The annual growth rate for total employment in the southern states (3.1 percent) significantly exceeded that for the United States (2.1 percent) which, in turn, significantly exceeded that for the east north central region (1.4 percent) and the Cleveland SMSA (0.6 percent).
- In all four of these areas, manufacturing did less well than other sectors. Manufacturing employment declined in Cleveland and the Great Lakes states and remained almost constant in the nation as a whole. Only the southern states showed a significant increase (1.9 percent annually).
- Although Cleveland SMSA employment increased in all other sectors, in every case its growth rate was exceeded by that of the east north central region which, in turn, was exceeded by the U.S. average. Again, southern states employ-

Table 2.3

1977 EMPLOYMENT AND 1967-77 RATES OF CHANGE IN EMPLOYMENT, CLEVELAND SMSA AND COMPARISON AREAS

Area	Total	Manufac- turing	Services	Retail & Wholesale Trade	Other Sectors
Number of Employees, 1977 (millions)					
Cleveland SMSA	.76	270.8	168.0	201.7	121.8
United States	67.18	19,647.0	15,249.0	18,492.0	13,789.0
East North Central Reg.	13.60	4,932.6	2,782.4	3,575.0	2,314.9
Southern States	11,586.3	3,738.1	2,332.0	3,157.2	2,359.0
Atlanta SMSA	686.2	131.3	159.0	230.7	165.2
Baltimore SMSA	671.9	161.2	163.6	197.3	149.8
Denver SMSA	548.3	104.9	137.2	169.0	137.2
Minneapolis SMSA	817.8	220.6	198.2	241.3	157.7
Pittsburgh SMSA	789.5	249.2	189.1	197.3	153.9
St. Louis SMSA	822.3	250.9	190.8	221.5	159.1
San Diego SMSA	406.1	78.9	114.5	125.1	87.6
Seattle SMSA	520.8	126.1	119.2	155.8	119.7
Annual Percent Change in Employment, 1967-77					
Cleveland SMSA	.6	-1.4	3.5	2.0	.1
United States	2.1	.1	4.3	3.1	2.0
East North Central Reg.	1.4	-.5	4.0	2.5	1.2
Southern States	3.1	1.9	5.6	4.4	3.1
Atlanta SMSA	4.8	1.2	7.5	5.1	3.1
Baltimore SMSA	.8	2.6	3.5	2.3	.9
Denver SMSA	5.0	3.6	6.2	5.1	5.0
Minneapolis SMSA	2.8	.9	5.3	6.6	1.8
Pittsburgh SMSA	-.4	-1.6	3.0	2.0	-3.6
St. Louis SMSA	.7	-1.6	3.5	2.1	.2
San Diego SMSA	5.7	2.8	6.7	6.3	6.6
Seattle SMSA	1.7	-2.7	5.4	3.6	2.3

SOURCE: Rand analysis of data from U.S. Department of Labor, Bureau of Labor Statistics (1979c and 1979d).

ment grew faster than national employment in every category.

- In all four areas, the service sector outperformed all others: wholesale and retail trade always ranked second, the "other" category third, and manufacturing fourth.

In comparing Cleveland's growth to that in the other metropolitan areas, the following conclusions are relevant:

- While there were differences, 1967-77 growth rates in the Cleveland SMSA and other northeast and north central metropolises were essentially in the same range. Growth in the sunbelt SMSAs was much faster, particularly in Denver and San Diego (whose annual increases exceeded five percent).
- In the SMSAs, the pattern of change among sectors was consistently similar to that we have noted for the nation and the two regions. In every case, the service sector grew most rapidly and the manufacturing sector either grew less rapidly or decreased.

Changes in Sector Shares

Among all of our comparison units, Cleveland had the highest share of total employment in manufacturing (43 percent) in 1967 (Table 2.4). Atlanta, Denver, and San Diego were the least manufacturing-oriented (ranging from 22 to 26 percent, respectively). The shares in services and trade were remarkably consistent. In all areas the 1967 service sector share ranged from 16 to 25 percent. Except for Atlanta, Denver, and San Diego, all of the 1967 shares in wholesale and retail trade fell in the 20 to 28 percent range.

Directions of change in sector shares from 1967 to 1977 were almost always the same. In all areas the percentage of total employment in services increased significantly and the share in manufacturing declined. Trade experienced a modest increase in all areas except the Denver SMSA where its share remained constant.

Consistency in Population and Employment Trends

It might at first seem surprising that Cleveland area employment increased during the 1970s whereas local population declined. The underlying forces that explain these changes, however, are quite consistent with those operating nationally over the period. Two are most important. First, the baby boom generation moved into the labor

Table 2.4

SECTOR SHARES OF TOTAL EMPLOYMENT, CLEVELAND SMSA AND COMPARISON AREAS, 1967-77

Area		Total	Manu- fact.	Services	Retail & Wholesale Trade	Other Sectors
		Percent of Total				
Cleveland SMSA	1967	100.0	43.4	16.6	23.0	17.0
	1977	100.0	35.5	22.0	26.5	16.0
United States	1967	100.0	35.7	18.5	25.0	20.8
	1977	100.0	29.3	22.7	27.5	20.5
East No. Central Reg.	1967	100.0	43.5	15.8	23.4	17.3
	1977	100.0	36.3	20.4	26.3	17.0
Southern States	1967	100.0	37.7	16.4	24.9	21.0
	1977	100.0	32.3	20.1	27.2	20.4
Atlanta SMSA	1967	100.0	25.6	16.9	30.8	26.7
	1977	100.0	19.1	23.2	33.6	24.1
Baltimore SMSA	1967	100.0	33.7	18.7	25.5	22.1
	1977	100.0	24.0	24.3	29.4	22.3
Denver SMSA	1967	100.0	22.0	22.4	30.5	25.1
	1977	100.0	19.2	25.0	30.8	25.0
Minneapolis SMSA	1967	100.0	32.4	18.9	27.5	21.2
	1977	100.0	27.0	24.2	29.5	19.3
Pittsburgh SMSA	1967	100.0	35.9	17.2	19.8	27.1
	1977	100.0	31.6	23.9	25.0	19.5
St. Louis SMSA	1967	100.0	38.5	17.7	23.5	20.3
	1977	100.0	30.5	23.2	26.9	19.4
San Diego SMSA	1967	100.0	25.7	25.6	28.9	19.8
	1977	100.0	19.4	28.2	30.8	21.6
Seattle SMSA	1967	100.0	37.6	15.9	24.9	21.6
	1977	100.0	24.2	22.9	29.9	23.0

SOURCE: Rand analysis of data from U.S. Department of Labor, Bureau of Labor Statistics (1979c and 1979d).

force, and second, a much larger percentage of all working age women sought employment. There was thus an immense increase in the absolute number of people wanting to work and, by and large, the national economy created jobs for them.

As a result the number of employed persons per thousand population increased in the United States as a whole, from 267 in 1967 to 296 in 1977. Traditionally, a higher proportion of the total population in the Cleveland area has been employed. In the Cleveland SMSA the number of workers per thousand population increased from 344 in 1967 to 383 in 1977. In both areas (the United States and the SMSA) the ratio increased at the same rate (by 11 percent over the decade).

Components of Change

Traditionally available data on employment show only the total number of jobs in specific sectors and industries at various points in time. Therefore, an analyst interested in change can examine only the net difference between the totals at the start and end of some period, as we have done earlier in this chapter. While obviously valuable, this approach does not convey a full understanding of the dynamics of job generation.

In the last few years, David Birch and his colleagues at M.I.T. have examined a data source that provides much more complete information on the process—a file created by the Dun and Bradstreet Corporation that traces the individual employment histories of roughly 80 percent of the nation's business establishments in the early 1970s. Use of this file enabled Birch to measure not only net employment change, but also the "components of change," i.e., gains and losses. Employment gains in an area occur when establishments are initially set up (births), expand, or move into the area from outside. Losses occur when establishments go out of business (deaths), lay off staff (contractions), or move out of the area.

Data from these studies for metropolitan Cleveland and all U.S. SMSAs (1969-72) are shown in Table 2.5. It is clear that net change numbers mask a tremendous amount of turnover that goes on each year in the economy. The Cleveland firms included in Table 2.5 actually suffered gross job losses three times the size of their ultimate net loss (179 per thousand initial employees vs. 60), but they also generated a substantial number of replacement jobs (119 per thousand initial employees). Summarizing national data for periods through 1976, Birch (1981) found a surprising degree of consistency in the gross loss rate. About eight percent of the jobs in the U.S. economy are terminated each year, implying that over a five-year period the economy has to generate replacement jobs equal to about half of the total at the start if it wants to come out even at the end. The point deserving emphasis is that in the 1970s the economy did that and more.

Table 2.5

COMPONENTS OF EMPLOYMENT CHANGE, CLEVELAND SMSA
AND ALL U.S. SMSAs, 1969-72
(Per thousand employees, 1969)

Type of Change	Cleveland SMSA		All U.S. SMSAs Total
	Total	Manufac- turing	
Total Employment, December 1969	1,000	1,000	1,000
Employment Losses			
Deaths of existing establishments	-99	-88	-117
Contractions of existing establishments	-79	-73	-98
Outmigration of establishments	-1	-1	-2
Total losses	-179	-162	-217
Employment Gains			
Births of new establishments	39	16	56
Expansions of existing establishments	79	53	120
Inmigration of establishments	1	1	2
Total gains	119	70	178
Net Change in Employment	-60	-92	-39
Total Employment, December 1972	940	908	961

SOURCE: Allman and Birch (1975).

While the data in Table 2.5 are partial and cover only the early part of the decade, they are enough to demonstrate that metropolitan Cleveland is not significantly different from the nation in this regard. We can be sure that even in manufacturing, which suffered a net decline in employment, there were many new jobs created, just not enough to offset gross losses. If this had not occurred, net declines would have been substantially greater than they turned out to be.

It is also important to note that the gross loss area for total Cleveland employment was not much different than that for all U.S.

SMSAs; in fact, it was somewhat lower than the average. Birch found that gross loss rates were quite similar in all parts of the country. High growth states and cities in the sunbelt lost about the same percentage of jobs each year as slow growth states and cities in the north. The differences in their performance occurred on the other side of the ledger: high growth areas generated many more new jobs. An obvious implication for economic development policy is that incentives for a higher level of job creating activity are more important in older industrial areas than attempts to reduce losses; significant turnover appears to be normal and inevitable in a healthy economy.

Also noteworthy is that the migration of business establishments played an insignificant role in local and national SMSA employment change in the early 1970s. Birch found that this was true in all parts of the country. Virtually all employment gains are created by births and expansions. Almost all losses occur from establishment deaths and contractions. An implication often drawn from this finding is that encouraging new firms to start up and existing firms to expand deserves much more emphasis in local economic development than efforts to get establishments now located elsewhere to pull up stakes and move.

Unemployment Rates

The unemployment rate is often used as a summary measure of a region's economic health. The measure has many imperfections (see, for example, Bloom and Northrup, 1976) but it is probably most useful in making comparisons between different areas over time as we have done in Fig. 2.5. There we have plotted quarterly unemployment rates for the Cleveland SMSA, the Detroit SMSA, and the United States as a whole from 1970 through 1980.

While the general business cycle pattern is evident for all three areas over the decade, there are surprising differences among them. The unemployment rates for the United States and for the Cleveland SMSA fluctuated in the four to eight percent range through the period. Most notable is that except for the recession periods, Cleveland's unemployment rate was significantly below the national rate. That this is not typical for older industrial centers is illustrated by the curve for Detroit, which sat higher than the curve for the United States throughout and peaked substantially above the U.S. and Cleveland rates in the recessions.

Thus, while most northern industrial areas have experienced roughly similar changes in employment over the past decade, the momentary effects of their problems have not always been the same. One

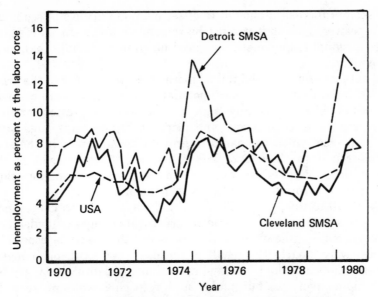

SOURCES: U.S. Department of Labor, Bureau of Labor Statistics and
Ohio Bureau of Employment Services, various years.

Fig. 2.5—Quarterly unemployment rates, Cleveland SMSA,
Detroit SMSA, and total United States, 1970-1980

factor that might explain the differences in the Cleveland and Detroit experiences is the difference in the industrial diversity of the two areas. This relationship will be examined in Chapter III.

SURFACE TRENDS

The picture we have painted in this chapter is disturbing, particularly when recent trends are compared with typical expectations of the 1960s. Then, even though problems in the central city were apparent, growth in the metropolis as a whole was to be counted on. Now we find that Cleveland and a number of other metropolitan areas have begun to lose population.

Perhaps more troubling for the Cleveland area is the recent absolute decline in manufacturing employment. Manufacturing accounts for such a large share of the area's work force that declines in that sector seem particularly threatening. The fact that employment in other sectors increased enough to offset manufacturing's losses is indeed a positive sign, but it must be remembered that in all of these sectors national employment increased much more rapidly than local employment.

The data we reviewed did tell us more about the nature of the problem. We found that neither local population nor employment changes were explained by unusually high loss rates (outmigration, or firm deaths and contractions) as some media accounts have suggested. Rather, at least when compared to growing urban areas in the sunbelt, metropolitan Cleveland falls behind on the other side of the ledger with low rates of inmigration and comparatively small employment increases from firm births and expansions.

Still, in all of this, it is difficult to find ways in which Cleveland's performance has been unique. Basic structural changes (sluggish performance in manufacturing and growth in other sectors, especially services) were clearly the result of national, not local, phenomena. The performance of the Cleveland area economy definitely lagged behind national averages, but in almost all respects it was similar to the performance of most older manufacturing centers in the northeast and north central regions.

What does this mean for Cleveland's future? Is the area destined simply to follow along with the rest of America's industrial heartland in a pattern of continued decline, or are there features of the local economy that create opportunities for a different path?

Surely, conjectures at this point would be premature. If there is anything the volatile 1970s have taught us, it is that projecting surface trends like those reviewed in this chapter implies considerable risk. We need to look deeper into the underlying structure of the metropolitan economy and to understand which industries are most important to the Cleveland area and why.

PART B

HOW THE CLEVELAND ECONOMY
WORKS

Efforts to deal with the problems facing the Cleveland metropolitan area will be more successful if they are based on a sound understanding of how the regional economy works and what exactly has been happening to it over the recent past. Part B treats the first of these questions. We begin in Chapter III by presenting a summary of some of the basic principles of regional economics and then proceed to use those principles to interpret some of the data available about the Cleveland economy. We based this discussion on two very general ideas. First, we assume that most large changes in the Cleveland economy are brought about by changes in sales of the things Cleveland exports to the rest of the nation and the world. Second, we are not as concerned with the regional economy per se as with the effects of changes in the regional economy on the lives of Cleveland area residents. Analysis of the metropolitan economy, therefore, should be aimed at determining how changes in the region's competitive position as an exporter could affect the quality of life in Cleveland.

III. CLEVELAND'S ECONOMIC RELATIONSHIPS

OVERVIEW

A summary understanding of the main steps in the process by which changes in exports affect the quality of life in a region is depicted in Fig. 3.1.

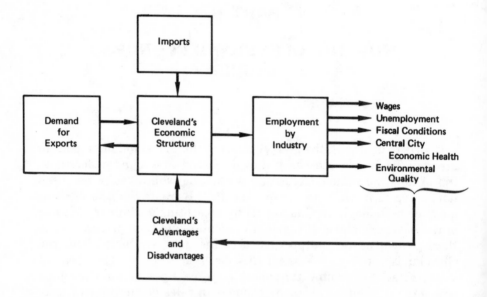

Fig. 3.1—Schematic of the Cleveland economy

The scheme begins with exports, and this reflects our assumption: to understand Cleveland's position as an exporter is to understand the key source of change in the regional economy. Economic changes in Cleveland can actually be stimulated by any number of events such as changes in local consumption patterns, increases in local production of items that had previously been imported, or even such events as the scheduling of the major league All Star Game in Cleveland. However, nothing we have found out so far about the Cleveland economy contradicts the presupposition that the competitive position in U.S. and world markets of the metropolitan area's major industries is the key determinant of its economic health.

Two general observations about exports will complete the preliminary discussion of this part of the schema. First, one usually thinks of exports as involving the shipment of goods out of the region. For the most part this is a correct view of Cleveland's exports, but it is also important to remember that services can be exported too. When a patient from Illinois comes to the Cleveland Clinic for surgery, or when a firm with headquarters in Atlanta holds a regional sales meeting at the Stouffer's Inn on the Square, services are being exported. Similarly, retail and wholesale sales can, in part, be export industries as can transportation and communication services.

Second, the interaction between sales of exports to the rest of the world and the health of regional economy works in two ways. This reflects two basic determinants of each Cleveland industry's sales to the rest of the world: worldwide (or United States, or north central regional, or Ohio) demand for the product in question *and* the price of goods produced in Cleveland compared with those produced elsewhere. The higher Cleveland's relative price, the smaller its share of the total market for a good or service. The prices of Cleveland's exports depend, in turn, on the advantages and disadvantages of doing business and living in the region—i.e., the local prices of productive inputs.

The next element of the schema is the regional economy. This box in the diagram represents two characteristics of the Cleveland economy: the structure of interindustry relationships and the local economic environment—the advantages and disadvantages mentioned above.[1]

What do we mean by "the structure of interindustry relationships?" When a Cleveland firm receives an order from outside the metropolitan area it must purchase inputs—labor, raw materials, semifinished goods, and, possibly, some new machines and new factory and office space. Some of these purchases will be from firms and individuals located outside the metropolitan area, that is, some inputs will be supplied through imports. However, most labor and any other inputs that are available at competitive prices locally will be purchased or rented from Cleveland firms and households. These local suppliers will then increase their production and buy some of their own inputs from other local firms, and so on. Furthermore, the employees whose jobs were generated by the new export will spend a large part of their wages in Cleveland, expanding activity in the retail sales industry and its local suppliers. Each new export, therefore, stimulates a whole

---

[1] Chapter IV is a discussion of Cleveland's environment for economic activity.

chain of economic exchanges and these exchanges, taken as a whole, are what we call "the structure of interindustry relationships."

In an economy as large as Cleveland's there are millions of such relationships. It is clearly impossible to comprehend the structure of the local economy in all its details. However, economists have developed a number of tools for organizing and aggregating data on these relationships and summarizing what the data mean. Later in this chapter we will explain and present a statistic that summarizes interindustry relationships in the Cleveland economy.

By this process each order for exports works its way through the Cleveland economy stimulating a specific mix of activities in other industries. Taken together, the region's exports generate all local activity, and the industrial composition of exports determines the industrial composition of the entire regional economy. Exports of steel, machine tools, medical services, convention facilities, and so on will stimulate a certain amount of employment in all other industries. Total employment and its industrial composition, in turn, generate all of the elements of the quality of life of the residents of Cleveland. Total employment and its composition determine the aggregate level of income in the metropolitan area, the unemployment rate, the level of tax revenues and, therefore, affect the quality of public services, economic conditions in the central city as compared with the suburbs, and so on. The quality of life, taken as a whole, determines the kinds of people who will be attracted to Cleveland and, therefore, affects how hard or easy it is for firms to hire labor. Hence, the quality of life, through what systems analysts call a "feedback mechanism," influences the competitive position of Cleveland firms in the world market.

Figure 3.1 presents an overview of how exports influence and are influenced by the quality of life in the region. The rest of this chapter fills in this general schema with Cleveland data. The next section describes one of the ways in which economists summarize the millions of relationships that make up the structure of the local economy and presents a statistic that summarizes these interactions. It concludes with an analysis of the hypothesis that, whatever the apparent complexity of Cleveland's economic structure, the regional economy is tied so closely to the automobile industry that the picture is really very simple. The following section uses the same economic tools to estimate the industrial composition of Cleveland's net exports for local industries. The final section examines the relationships along some of the arrows on the righthand side of Fig. 3.1.

SUMMARIZING THE STRUCTURE OF THE CLEVELAND ECONOMY

When exports to the rest of the world by a firm located in Cleveland increase, as noted previously, some proportion of the inputs used by the exporting firm to increase production will be purchased locally. Other inputs will be imported from outside the metropolitan area. Among all inputs—labor, raw materials, semifinished goods, office space, factory space, machines, etc.—the most important to the community is labor. Most labor is "purchased" locally and most of the income labor receives is spent locally on consumer goods. Hence, to a large extent, the degree of stimulus provided to the local economy by an increase in exports by a given firm depends on what proportion of the firm's inputs consists of labor. Other inputs may also be purchased locally. Which inputs and what proportion of total inputs are purchased locally depend on the nature of the firm's production technology and the industrial composition of the local economy. Exports by firms that use a large proportion of inputs that happen to be produced in large proportions locally will stimulate the local economy more than will exports by firms that use a lot of imported inputs.

Economists at the U.S. Department of Commerce have developed a method for combining information about the production technology of firms in different industries and about the specific industrial composition of regional economies into a tool that allows us to summarize the stimulus generated by new export business for Cleveland's major industries.[2]

The Commerce Department method assumes that Cleveland firms in a given narrowly defined (usually four-digit) industry use the same production technology—that is, the same mix of labor, machines, raw materials, telephone calls, business trips, and so on—as the average U.S. firm in the same industry in 1972. They assume further that all labor is purchased locally and that Cleveland firms producing productive inputs (raw materials, semifinished goods, business services) export their products only after all local demand is met. This last point should be explicated a bit further. Consider the input classified as "metal forming machine tools" (SIC 3541). Cleveland firms, given their current level of operations, will want to purchase a certain value of metal forming machine tools each year. If this is less than or equal to the total value of such machine tools produced in Cleveland, then it is assumed that all local demand for this input will be met by local

---

[2]The Commerce Department's techniques for regionalizing the 1972 U.S. input-output table are described and evaluated in Cartwright, Biemiller, and Gustely (1981). A description of how we used the Commerce Department's Cleveland I-O Table to perform the computations presented in this report is found in Appendix C.

machine tool manufacturers. It is also assumed that if there is any excess over local demand for metal forming machine tools produced by Cleveland firms in SIC 3541 it will be exported. By contrast, if local firms in SIC 3541 produced fewer machine tools than are required as inputs by other local firms, all local production is assumed to be sold locally and, in addition, some machine tools are imported. These assumptions allow us to estimate the effects on the local economy as a whole of any given increase in the value of exports by any given local industry without actual observations of how much each Cleveland firm purchases or sells locally.

These somewhat unrealistic assumptions—that Cleveland technology today is the same as the 1972 U.S. average and that Cleveland firms will not buy machine tools from other cities as long as total local production exceeds total local demand—may render the figures in Table 3.1 somewhat inaccurate. Small differences across sectors are probably spurious, but the assumptions are probably realistic enough to lend credibility to the estimates of gross differences across sectors.

One way of summarizing all of the information generated by the Commerce Department's approach to regional input-output analysis is to compute a summary statistic for each industry called a "multiplier." A multiplier indicates how much total local income will be generated by an increase in export business for an individual industry. A multiplier of, say, 1.3 for industry I, indicates that if export sales of industry I increase by $1 million, total revenues of all Cleveland firms will increase by $1.3 million. Multipliers for Cleveland industries as estimated by the Commerce Department method are reported in Table 3.1.

Inspection of this table immediately indicates one thing: many of the highest multipliers are found among Cleveland's "anchor industries"—the durable goods manufacturing sectors—indicating that the heavy industrial sectors are able to purchase a large proportion of their inputs locally. That is, Cleveland is able to manufacture durable goods essentially from start to finish. This is in marked contrast to the typical U.S. metropolitan area in which the highest multipliers tend to be found among the service sectors.

Data on multipliers for the same industries in the United States as a whole (from Pascal and Gurwitz, forthcoming) show that those sectors with the highest multipliers in Cleveland do not, on average, generate the most stimulus elsewhere. We found that the rank order correlation between Cleveland SMSA and average U.S. multipliers was only 0.44. In other words, Cleveland's economic structure is different from the average region's, and this difference is summarized by the uniquely stimulative role of the durable goods manufacturing industries in the local economy.

Table 3.1

EARNINGS MULTIPLIERS FOR CLEVELAND
SMSA INDUSTRIES, 1978

Industry	Earnings Multiplier
Durable Goods Manufacturing	
Primary Metals	2.55
Fabricated Metals	2.74
Nonelectrical Machinery	2.70
Electrical Machinery	2.49
Motor Vehicles	2.71
Other Transport Equipment	2.88
Instruments	2.55
Miscellaneous Manufactures	2.61
Nondurable Goods Manufacturing	
Stone Products	2.13
Textiles	2.07
Apparel	1.94
Paper Products	2.11
Printing	2.51
Chemicals	2.41
Rubber Products	2.46
Lumber Products	2.60
Food Processing	2.42
Sales	
Retail Sales	2.33
Eating and Drinking Est.	2.42
Wholesale Sales	2.43
Services	
Finance	2.61
Insurance	2.89
Leasing	1.50
Hotels	2.40
Personal Services	2.76
Business Services	2.44
Health Services	2.31
Other	
Transportation	2.51
Communications	2.01
Utilities	1.92
Construction	2.69
Agriculture	2.18

SOURCE: Rand analysis of Cleveland SMSA input-output relationships based on data from U.S. Department of Commerce, Bureau of Economic Analysis. (See Appendix C.)

METROPOLITAN CLEVELAND'S EXPORTS

Multipliers measure the degrees to which exports by different industries stimulate the metropolitan economy. This, though, tells only part of the story of how regional economic change has taken or could take place. We see from Table 3.1, for example, that exports of financial services could provide a relatively high degree of stimulus to the Cleveland economy. A multiplier of 2.61 does not indicate whether, in fact, this industry does bring income into the metropolitan area. If Cleveland's financial sector—its banks, holding companies, brokerage houses, and so on—actually provides services only to Clevelanders, then the multiplier represents an unrealized potential. This section, therefore, goes on to estimate the degrees to which different industries have brought income into the metropolitan area by exporting their products over the 1970s.

In addition to indicating Cleveland's export specialties and the recent changes in this region's role in the U.S. and world economies, this analysis also suggests, in part, which type of export earnings would be easiest to generate in the near future. Presumably it would be easier for the region to generate earnings by continuing to sell things non-Clevelanders are already used to coming to Cleveland to buy than to market products and services for which the region is less well known. The latter is not impossible, but the cost of marketing would be much higher to induce people to take their winter vacations in Cleveland than to induce them to come there to buy their machine tools.

Table 3.2 presents our findings about the composition of Cleveland's exports.

Before going on to discuss individual findings it may be useful to state precisely what each number of the list represents. Table 3.2 tells us, for example, that in 1978 there were 6,040 more employees in the instruments manufacturing industry than were needed to produce enough instruments to meet the demand by local firms and households for these products. The figure 6,040 was 92 percent of total employment in this industry in Cleveland in 1978. By way of contrast, Cleveland chemical manufacturers, even though they employed 11,209 employees in 1978, would have had to hire 15,729 more workers to satisfy the entire local demand for their products.

The phrasing of the last paragraph reveals a limitation of the input-output approach and, indeed, of any aggregative tool of economic analysis. Each sector included in the model is assumed to produce a single, perfectly uniform product. Thus, there is only one "chemical" and only one type of "transportation vehicle." The model does not admit the possibility that Cleveland might both export and import

Table 3.2

TOTAL EMPLOYMENT AND EXPORT EMPLOYMENT IN CLEVELAND SMSA INDUSTRIES, 1978

Industry	Total Employment	Estimated Export Employment	Percent Export Employment
Durable Goods Manufacturing			
Primary Metals	30,661	2,706	9
Fabricated Metals	43,832	34,253	78
Nonelectrical Machinery	45,116	36,159	80
Electrical Equipment	22,065	18,274	83
Motor Vehicles	22,088	9,078	41
Other Transport Equipment	5,875	5,111	87
Instruments	6,562	6,040	92
Miscellaneous Manufactures	4,166	3,904	94
Nondurable Goods Manufacturing			
Stone Products	4,295	1,789	42
Textiles	1,970	1,771	90
Apparel	8,091	-301	--
Paper Products	4,692	1,416	30
Printing	13,927	-2,047	--
Chemicals	11,209	-15,729	--
Rubber Products	11,224	-7,673	68
Lumber Products	3,745	3,369	90
Food Processing	8,909	-21,168	--
Sales			
Retail Sales	106,930	18,338	17
Eating and Drinking Est.	40,424	3,079	8
Wholesale Sales	60,748	11,226	18
Services			
Finance	14,882	5,464	37
Insurance	15,650	15,650	(a)
Leasing	10,531	-35,930	--
Hotels	7,594	5,860	77
Personal Services	9,505	-7,882	--
Business Services	47,247	14,879	36
Health Services	52,170	12,710	24
Other Services	41,512	-6,724	--
Other			
Transportation	26,782	-4,117	--
Communications	12,808	-5,513	--
Utilities	8,372	-16,347	--
Construction	33,738	19,220	56
Agriculture	1,516	1,381	91

SOURCE: Rand analysis of Cleveland SMSA input-output relationships based on data from U.S. Department of Commerce, Bureau of Economic Analysis. (See Appendix C.)

NOTE: A negative sign indicates that the industry is a net importer.

[a]Probable error in the data.

transportation vehicles. Thus, while a very large percentage of the output of the Ford plant in Cleveland might be shipped to other parts of the country, the model indicates that only 41 percent of employment in the motor vehicle manufacturing industry is devoted to producing for export. What, then, do these numbers really mean?

When we say that some number or some percentage of employees in sector I is producing for "export" what we mean, more precisely, is that, given what we know about employment levels in other industries in the Cleveland area, there is still an unexpectedly large number of employees in sector I in Cleveland. Consider the case of the fabricated metals industry. One would ordinarily expect that a region whose economic base was heavy industry would have a large fabricated metals sector because fabricated metals are both important inputs and outputs of heavy industrial processes. What the numbers in Table 3.2 indicate is that even given the high levels of employment in the primary metals, nonelectrical machinery, motor vehicles, and other heavy manufacturing sectors, there is still a high concentration of fabricated metals employment in Cleveland. In fact, there were some 34,253 more such employees than one would expect in that industry, if only local needs were being met.

By contrast, given the heavy concentration of industries using steel, aluminum, and so on, even some 30,000 workers in the primary metals industry produce only a few more of their products than are used locally. This is not to say that almost as much steel as Republic and Jones and Laughlin produce accumulates in Cleveland each year, but that this steel is processed further and is exported from Cleveland as auto parts, machine tools, medical instruments, and so on.

One general impression of the Cleveland economy that emerges from the data in Table 3.2 is of substantial economic diversity. Cleveland produces some of almost everything, with the exception of such patently nonmetropolitan activities as agriculture and mining,[3] and exports substantial amounts of a large number of things to the rest of the world. This diversity is a characteristic that Cleveland shares with many of the other major metropolitan areas of the United States. In other words, by no stretch of the imagination can Cleveland be thought of as a "mill town." This diversity offers two distinct benefits to the metropolitan economy. First, the diversity acts as a cushion against fluctuations in the national economy. At any point in the national business cycle there is probably at least one industry that is doing well and can, therefore, to some extent, support the rest of the local economy. The relatively low average unemployment rate

---

[3]There are so few observations of firms in these industries in Cleveland that any "results" reported in the table must be viewed as spurious.

enjoyed by Cleveland as compared with some other cities in the northeast-north central region is, in part at least, probably the result of this diversity of the local economy (see Chapter II). The second advantage of diversity is that it offers a wide variety of opportunities for economic development. Increases in U.S. or worldwide demands for a wide variety of products could be translated into growth for the regional economy, given the right combination of local policies and a large enough cadre of local entrepreneurs. In other words, there are relatively few paths of economic development for which Cleveland would have to start from scratch.

At the same time as it illustrates Cleveland's basic economic diversity, Table 3.1 also gives us a more specific indication of the metropolitan area's relative economic specialty. Table 3.1 focused our attention on the traditional anchor industries as likely sources of stimulus to general economic development. Table 3.2 allows us to distinguish among the anchor industries and suggests that Cleveland's particular specialties are fabricated metals, nonelectrical machinery, and, to some extent, electrical equipment. The export employment figures for the other two traditional anchor industries are, in fact, somewhat surprising. Neither primary metals nor transportation vehicles employs a large number or large proportion of export employees. While these industries may, in fact, be heavily concentrated in Cleveland (see Chapter V), they are not much more heavily concentrated in this region than one would expect, given the general local density of durable goods manufacturing industries. This finding allows us to move beyond the general characterization of Cleveland as a center of durable goods manufacturing and to specify that this economy's specific role in the U.S. economy—its economic specialty—is as an exporter of semifinished goods (fabricated metals) and producers' durables (nonelectrical machinery, electrical equipment, and instruments). Cleveland is a "factory town," but it is a factory town that buys things from and sells things to other factory towns rather than directly to consumers.

Additional insights into Cleveland's role as an exporter are revealed when we observe average annual growth rates in total and export employment in each of the industries between 1972 and 1978. These figures are presented in Table 3.3.

This table indicates that within the durable goods manufacturing sector Cleveland was becoming more specialized over the 1972-78 period. Both total and export employment in primary metals, electrical equipment, and transportation vehicles were declining, whereas total and export employment in fabricated metals and nonelectrical machinery were increasing. This trend has two meanings. First, it means that Cleveland was becoming a more specialized manufacturing cen-

Table 3.3

AVERAGE ANNUAL GROWTH RATES IN TOTAL
AND EXPORT EMPLOYMENT, CLEVELAND
SMSA INDUSTRIES, 1972-78

Industry	Average Annual Growth Rate (%)	
	Total Employment	Estimated Export Employment
Durable Goods Manufacturing		
Primary Metals	-2.1	-16.0
Fabricated Metals	2.5	2.9
Nonelectrical Machinery	1.8	1.9
Electrical Equipment	-1.6	-2.0
Motor Vehicles	-3.3	-8.6
Other Transport Equipment	-1.1	-1.1
Instruments	9.2	9.7
Miscellaneous Manufactures	0.3	0.4
Nondurable Goods Manufacturing		
Stone Products	-2.1	6.7
Textiles	-10.6	-11.0
Apparel	0.6	(a)
Paper Products	-0.7	-8.2
Printing	-2.2	(a)
Chemicals	-6.5	(a)
Rubber Products	6.9	10.3
Lumber Products	-1.6	-2.2
Food Processing	-0.1	(a)
Sales		
Retail Sales	2.4	4.1
Eating and Drinking Est.	5.9	(a)
Wholesale Sales	1.1	-2.1
Services		
Finance	1.0	0.4
Insurance	2.8	2.8
Leasing	2.2	(a)
Hotels	0.7	3.6
Personal Services	-1.3	(a)
Business Services	5.8	17.0
Health Services	4.7	18.0
Other Services	4.5	(a)
Other		
Transportation	3.2	(a)
Communications	0.3	(a)
Utilities	19.6	(a)
Construction	5.2	7.5
Agriculture	7.2	7.7

SOURCE: Rand analysis of Cleveland SMSA input-output
relationships based on data from U.S. Department of
Commerce, Bureau of Economic Analysis. (See Appendix C.)

[a]Industry is a net importer.

ter and, hence, the prospects for the local economy were becoming riskier. For example, the possibility that a large proportion of the U.S. market for machine tools might be captured by foreign manufacturers was a relatively more threatening prospect to the Cleveland economy in 1978 than in 1972. At the same time, the fact that the sale of the Cleveland nonelectrical machinery and fabricated metals industries presumably increased while activity in the other heavy manufacturing industries was decreasing indicates that Cleveland's major export industries serve a diverse set of customers. Presumed decreases in sales to the automobile industry were apparently more than made up for by increases in sales to other consuming industries.

These trends are not consistent with the hypothesis that the Cleveland area economy as a whole is dominated by the automotive industry. The hypothesis is noted often enough, however, that we thought it merited further testing. We studied the relationship between month-to-month variations in U.S. automobile and truck production from 1975 to 1981, and local unemployment rates in several metropolitan areas (a complete description of the test and its results is given in Appendix D). In Detroit, the two variables were highly correlated; declines in auto production were consistently associated with large increases in unemployment. In the Cleveland area, the association existed but it was not as strong. In fact, the analysis suggested that Cleveland is somewhat less sensitive to that industry than other metropolitan areas not ordinarily thought of as auto towns: Pittsburgh and Indianapolis. We conclude that while automotive production is very important to the Cleveland area's economic base, the diversity of that base prevents it from being the sole influence.

A second pair of notable figures from Table 3.3 are the growth rates of export employment in the business and health services industries. The apparent growth of "exports" by the health services sector, presumably associated with the care of out-of-town patients in Cleveland's major research and teaching hospitals (see Chapter IX), may, in fact, be spurious. Over the decade of the 1970s the proportion of the average household's income devoted to purchase of health services increased markedly (again, see Chapter IX). Because this change in household spending behavior was not reflected in the methodology by which we computed export employment, this change in household expenditure behavior would show up as an increase in export employment. Consequently, we should not make too much of the apparent substantial increase in export employment in the health services industry.

The increase in export employment in the business services industry is another matter. It is large and there is less reason to think that it is spurious.[4] It would be too much to say, however, that the service sectors, taken as a whole and led by business services, are replacing the older anchor industries as the export base of the Cleveland economy. Exports of machinery and fabricated metals would have to decline substantially, which they have not done, and sectors other than business services (finance and communications, for example) would have to grow substantially, which they have not, if services were to assume durable goods manufacturing's traditional role in Cleveland's economy. The trend in business services is worth monitoring, however. This is a diverse sector including such component industries as local building maintenance and international management consulting. More analysis would have to be undertaken before we could determine what the rapid growth of this sector means for the Cleveland economy.

In fact, Table 3.3 raises a number of questions that cannot be answered without more detailed analysis. We do not know the reasons for and implications of rapid increases in employment in the rubber products, instruments, and utilities industries. Even some of the smaller numbers generate interesting questions. Export employment in the retail sales sector appears to be growing more rapidly than total employment in that industry. Does this reflect an increase in Cleveland's role as a regional shopping center or is this another example of spurious exporting? Answering all of these questions must be reserved for future work.

THE REGIONAL ECONOMY AND REGIONAL WELFARE

As noted in the introduction to this part of the report, we view the economy of the Cleveland metropolitan area as only a means to the end of a good life for the residents of the region. If the quality of regional life were perfectly measured by gross regional income or the total number of jobs available in the metropolitan economy, our analysis of how the regional economy works could end here. We would simply recommend that community leaders adopt policies that will

---

[4]It may be that, just as households have increased the proportion of their income devoted to health services, firms across all industries have begun purchasing more business services per unit of output. If this is the reason for the increase in business service activity in Cleveland then the increased exports are also spurious. We have evidence of a change in household behavior with respect to medical care, but no evidence either way about why business service activity was increased. Therefore, the apparent increase in business service exports presents a more intriguing prospect for exploitation aimed at stimulating regional economic growth.

encourage exports by those local industries that already have a national or worldwide reputation and that stimulate a great deal of growth in the local economy. But regional well-being has more aspects than just the total number of jobs or total income. Employment and income are important, maybe even most important, but so are all of the other effects of different patterns of regional growth and decline that appeared on the righthand side of Fig. 3.1. Furthermore, even if we did not care about such outcomes as the fiscal condition of local governments, the regional unemployment rate, or the relative economic health of the central city as ends in themselves, they would be important because they can affect prospects for general economic development.

The analytical framework presented here could accommodate any number of factors, but because of limitations on readily available data, we have treated only three important outcomes in a fairly simple manner. The three outcomes we will discuss are: the relative economic health of the central city as compared with the suburbs, employment of blacks, and employment of youth. Another important effect of economic change, the average wage rate, will be discussed in some detail in the next chapter. A brief discussion of why each of these measures is important will precede a presentation of the data and a discussion of the results.

The Relative Economic Health of the Central City

From the point of view of most policymakers with a regional orientation, the City of Cleveland is the most important part of the metropolitan area. It is by far the largest jurisdiction in the region. Furthermore, while far from holding a monopoly on the region's social problems, the city generally has a more severe fiscal situation, a more troubled public school system, higher unemployment, a higher crime rate, and more poverty than even the most troubled suburban jurisdiction. Finally, the economic condition of the central city is important to all residents of the metropolitan area, even to those who live, work, and play entirely in the suburbs. The image that the Cleveland metropolitan area projects to the rest of the nation and the world is determined in large part by economic conditions in the central city. When all one finds out about Cleveland through the national media is that the city government is in default and that the city is run down, it may become difficult for firms located in Parma to attract high quality personnel from elsewhere and property values even in Shaker Heights may be hurt. Consequently, decisionmakers throughout the metropolitan area will want to know not only what the effects of their choices will be on the metropolitan economy as a whole, but also on economic conditions in the City of Cleveland.

For a variety of reasons economic activity has been shifting away from central cities all over the country for most of the post-World War II period. However, certain industries—financial institutions, legal services, membership organizations, etc.—still continue to choose central city locations more often than not. In Table 3.4 we present data on which Cleveland industries were most heavily concentrated in the central city in 1970. The 1970 data are the most recent available for all industries until the 1980 Census results for such variables are released. Because the general trend of movement by all industries to the suburbs has continued during the 1970s, all of the figures in Table 3.4 are probably higher than the current figures. However, the table does illustrate the differences across industries, and there is no reason to suspect that interindustry differences have changed markedly over the last decade.

Employment of Blacks and Youth

Economists distinguish among types of unemployment: voluntary, cyclical, and structural. Those who are "voluntarily" unemployed are intentionally between jobs for a short period of time. The voluntarily unemployed can easily find work, and are, therefore, not usually of much concern to policymakers. The cyclically unemployed are victims of a national business cycle. Laid-off auto workers who expect to be called back to the plant within a fairly short period of time fall into this category. There is little that policymakers in Cleveland can do to affect the timing or severity of national business cycles. However, there are steps that might be taken to reduce the vulnerability of the regional economy to national economic fluctuations. Recent econometric analyses (Victor and Vernez, 1981) have indicated that metropolitan areas with relatively high concentrations of employment in the service sectors, as opposed to the manufacturing sectors, are less sensitive to cyclical changes in the national economy.

The type of unemployment most subject to remediation at the regional level is structural unemployment. Structural unemployment—in other words, long-term unemployability—arises for several reasons. Some workers cannot supply the productive skills local employers are seeking. The skills of other workers may be insufficient to produce enough to permit them to be paid the minimum wage rate. Still others may be victims of racial or age discrimination. There are several instruments that local policymakers can apply to reducing structural unemployment. Well-designed training programs have

Table 3.4

ESTIMATED RACIAL, AGE, AND LOCATIONAL COMPOSITION OF EMPLOYMENT IN CLEVELAND SMSA INDUSTRIES, 1970

Industry	Percent of Industry Employment		
	Central City	Black	Youth
Durable Goods Manufacturing			
Primary Metals	52	14	11
Fabricated Metals	31	5	14
Nonelectrical Machinery	37	5	19
Electrical Equipment	30	3	13
Motor Vehicles	41	19	9
Other Transport Equipment	31	0	23
Instruments	37	0	0
Miscellaneous Manufactures	57	14	29
Nondurable Goods Manufacturing			
Stone Products	27	0	9
Textiles	67	0	0
Apparel	100	0	29
Paper Products	0	50	0
Printing	58	0	6
Chemicals	47	13	13
Rubber Products	62	5	19
Lumber Products	67	0	33
Food Processing	64	18	37
Sales			
Retail Sales	37	8	33
Eating and Drinking Est.	48	11	45
Wholesale Sales	47	7	14
Services			
Finance	60	10	40
Insurance	58	7	15
Leasing	43	14	0
Hotels	69	23	54
Personal Services	29	33	37
Business Services	67	10	19
Health Services	53	11	9
Other Services	20	0	50
Other			
Transportation	44	6	19
Communications	78	22	39
Utilities	73	9	18
Construction	33	9	27
Agriculture	100	0	43

SOURCE: U.S. Department of Commerce, Bureau of the Census, 1970 Census Public Use Sample.

been useful in some places, for example. The analysis presented in this report focuses on the effects of industrial composition of total metropolitan employment on the number of jobs for blacks and workers under 25 years of age. These two groups tend to have much higher structural unemployment rates than older or white workers. Certain industries, either because they require job skills possessed by black workers or young workers or because their traditions are less discriminatory (e.g., the auto industry), tend to hire larger proportions of the groups of workers who are most likely to be structurally unemployed.

Beyond a general concern with structural unemployment, there is another reason to be concerned with creating jobs for young people. If metropolitan area leaders wish to reduce the net outmigration of population from Cleveland and if young people are more likely to migrate than older people (see Chapter II), creating jobs for youth may be one way of stabilizing regional population.

Again, we have measured each industry's potential contribution to alleviating the problem of structural unemployment among blacks and youth by the proportion of such workers in the industry's work force in 1970. The last decade has seen some reduction of racial discrimination in the labor market and has witnessed the influx of the "baby boom" generation into the labor force. It is likely, therefore, that the work forces of all industries include larger proportions of black and young workers now than they did in 1970. However, as with central city employment, there is no reason to believe that interindustry differences have altered much since 1970.

Table 3.4 presents the proportions of blacks and youth in the work forces of Cleveland's major industries in 1970 and the proportion of total industry employment located in the central city.

Before discussing these data, two important distinctions should be made. First, the figures showing black employment, for example, do not measure the distribution of metropolitan Cleveland's black labor force across industries. Instead, they represent the percentage of each particular industry's labor force that is black. Second, the figures showing central city employment do not indicate the percentage of industry employees who are central city residents. Instead they indicate the proportion of industry jobs that are located in the central city. So when we speak of a particular sector being concentrated in the central city, we do not necessarily mean that that sector employs large numbers or proportions of central city residents.

Table 3.4 indicates three things about how the Cleveland economy and the Cleveland political economy work. First, we see that the central city economy is apparently as diverse as the economy of the metropolitan area as a whole. Almost every industry is represented in the central city in substantial proportions. This lack of specialization of the central city economy—the City of Cleveland is not just the metropolitan area's service center—is good news for those called upon to devise development plans for the metropolitan area. Policies designed to encourage the growth of almost any industry, including all of the anchor industries, appear as likely to help the central city, at least to some extent.

The figures on black employment and, to a lesser extent, on youth employment tell a very different story. In the previous section of this chapter we developed several kinds of evidence that the fabricated metal and nonelectrical machinery industries were especially worthy of the attention of Cleveland area policymakers. However, these two industries employ very small proportions of blacks. In other words, these two industries constitute a major strength of the Cleveland economy and can contribute substantially to general local economic growth, but they cannot be relied upon to solve all metropolitan area problems. Specifically, growth of these industries will not be an effective means of reducing structural unemployment in the black community, unless the sectors change their hiring practices.

Indeed, when one inspects the figures, it is clear that black employment is concentrated in a small number of industries, especially when we compare these figures with the percentage of employment in the central cities. This suggests, in turn, that overall economic growth may not be sufficient to meet the needs of the black community effectively. A development strategy that is more fully responsive to those needs would require three elements: immediate job creation, affirmative action, and training.

Immediate job creation for blacks would involve support for some of the sectors that employ large proportions of minority workers. However, longer-range efforts should concentrate on moving increasing numbers out of low-paying, low-status occupations. Affirmative action will be important, but training aimed at preparing minorities for new jobs in promising industries and emerging technical fields deserves emphasis.

SUMMARY

This chapter was organized around a schematic overview of the Cleveland economy that illustrated how changes in exports to the rest of the United States and the world affected a number of dimensions of metropolitan welfare. A change in export sales by a local industry stimulates activity in a number of other local industries. The relative stimulative effects of industries are measured by multipliers. We computed such multipliers for Cleveland industries using a methodology developed by the U.S. Commerce Department. We found, in general, that greater exports by Cleveland's traditional anchor industries—primary metals, fabricated metals, nonelectrical machinery, and motor vehicles—stimulated more local growth than export increases for most other industries. Exceptions to this general rule were the retail sales industry and two of the service industries: medical and business services.

We also applied the Commerce Department methodology to estimating the industrial composition of Cleveland's total exports. A tabulation of the results indicated that Cleveland had a highly diverse economy—that it produced some of almost everything and exported many different things. The analysis also indicated that among the anchor industries the largest exporters, by far, were fabricated metals and machine tools. In other words, we concluded that Cleveland's greatest comparative advantage is as a supplier of semifinished goods and producers' durables. We also tested the possibility that all of Cleveland's anchor industries were, essentially, no more than suppliers of the automobile industry. We concluded that the health of the U.S. automobile industry was, indeed, very important to the Cleveland economy, but that it would be a mistake to think of Cleveland as solely an "auto town."

A further analysis of changes in total and export employment by industry between 1972 and 1978 indicated that, among the durable goods manufacturing sectors, Cleveland was becoming more specialized in fabricated metals and nonelectrical machinery. This analysis also uncovered rapid growth in Cleveland's export of business services.

Finally, we reported some statistics that indicate how different industries might contribute to the solution of different metropolitan problems. We discovered a general commonality of economic interest between the central city economy and the metropolitan economy as a whole. However, we found blacks may not share equally when new jobs are created in some of metropolitan Cleveland's anchor industries.

IV. METROPOLITAN CLEVELAND AS AN ENVIRONMENT FOR ECONOMIC ACTIVITY

INTRODUCTION

The previous chapter developed some insights into what Cleveland's economic specialties are by observing what people from outside the metropolitan area come to Cleveland to buy. We concluded that the region's chief specialties are as a manufacturer of durable goods, particularly of semifinished goods and producers' durables, and, to a growing extent, business services. This chapter examines Cleveland's advantages and disadvantages as a location for economic activity in a different way. Instead of observing what people come to Cleveland to buy, we will look directly at a number of the characteristics of the metropolitan area that affect its attractiveness as a place to do business, to produce and market goods and services.

This review is important for two reasons. First, an understanding of the metropolitan area's particular advantages and disadvantages as a location for enterprise is essential in providing a clear sense of future prospects generally. Second, at least some of the characteristics that determine an area's attractiveness for business can be changed by concerted community action, thus the data are important in the consideration of economic development policy.

This chapter consists of three main parts. First, we present a framework for organizing information about basic metropolitan characteristics. Second, we examine data on aspects of the Cleveland area's location and internal environment that have important effects on business investment decisions. Finally, we review selected information on metropolitan Cleveland's attractiveness as a place to live that affects the location decisions of workers as well as entrepreneurs.

In this analysis we do not attempt to be exhaustive, but rather, we concentrate on those factors that the literature on industrial location suggests are most important. The list of factors that play some role in investment decisions, according to that literature, is a very long one. The data required for a solid evaluation of many of them do not exist; efforts to obtain a full accounting would have been much beyond the scope of this study. Fortunately, however, we do not need to understand all the factors to sort out the basics.

Similarly, as we put Cleveland's attributes in context in this chapter, we limit our choice of comparison areas to the eight SMSAs noted in Chapter II that are in the same basic size class. Comparisons with other areas (e.g., New York City or Taipei) might be of interest, but comparing Cleveland with all other locations of possible interest would have been confusing at the very least. Our focus on other metropolitan areas of a similar size recognizes that there are obvious limits to what the Cleveland area can become; it cannot become a southern rural county or the nation's leading financial center. It can, however, improve its competitive position by becoming more effective as a leading regional metropolis.

A FRAMEWORK FOR ASSESSMENT

An assessment of the advantages and disadvantages of any region as a location for economic activity must begin with some notion of why firms and households might choose one location over another. Much has been written on this subject, although there are many more theoretical essays than reliable quantitative studies of location decisions and their outcomes. The view we summarize below is consistent with what we consider the most relevant components of that literature as reviewed and synthesized by Vaughn (1977).

Determinants of Firm Location

Firms choose locations primarily with the objective of maximizing profits. Other motives may enter firm managers' decision processes, most notably the managers' own subjective preferences, but over the long run, locations that generate higher than average profits for firms should enjoy higher than average growth rates. Profits, in turn, are determined by the quantity of its product a firm can sell, the price at which it can be sold, and the prices of inputs the firm uses in production. An analysis of the location choices, as opposed, say, to the technological or product mix choices of firms should focus on two major determinants of geographic differences in levels of sales and prices: transportation costs and interregional differences in wages. Firms producing products that are inexpensive to transport and require very little labor to produce can locate almost anywhere. Firms producing products that are expensive to ship by a labor-intensive process choose their locations very carefully. During the post-World War II period real transportation costs have dropped for almost all products, as a result of the completion of the interstate highway system and the decrease in the price of air transport. This reduction in transportation costs has been one of the major causes of the faster relative economic growth rates of the remote population centers of the sunbelt. However, for many products, transportation costs remain an important determinant of firm behavior.

The closer a firm is to its source of supply, the lower, in general, will be the transportation costs built into the prices of its inputs. The closer the firm is to concentrations of its customers, the greater, in general, the volume of its sales at any given price. However, the closer a firm is to its competitors, the lower the price it will be able to charge. For all of these reasons, one of the characteristics of a region that determines its desirability as a place to do business is its location relative to other concentrations of economic activity.

The second major determinant of firm profits is the prices of inputs, most notably, the price of labor. Wage rates vary across metropolitan areas for a variety of reasons that will be discussed in more detail below. From the point of view of firms, however, the fact of these variations is more important than their causes. If identical labor can be purchased more cheaply in one place than another, everything else being equal, firms will choose the location where wages are low.

The availability and price of other inputs also matters to firms. Availability of energy supplies is becoming more of a concern to many industries. For large firms with access to national capital markets, the local availability of loans probably does not matter, but for smaller firms the level of deposits at local banks may make a difference. Finally, the price and availability of office space may influence the location choices of some firms.

Our assessment of Cleveland's advantages and disadvantages as a location for industries, then, will amount to a comparison of this region with a group of competitive metropolitan areas on several dimensions that affect firm profits. We give most emphasis to two dimensions: Cleveland's geographic location relative to other economic activities and local wage rates.[1]

We then discuss several other factors briefly. For some, we draw preliminary conclusions based on relatively simple comparisons (energy availability and capital availability). For others, where independent analysis was either impossible or inappropriate, we note either readily apparent effects or discuss why influences are difficult to determine (the size and composition of the labor force, water availability, state and local taxes, local public services, and infrastructure).

---

[1]Wage rates in Cleveland will be compared with U.S. and southern state averages in addition to the other metropolitan areas' wage rates.

Determinants of Household Location

Workers and their households also choose locations. Americans move fairly long distances fairly frequently. For example, between 1965 and 1970 almost 34 million[2] Americans, about 17 percent of the population, moved across state boundaries (Wattenberg, 1976). In general, they move with the combined motivations of finding a better, or better paying, job and improving the quality of their lives. These two motives interact. Households may be willing to trade off some of their quality of life objectives if the jobs in a region pay especially well. By contrast, they may be willing to take a lower paying job in a region where the lifestyle particularly suits the household's tastes. At least part of the regional wage differential can, therefore, be thought of as a "premium" price paid to local workers to compensate them for some disadvantage of living in the region or, by contrast, a "discount" offered by workers in exchange for some regional amenity. Evidence has been reported in the economic literature (Greenwood, 1975; Henderson, 1982) that workers are compensated for interregional differences in costs of living and in such amenities or disamenities as climate and crime rates. Furthermore, although it is difficult to test these assertions empirically, it is to be expected that such factors as environmental quality and the quality of cultural institutions are reflected in regional wage differences.

The second group of advantages and disadvantages, therefore, are the characteristics that are likely to attract households to or repel them from the Cleveland metropolitan area. These factors are important for two reasons: they are direct indicators of the current quality of local life and, as such, they help determine regional wages.

THE CLEVELAND ENVIRONMENT AS A LOCATION FOR FIRMS

This section and the next consist of a series of tables and charts in most cases comparing Cleveland, on a number of dimensions, with eight other metropolitan areas of similar size. These metropolitan areas are Atlanta, Baltimore, Denver, Minneapolis, Pittsburgh, St. Louis, San Diego, and Seattle.

---

[2]This double counts those who moved twice.

Cleveland's Location

Tables 4.1 and 4.2 present data that describe Cleveland's comparative advantages among the sample cities with respect to location. The figures in these tables were computed in the following way. We drew circles of 250 and 500 miles radius (easy and feasible overnight trucking radii, respectively) around each of the sample cities and identified the other metropolitan areas that lay within those circles. Then we computed the total metropolitan population, disposable income, and employment in a number of broadly defined industrial sectors within 250 and 500 miles of each sample metropolitan area. The totals within 250 and 500 miles were then compared with the totals for those variables for all U.S. metropolitan areas. We found, for example, that 34.6 percent of all U.S. metropolitan nondurable manufacturing employment was located within 250 miles of Baltimore in 1970 and that only 0.4 percent of total U.S. metropolitan service sector employment was located within 500 miles of Seattle in 1976.

Before we discuss the implications of these figures, recall that location close to other centers of economic activity may be a mixed blessing. It is advantageous to be near one's customers and suppliers, but it is disadvantageous to be too close to one's competitors. However, when we compare similar cities on this dimension, the disadvantageous aspects of central locations "cancel out" in a sense. Even though Cleveland, in some sense, suffers because it is near Pittsburgh, a serious competitor as we shall show, by the same token Pittsburgh suffers the disadvantage of being close to Cleveland. Consequently, we will treat location close to other activities as an unambiguous advantage. The higher the percentage of any given industry that lies close to a metropolitan area, the more advantageous that location will be to firms doing business with that industry.

For convenience of interpretation we have underlined each number in Tables 4.1 and 4.2 that is larger than the equivalent figure for Cleveland. It is apparent that Cleveland has a clear locational advantage over most of the cities in this group. Only Pittsburgh lies within 500 miles of a larger proportion of the activities treated here in most categories, and Cleveland lies within 500 miles of a larger proportion of total metropolitan service sector activity than any of the other cities in the sample.

However, when we measure the proportions of activity that lie within "easy" overnight trucking distance from these cities (250 mile radius), we find that the Cleveland area has little distinct advantage over the other northeast north central cities. On this criterion, Cleveland ranks second best with respect to durable goods manufactures, third best with respect to our measure of four other activities, and

Table 4.1

PERCENT OF U.S. METROPOLITAN POPULATION, INCOME, AND EMPLOYMENT
WITHIN 250 MILE RADIUS OF SELECTED SMSAs

	Cleveland	Atlanta	Baltimore	Denver	Minneapolis	Pittsburgh	St. Louis	San Diego	Seattle
Population									
1978	13.9	5.8	24.9	1.3	2.6	20.2	12.9	8.8	2.6
1970	14.8	5.5	26.6	1.2	3.0	21.3	13.3	8.3	2.5
Total Income									
1976	13.9	4.9	26.8	1.3	2.9	20.8	13.3	8.8	2.6
1970	14.4	4.6	29.2	1.2	2.9	21.7	13.8	8.9	2.5
Employment by Sector									
Total Nonag.									
1976	15.6	6.1	29.6	1.2	2.7	23.6	15.5	10.0	3.6
1970	13.6	4.7	27.2	0.9	2.6	20.9	14.0	8.1	2.8
Durable									
1976	25.1	3.6	21.8	0.7	2.3	27.9	16.7	10.4	3.2
1970	25.2	3.8	24.6	0.6	2.6	29.3	18.7	10.0	1.7
Nondurable									
1976	12.6	8.1	30.2	0.9	2.7	20.9	14.1	7.4	1.7
1970	12.3	8.1	34.6	0.7	2.6	21.8	16.3	6.1	1.0
Wholesale Trade									
1976	13.6	6.3	28.1	1.4	2.8	20.6	16.2	10.4	2.4
1970	12.8	6.4	31.0	1.4	3.4	19.8	18.0	9.6	2.1
Finance									
1976	10.4	5.2	29.8	1.2	2.4	17.6	13.8	8.2	3.6
1970	10.3	4.7	32.8	1.0	2.8	17.8	14.6	7.9	3.3
Service									
1976	16.9	1.7	23.4	1.9	0.3	18.5	16.2	16.9	1.3
1970	15.9	1.4	31.3	1.6	0.3	23.1	15.9	15.4	1.0

SOURCE: Rand analysis of data from U.S. Department of Labor, Bureau of Labor Statistics (1979c), and data from U.S. Department of Commerce, Bureau of the Census (1980c).

Table 4.2

PERCENT OF U.S. METROPOLITAN POPULATION, INCOME, AND EMPLOYMENT
WITHIN 500 MILE RADIUS OF SELECTED SMSAS

	Cleveland	Atlanta	Baltimore	Denver	Minneapolis	Pittsburgh	St. Louis	San Diego	Seattle
Population									
1978	50.6	22.1	43.7	4.4	15.5	55.9	32.4	14.3	2.8
1970	53.4	21.8	46.3	4.1	16.0	58.8	33.2	13.5	2.7
Total Income									
1976	52.7	19.9	44.6	4.1	15.8	57.7	32.0	14.7	2.8
1970	56.1	19.4	48.0	3.7	16.4	61.4	32.7	14.6	2.7
Employment by Sector									
Total Nonag.									
1976	59.5	23.3	49.7	4.6	17.7	64.9	36.5	16.3	3.1
1970	53.1	18.6	44.8	3.5	16.0	57.8	31.6	13.1	2.4
Durable									
1976	60.7	19.8	49.2	3.1	22.3	64.1	44.8	14.8	2.4
1970	64.4	20.9	51.9	2.3	23.0	67.8	46.0	13.8	1.0
Nondurable									
1976	60.5	23.6	54.0	3.0	16.6	66.1	32.8	11.6	1.4
1970	65.1	22.9	57.9	2.2	16.6	70.4	33.1	9.8	1.8
Wholesale Trade									
1976	53.6	21.8	42.6	5.4	18.0	56.2	35.2	17.0	1.8
1970	56.1	30.3	43.8	4.3	19.2	58.2	35.7	15.5	1.6
Finance									
1976	53.1	19.0	45.7	4.3	15.0	58.4	29.6	14.2	3.0
1970	56.1	17.7	48.7	3.8	15.8	60.6	29.8	13.3	2.8
Services									
1976	49.3	16.4	37.9	6.1	16.5	49.1	35.8	27.0	0.4
1970	56.0	15.1	44.4	5.1	16.2	37.5	33.3	24.2	0.4

SOURCE: Rand analysis of data from U.S. Department of Labor, Bureau of Labor Statistics (1979c),
and data from U.S. Department of Commerce, Bureau of the Census (1980c).

fourth best, after Pittsburgh, Baltimore, and St. Louis, with respect to the remaining three activities.

These tables reveal two other items of note. First, the comparison of 1970 and 1976 figures suggests some somewhat surprising conclusions about changes in the Cleveland area's comparative locational advantage. When we look at Table 4.2, we find that the proportions of all but two activities within 500 miles of Cleveland decreased between 1970 and 1976 or 1978. The two exceptions are durable and nondurable manufactures. However, considering so much recent publicity about the shift of economic activity to the sunbelt, these changes seem surprisingly small. The general locational advantage of northeastern and north central cities did not change markedly. These large regions are still the economic heartland of the United States and shifts to the sunbelt will have to continue at a very rapid rate for a very long time before that basic characterization is altered.

An unexpected finding is also revealed in Table 4.1. We see that the proportions of only three of the eight activities within 250 miles of Cleveland decreased between 1970 and 1976. Cleveland's relative locational advantage with respect to the five other activities improved slightly or remained stable over the period. Furthermore, the overall improvement in Cleveland's position in this regard contrasted with what happened to Cleveland's main competition. Baltimore, Pittsburgh, and St. Louis all lost ground in many of the categories where Cleveland gained. For example, while the proportion of service sector employment within 250 miles from Cleveland increased six percent between 1970 and 1976, from 15.9 percent to 16.9 percent, the proportion of such activity within 250 miles of Baltimore decreased by 25 percent. The similar figure for Pittsburgh was a 20 percent decrease. Only further analysis would indicate definitively just why recent trends have increased this particular aspect of Cleveland's locational advantage.

The final point revealed by these figures provides further confirmation of the contention that Cleveland's greatest comparative advantage lies in durable goods manufactures. A greater concentration of this activity lies within both 250 and 500 miles of Cleveland than any other activity, and Cleveland consistently ranks second on this dimension, exceeded only by Pittsburgh.

Cleveland's Wages

Wages vary for a number of reasons. Some of the reasons that Cleveland's wages tend to be higher than the national average will be assessed in the next section of the chapter. In this section, we present evidence that Cleveland wages are, indeed, high by national standards, but that industry-by-industry and occupation-by-occupation wage differentials are far from uniform.

Table 4.3 compares Cleveland SMSA average manufacturing wages with the eight other similarly sized metropolitan areas, and Table 4.4 presents comparisons of Cleveland manufacturing wages with the national average and the average for nine southern states for a larger number of highly detailed sectors. We cannot explain all of the variation across industries in Table 4.4, but these data can be used to make some points about Cleveland's attractiveness to different types of firms.

As Table 4.3 indicates, Cleveland's hourly manufacturing wages tend to be high, even in comparison with other metropolitan areas of similar size. Only Pittsburgh's average wages exceed Cleveland's. However, these differences across cities are misleading indicators of Cleveland's true competitive position with respect to wages for three reasons. First, metropolitan averages are affected by the industrial composition of local employment. One reason Pittsburgh and Cleveland top the list in Table 4.3 is the large proportion of employers in the high-paying durable goods manufacturing industries in their work forces. The data do not mean, in other words, that all employers must pay 30 percent more per hour in Cleveland than in Atlanta. Hence, an industry-by-industry comparison of wages is required.

Table 4.3

AVERAGE MANUFACTURING WAGES IN NINE
METROPOLITAN AREAS

SMSA	Hourly Wages per Production Worker (1972) ($)
Cleveland	4.74
Atlanta	3.65
Baltimore	4.31
Denver	4.46
Minneapolis	4.39
Pittsburgh	4.87
St. Louis	4.50
San Diego	4.45
Seattle	4.72

Table 4.4

MANUFACTURING WAGE COMPARISONS

Industry	Employment (000s)	Average Wage per Production Worker Hour				
		Clev. SMSA Average, 1977 ($)	Ratio-Clev. SMSA to U.S. Average		Ratio-Clev. SMSA to South. St. Avg.	
			Ratio 1977	% Change in Ratio, 1967-77	Ratio 1977	% Change in Ratio, 1972-77
TOTAL MANUFACTURING	265.4	7.06	1.20	1.7	1.53	-2.0
Major Durable Goods Manufacturing						
33 PRIMARY METAL INDUSTRIES	29.2	8.86	1.10	5.1	1.31	2.8
331 Blast Fur. & Basic Steel Prod.	14.1	9.88	1.04	1.7	1.56	7.4
332 Iron & Steel Foundries	7.1	9.36	1.33	12.9	1.63	-5.3
3341 Sec. Nonferrous Metals	1.2	6.63	1.11	7.2	N/A	N/A
335 Nonferrous Rolling & Drawing	2.1	6.89	1.01	-7.2	1.24	-10.4
3351 Copper Rolling & Drawing	1.2	8.00	1.19	6.2	N/A	N/A
335X Other Nonfer. Rol. & Drawing	.9	5.56	.81	-20.9	N/A	N/A
336 Nonferrous Foundries	3.5	6.43	1.10	4.7	N/A	N/A
3361 Aluminum Foundries	2.7	6.70	1.09	3.0	N/A	N/A
336X Other Nonferrous Foundries	.8	5.64	1.07	14.0	N/A	N/A
33X Other Prim. Metal Industries	1.2	5.65	.74	-29.2	N/A	N/A
34 FABRICATED METAL PRODUCTS	44.7	6.83	1.12	1.8	1.34	-3.5
342 Cutlery, Hand Tools, & Hdwe.	1.6	5.13	.87	-22.7	1.10	-6.6
343 Plumb., Heat., Exc. Electric	1.4	6.00	1.14	9.4	1.34	-0.7

Table 4.4 (Continued)

| Industry | Employment (000s) | Average Wage per Production Worker Hour | | | | |
| | | Clev. SMSA Average, 1977 ($) | Ratio-Clev. SMSA to U.S. Average | | Ratio-Clev. SMSA to South. St. Avg. | |
			Ratio 1977	% Change in Ratio, 1967-77	Ratio 1977	% Change in Ratio, 1972-77
Major Durable Goods Manufacturing (Continued)						
344 Fab. Structural Metal Products	5.6	5.68	.99	-7.1	1.09	-13.1
3441 Fabricated Structural Metal	1.0	6.23	1.07	6.5	1.24	-6.2
3443 Fab. Pl. Wk. (Boiler Shops)	.8	6.67	1.02	-7.2	1.04	4.3
3444 Sheet Metal Work	2.2	5.31	.91	-8.9	1.09	-7.6
3444X Other Fab. Structural Metal	1.6	5.32	1.09	-6.2	N/A	N/A
345 Screw Mach. Prod., Bolts, etc.	6.7	6.17	1.06	.4	N/A	N/A
3451 Screw Machine Products	2.4	5.05	.95	-8.6	N/A	N/A
3452 Bolts, Nuts, Rivets, & Washers	4.3	6.80	1.09	5.7	N/A	N/A
3471 Plating and Polishing	1.6	4.60	1.04	.8	1.10	-10.1
349 Misc. Fabricated Metal Products	6.7	5.66	.99	-9.0	1.11	-11.3
3494 Valves and Pipe Fittings	2.8	5.88	.97	-8.2	1.15	-2.9
349X Other Misc. Fab. Metal Prod.	3.9	5.50	1.00	-10.9	N/A	N/A
34X Stamp. & Other Fabricated Metals	21.1	7.87	1.13	-2.0	N/A	N/A
35 NONELECTRICAL MACHINERY	44.0	6.88	1.05	-3.6	1.33	-7.5
353 Construc. & Related Machinery	10.4	7.56	1.05	-5.3	1.37	-3.2
354 Metalworking Machinery	14.3	6.69	1.01	-3.2	1.33	1.6
3542 Mach. Tools Metal Form. Types	1.2	6.69	1.00	4.6	N/A	N/A
3544 Spec. Dies, Tools, Jigs, Fixture	3.3	6.32	.92	-10.1	1.05	-10.8
3545 Machine Tool Accessories	4.1	6.48	1.04	-.9	N/A	N/A
354X Other Metalworking Machinery	5.7	7.18	1.10	-1.0	N/A	N/A

Table 4.4 (Continued)

| | Employ-ment (000s) | Average Wage per Production Worker Hour | | | | |
| | | Clev. SMSA Average, 1977 ($) | Ratio-Clev. SMSA to U.S. Average | | Ratio-Clev. SMSA to South. St. Avg. | |
Industry			Ratio 1977	% Change in Ratio, 1967-77	Ratio 1977	% Change in Ratio, 1972-77
Major Durable Goods Manufacturing (Continued)						
355 Special Industry Machinery	4.9	7.18	1.17	7.9	1.44	0.1
3559 Special Industry Machinery, NEC	3.7	7.31	1.13	11.6	1.43	1.1
355X Other Special Industry Machinery	1.2	6.69	1.12	-4.2	N/A	N/A
356 General Industrial Machinery	3.8	6.52	1.01	-5.1	1.33	-4.1
3564 Blowers and Fans	.5	5.33	.93	-7.9	N/A	N/A
3567 Industrial Furnaces and Ovens	.4	5.00	.83	-17.2	N/A	N/A
3569 Gen. Industrial Machinery, NEC	.8	6.09	1.06	-1.7	1.33	-8.0
356X Other Gen. Industrial Machinery	2.1	7.17	1.06	-3.0	N/A	N/A
358 Refrigeration & Service Machinery	1.0	5.00	.83	-24.4	1.02	-12.8
35X Other Machinery, Exc. Electrical	9.6	6.67	1.03	-4.5	N/A	N/A
36 ELECTRICAL MACHINERY	21.7	6.43	1.15	5.8	1.38	1.6
361 Electric Distributing Equipment	.7	4.60	.82	-8.7	0.98	-7.0
362 Electrical Industrial Apparatus	7.3	8.53	1.51	15.2	1.78	-8.4
3621 Motors and Generators	1.5	6.31	1.15	15.7	N/A	N/A
3622 Industrial Controls	1.9	6.61	1.20	3.8	N/A	N/A
362X Other Elec. Industrial Apparatus	3.9	10.42	1.71	.5	N/A	N/A
363 Household Appliances	2.1	4.97	.89	-13.4	1.23	-19.2
364 Elec. Light. & Wiring Equipment	4.7	5.45	1.03	-6.4	1.14	5.3
369 Misc. Electrical Equip. Supplies	4.2	5.89	.96	-9.2	1.23	-4.0
36X Other Electric & Electronic Equip.	2.7	4.85	.87	15.3	N/A	N/A

Table 4.4 (Continued)

Industry	Employ-ment (000s)	Clev. SMSA Average, 1977 ($)	Average Wage per Production Worker Hour			
			Ratio-Clev. SMSA to U.S. Average		Ratio-Clev. SMSA to South. St. Avg.	
			Ratio 1977	% Change in Ratio, 1967-77	Ratio 1977	% Change in Ratio, 1972-77
Other Manufacturing (Continued)						
27 PRINTING AND PUBLISHING	12.9	6.76	1.06	3.5	1.27	-0.6
2711 Newspapers	4.1	8.32	1.16	-2.6	1.52	-1.4
2721 Periodicals	1.1	4.50	.80	-31.4	0.94	-50.1
273 Books	.3	1.67	.30	-73.5	0.36	-77.2
278 Blankbooks and Bookbinding	.6	5.30	1.12	4.6	1.28	0.1
2791 Typesetting	.3	6.40	.91	-6.7	1.02	-17.7
27X Other Printing and Publishing	6.5	6.67	1.05	9.8	N/A	N/A
28 CHEMICALS AND ALLIED PRODUCTS	9.6	6.47	.95	-3.3	1.02	-5.6
281 Industrial Inorganic Chemicals	1.8	7.05	.95	-9.3	1.00	-20.1
282 Plastics Materials & Synth.	1.0	6.44	.92	4.5	0.98	-5.6
284 Soap, Cleaners, & Toilet Goods	.6	5.29	.89	7.1	1.11	20.4
28X Other Chemicals & Allied Prod.	6.2	6.43	.94	-4.0	N/A	N/A
29 PETROLEUM AND COAL PRODUCTS	1.8	5.87	.69	-28.7	1.04	-15.5
30 RUBBER AND PLASTIC PRODUCTS	9.6	4.74	.90	-6.3	0.90	-8.9
32 STONE, CLAY AND GLASS PRODUCTS	4.6	6.22	1.04	-3.8	1.19	-7.9

Table 4.4 (Continued)

Industry	Employment (000s)	Clev. SMSA Average, 1977 ($)	Ratio-Clev. SMSA to U.S. Average		Ratio-Clev. SMSA to South. St. Avg.	
			Ratio 1977	% Change in Ratio, 1967-77	Ratio 1977	% Change in Ratio, 1972-77
Other Manufacturing (Continued)						
3272　Concrete Products, NEC	.4	6.43	1.25	14.2	1.51	8.3
3273　Ready-Mixed Concrete	.8	7.08	1.16	-27.6	1.45	-17.1
32X　Other Stone, Clay, & Glass Prod.	3.4	5.98	.98	-.7	N/A	N/A
38　INSTRUMENTS AND RELATED PRODUCTS	6.6	5.21	.94	-3.6	1.19	-14.6
382　Measuring & Controlling Devices	5.3	5.38	.99	-2.0	1.20	-15.8
38X　Other Instr. & Related Products	1.3	4.72	.85	-6.9	N/A	N/A
39　MISC. MANUFACTURING INDUSTRIES	4.1	4.69	1.07	-4.7	1.22	-6.6
395　Pens, Pencils, Off. & Art Supp.	.3	4.75	1.07	6.5	1.28	-15.8
399　Miscellaneous Manufactures	2.6	4.89	1.04	-1.0	1.22	0.0
39X　Other Misc. Mfg. Industries	1.2	4.28	1.02	-22.9	N/A	N/A

SOURCE: Data file compiled from Census of Manufactures records (see Appendix B).

Second, a comparison of manufacturing wages across only similarly sized metropolitan areas presents a particularly incomplete view of the options available to manufacturing employers. More and more often Cleveland's competition is not Pittsburgh or St. Louis, but rural towns, particularly those in the sunbelt. A more precise illustration of Cleveland's competitiveness with respect to wages is revealed by Table 4.4 which presents industry-by-industry comparisons with the U.S. average and, to pick an important example of the competition, nine southern states[3] with high growth rates in manufacturing employment.

Even the most detailed data available do not enable us to correct for the third possible source of imprecision in our comparisons. The data we have do not reflect differences in fringe benefit payments to employees. Differences in these packages, reflecting differences in workman's compensation laws, medical costs and local medical insurance standards, etc., are reported to be substantial. Without precise data we can do no more than point out that these factors probably increase the differences between Cleveland and the national or southern averages.

When we examine Table 4.4 we see first that in 1977, the average wage per production worker hour for all Cleveland manufacturing employees was 20 percent above the national average and 53 percent above the southern states average.[4] This does not mean, however, that the average Cleveland manufacturing employer pays his employees that much more than his competitors in other locations. Cleveland's concentration of employment in high wage durable goods industries brings up the average for the metropolitan work force as a whole. Considering the gaps industry by industry (i.e., not weighted by employment), the differences are not as pronounced: the Cleveland area average is six percent above the national average and 25 percent above that for the southern states. Still, such gaps are obviously significant to entrepreneurs seeking locations for new investment.

Table 4.4 also shows how Cleveland area manufacturing wages have been changing in relation to those of their counterparts elsewhere. The columns marked "% change in ratio" contain measures of this shift. For example, the entry for fabricated metal products in that column (Cleveland SMSA, southern states comparison) is −3.5. This means that the ratio of the Cleveland area to southern states averages in 1977 (1.34) was 3.5 percent below what it had been in 1972. In

---

[3]Alabama, Arkansas, Florida, Georgia, Mississippi, North Carolina, South Carolina, Tennessee, and Virginia—see the discussion of this selection in Chapter II.

[4]A figure of 1.20 in the column reporting the ratio of Cleveland wages to the national average indicates that Cleveland exceeds the national average by 20 percent.

other words, wages in the two areas were converging in this industry, albeit quite slowly.

Looking at the total for all industries we see that during the 1970s the wage gap between the Cleveland SMSA and the U.S. average actually increased slightly, and the gap between local and southern states wages decreased slightly. Clearly, there was no sign of any marked convergence in wages overall.

Emphasizing the totals, however, masks one of the important messages from Table 4.4—that there is considerable diversity in these measures among the narrowly defined industries. For example, the average local wage for the special industry machinery industry (SIC 355) was 17 percent higher than the national average and 44 percent higher than the southern states average for that industry; the gap had been widening. In contrast, the Cleveland area wage for SIC 3544 (special dies, tools, jigs, and fixtures) was eight percent below the national average and only five percent above the southern states average; local wages in that industry had been increasing less rapidly than those in the other areas.

Wages vary across metropolitan areas by occupation as well as industry. The figures in Table 4.5 (selected occupations only) point in the same direction as the industrial breakdown. Workers in most occupations receive somewhat higher wages in Cleveland than in the nation as a whole. There are some exceptions, and some of these are surprising. Several Cleveland industrialists mentioned to us a shortage of electronic technicians, for example. If this were true, and if there were no impediment to markets' adjusting, we would expect to find electronic technicians paid a relatively high wage in Cleveland. In fact they are not. This suggests either that the shortage is spurious, which is unlikely, or that there is something wrong in local markets for this occupation. The issue warrants further investigation.

Whether expressed by industry or by occupation, the evidence points to the conclusion that Cleveland area wages are high by national standards overall. The gap is substantially wider when metropolitan Cleveland is compared with one of its major competitors for industrial growth, the southern states. Unfortunately, detailed data were not available for rural areas and small towns in those states. We suspect that the wage gap compared to such areas would have been yet wider.

There are a number of factors that offer possible explanations for this gap. The analysis that would be required to assess their relative importance was beyond the scope of this study, but all deserve note. First, we emphasize that the numbers we have presented do not explicitly account for differences in the mix of worker skills in different areas. If the typical worker in a local industry is better trained than

Table 4.5

WAGE COMPARISONS BY OCCUPATION GROUP, 1980

	Cleveland Wages	
Occupation	Average Wage ($)	Percent of National Average
Office Workers	(weekly)	
Secretaries	266.00	86
Stenographers	271.00	109
Transcribing Typists	175.50	91
Typists	204.00	108
File Clerks	167.00	103
Messengers	180.00	105
Switchboard Operators	212.50	111
Receptionists	186.50	100
Order Clerks	237.00	107
Accounting Clerks	220.00	102
Payroll Clerks	227.50	99
Key Entry Operators	215.00	104
Maintenance, Toolroom and Powerplant Workers	(hourly)	
Maintenance Carpenters	10.45	112
Maintenance Painters	10.88	107
Maintenance Machinists	9.89	101
Maintenance Mechanics	10.95	115
Vehicle Maintenance Mechanics	9.95	102
Maintenance Pipefitters	11.35	108
Maint. Sheet Metal Workers	10.87	102
Millwrights	11.52	107
Maintenance Trades Helpers	8.39	109
Machine Tool Operators	10.62	104
Tool and Die Makers	10.66	103
Stationary Engineers	11.22	119
Boiler Tenders	10.18	125
Professional and Technical Workers	(weekly)	
Computer Systems Analyst	461.00	101
Computer Programmers	373.50	106
Computer Operators	275.00	105
Computer Data Librarians	224.00	97
Electronics Technicians	301.50	84
Registered Indus. Nurses	360.00	105

Table 4.5 (Continued)

Occupation	Cleveland Wages	
	Average Wage ($)	Percent of National Average
Material Movement and Custodian Workers	(hourly)	
Truck Drivers	9.75	112
Shippers	7.59	112
Receivers	7.49	112
Warehousemen	7.00	98
Order Fillers	7.38	112
Shipping Packers	7.16	122
Material Handlers	8.05	113
Forklift Operators	8.42	108
Power-truck Operators	9.00	119
Guards	4.64	105
Janitors	5.55	114

SOURCE: U.S. Department of Labor, Bureau of Labor Statistics (1980 and 1981).

his counterpart elsewhere, one would expect a difference in wages. To pin down the influence of this factor, new data would have to be collected; presently available sources do not provide wage information for narrowly defined industries in different areas, further broken down by occupation and skill level.

A second factor, by far the most publicized, is unionization. Ohio shares with the Great Lakes States generally a high rate of unionization compared to much of the sunbelt. Ohio has also had a high percentage of work time lost due to work stoppages, even in comparison to many other industrialized states. (See U.S. Department of Labor, 1979a, 1979b, and 1980.)

The influence of two other factors is less often thought about. One has to do with the heavy local concentration of employment in the durable goods industries (high wage industries virtually everywhere). This means that local firms in industries that pay lower wages than the durable goods manufacturers nationally must compete for labor at a higher rate in the Cleveland labor market. The other relates to our earlier discussion about amenities and disamenities of the Cleveland area as a place to live. We noted there that disamenities in the living environment as it is viewed by workers (ranging from cost of living differences to crime rates) may work to require compensating local wage premiums.

Although the interrelated effects of these factors are not well understood, we can draw some general conclusions about the impacts of the wage gaps we have discussed on future economic development in the Cleveland area. Obviously, in production processes where large gaps exist and other factors such as skill levels are in balance, entrepreneurs will choose to invest where labor costs are lower. The persistence of large differences in wages between metropolitan Cleveland and competitive areas will no doubt cause the Cleveland area to lose investment it might have otherwise attained.

It would be a mistake, however, to assume that because a wage gap exists "in general" that the Cleveland area can gain no further growth in manufacturing. First, we have noted that there is considerable diversity among Cleveland industries in these wage comparisons. According to our data, wage differences for some local industries are small or nonexistent.

More important, all firms are not equally sensitive to labor costs in relation to other factors in deciding where to locate new investment. In his study of location decisions of multi-plant firms Schmenner (1980) shows that some industries are able to tolerate higher wage bills to achieve other locational advantages. Thus where other attributes of the Cleveland environment are especially attractive to such industries, local growth may occur despite high wages. This point would not carry much weight if recent trends showed industry growth to be closely correlated with low wages, but as we shall see in Chapter V, that correlation does not appear. A number of industries that grew in the Cleveland area in the 1970s had average wage rates much higher than their counterparts in other regions.

Other Location Factors

Below we note other characteristics of the metropolitan Cleveland environment that influence business location decisions and offer a summary evaluation of their likely effects. Where insufficient information is available to support judgments, we indicate needs for additional research.

The Labor Force. The size and diversity of the Cleveland area labor force must be regarded as a local advantage, particularly for manufacturing. The Cleveland SCSA's total manufacturing work force in 1980 (369,000) was still larger than the totals for 30 states (including, for example, Alabama, Colorado, Kentucky, Maryland, and Washington). The industrial diversity we have noted also has been reflected in the diverse experiences and skills of local workers. A detailed analysis of local labor force characteristics is warranted, but was not possible in this study because the only suitable and recent data on this subject (from the 1980 Census) have not been released. When they are, an understanding of local strengths and weaknesses in particular industries and occupations can be obtained.

Availability of Energy and Water. The Cleveland area has some substantial advantages in both of these areas. First, the State of Ohio enjoys a relatively secure energy supply, and this factor has become increasingly important in firm's decisionmaking since the 1973 oil embargo and the gas shortages of 1979. Sixty-one percent of Ohio's total energy consumption is supplied by coal and natural gas. This figure is higher than for any other state in which our comparison SMSAs are located. The next highest figure was 52 percent in Missouri. This does not mean that Clevelanders would not have to scramble for supplies in a crisis; only that they might not have to scramble as hard as some of their competitors. Second, Cleveland's direct access to unlimited supplies of fresh water is an important asset, particularly considering the constraining role the lack of water may play in the 1980s in parts of the sunbelt.

Availability of Capital. Because larger firms have access to national capital markets, the availability of capital generally is not regarded as an important location factor in economic development. Local capital may be more important for smaller firms, however. We found that bank deposits per capita in our comparison SMSAs were not much different than the figure for Cleveland ($5,313), although the figures for Atlanta, Minneapolis, Pittsburgh, and Seattle were somewhat higher. This evidence does not suggest that capital represents either an advantage or a disadvantage with respect to future growth.

State and Local Taxes. Much has been made of tax advantages in economic development programs, but recent literature on firms' location decisions suggests they are not often the determining factor compared to transportation and labor costs (see, for example, Schmenner, 1980). Nonetheless, as a variable that can be influenced locally, they deserve attention. Although results vary depending on the measures used, recent analysis indicates that personal tax burdens in Cleveland are below average compared to other large cities (Greater Cleveland Growth Association, 1979, and Government of the District of Columbia, 1981). Cleveland's position with respect to business taxation is less clear, because of the role of Ohio's Corporate Franchise Tax (on net worth). Analysis to clarify the effects of this tax in relation to others appears warranted.

Local Services and Infrastructure. Much of the literature on business location decisions assigns some weight to the quality of local public services and infrastructures, but there has been little detailed or systematic analysis of their effects. An authoritative study of infrastructure problems in the Cleveland area is now under way (see Humphrey et al., 1979); additional analysis may be required to shed light on how particular problems affect the requirements of different kinds of firms. There has been much discussion of public service levels of late, in the local press and elsewhere, often noting problems in the city (particularly the public school system) in contrast to high quality services in the suburbs. Again, additional analysis would be needed to determine effects on business decisions.

THE CLEVELAND ENVIRONMENT AS A LOCATION FOR PEOPLE

The factors discussed below do not often appear explicitly in the calculations made by firms when they select locations for new plants or decide where to expand and contract operations. They are nonetheless important in the personal decisions made by entrepreneurs as well as their workers.

Data comparing Cleveland with eight other metropolitan areas along a number of dimensions are presented in Tables 4.6 and 4.7.

The six items listed in Table 4.6 represent different aspects of Cleveland's "noneconomic" quality of life. It should come as no surprise that Cleveland does not rank well among metropolitan areas of similar size with respect to climate. Only Pittsburgh and Seattle with less sunshine but slightly warmer temperatures are close competitors in this regard, and the climate of neither of those cities enjoys a particularly favorable reputation.

Air quality remains a problem in the Cleveland area, one of the Environmental Protection Agency's "nonattainment areas." Baltimore, Pittsburgh, St. Louis, San Diego, and Seattle also share that classification. Of those SMSAs for which comparable data are available, only Pittsburgh's air quality was unhealthful or hazardous more days between 1976 and 1978 than Cleveland's. However, some comfort may be taken from the fact that among the cities with the worst air pollution, Cleveland ranked third worst in 1976 and fifth worst in 1980. In other words, Cleveland's air quality is improving faster than average among cities with difficult pollution problems.

The number of bound volumes in the municipal public library is presented in Table 4.6 as one indicator of one of Cleveland's clearest

Table 4.6

COMPARISON OF CLEVELAND AND EIGHT OTHER SMSAs AS RESIDENCES

Item	Cleve.	Atlanta	Balt.	Denver	Minnea.	Pitts.	St. Louis	San Diego	Seattle
Average Daily Temperature, °F	49.7	60.8	55.0	50.1	44.1	50.4	55.9	61.7	51.1
Hours with Sunshine, as a % of Possible	52	61	57	70	58	49	59	73	49
No. of Days with Unhealthful Air (1976-1978)	145	--	60	--	--	168	136	52	82
Millions of Volumes in Public Library	2.7	1.0	2.2	1.7	1.5	2.0	1.4	1.6	1.5
Total Crime per Million Population (1980)	563	758	747	836	614	349	649	704	786
Total Violent Crime per Million Population (1980)	79	84	116	64	36	38	77	63	56

SOURCES: Newspaper Enterprise Association, Inc. (1980), U.S. Department of Justice (1980), U.S. Department of Commerce, Bureau of the Census, *Statistical Abstract of the United States*, 1980.

Table 4.7

ANNUAL COSTS OF AN INTERMEDIATE BUDGET FOR A 4-PERSON FAMILY, AUTUMN 1976

(Dollars)

Location	Total	Food	Housing	Transport	Clothing	Personal Care	Medical Care	Income Taxes	Low Budget	High Budget
Cleveland	16,412	3,893	3,966	1,421	1,196	431	889	2,043	10,023	23,486
Atlanta	14,830	3,767	3,169	1,338	1,133	356	847	1,775	9,222	21,410
Baltimore	16,195	3,720	3,578	1,347	1,146	350	938	2,621	10,280	23,715
Denver	15,906	3,689	3,594	1,383	1,390	333	836	2,209	9,765	23,078
Minneapolis	16,810	3,776	3,692	1,360	1,154	375	816	3,124	10,085	24,556
Pittsburgh	15,515	3,966	3,336	1,348	1,079	347	786	2,157	9,697	22,418
St. Louis	15,623	3,957	3,490	1,467	1,092	360	776	2,005	9,612	22,437
San Diego	15,989	3,582	3,835	1,453	1,126	339	1,079	2,022	10,007	23,687
Seattle	16,204	3,948	3,909	1,405	1,274	390	971	1,774	10,770	22,935
Metro. U.S.	16,596	3,917	3,952	1,411	1,150	362	929	2,328	10,041	24,492
Nonmetro. South	13,885	3,506	3,050	1,357	1,067	328	767	1,570	8,828	19,442
Cleveland exceeds 8-city average by:	3%	2%	10%	2%	2%	18%	1%	-20%	1%	2%

SOURCE: U.S. Department of Labor, Bureau of Labor Statistics (1979a).

advantages. The same set of values that directed Clevelanders to support the public library substantially more than residents of the other cities also generated support for all of the areas well-known cultural institutions. There is no way to measure the advantage gained by the quality of Cleveland's orchestra, the breadth of its theater, or its many other cultural activities, but these are factors that clearly set the Cleveland area apart from other regional centers in the same general size class.

It is notoriously difficult to compare crime rates across cities. The figures reported in Table 4.6 represented crimes reported to police. If residents of different metropolitan areas are more or less likely to report any given crime—and this likelihood is known to vary—the statistics are misleading. However, if the figures can, in fact, be relied on, they reveal a mixed picture. Total crime in Cleveland is on the low side, but violent crime is comparatively high. As with air pollution, though, the time trends are more encouraging than the "snapshot" view. Both the total and violent crime rates were increasing at a substantially lower rate in Cleveland than in the average of the eight other cities.

Table 4.7 presents comparative data on various elements of the cost of living in our eight sample cities, in the metropolitan United States, and in the nonmetropolitan south. The cost of maintaining an "intermediate" standard of living for an urban family of four in Cleveland was less than three percent above the eight-city average. This is a trivial difference, and in fact, the Cleveland figure was slightly below the average cost of living in all U.S. metropolitan areas. Cleveland's cost of living disadvantage over the nonmetropolitan south is more substantial, amounting to about 18 percent. Most components of the standard of living follow the same pattern, with Cleveland figures falling slightly above the average for the nine SMSAs. The notable exceptions are income taxes, personal care, and, surprisingly, housing costs. The low income tax figure probably reflects Ohio's tradition of a relatively small public sector. We have not looked into the causes of the relatively high cost of personal services in Cleveland, but, in any case, it represents only a small proportion of the typical family's budget. The high cost of housing reported by the Bureau of Labor Statistics is perplexing. The general impression in Cleveland and, indeed, around the country (Boyer and Savageau, 1982) is that the price of housing is relatively low in Cleveland. There are two obvious candidate explanations for this observation and probably several less obvious ones. First, because the figures in Table 4.7 are for 1976, they probably do not reflect the rapid inflation in housing prices that took place in some regions in the late 1970s. Indeed, more recent figures on the average sale prices of homes indicate that Cleveland's average of

$61,800 in 1980 was about 17 percent *below* the nine-SMSA average, suggesting that recent housing price inflation has not hit Cleveland as badly as most other similarly sized SMSAs. The second explanation works in the opposite direction. The housing cost figures reported by the BLS include the cost of heating the house. With comparatively cold winters, the high cost of home heating may be significant in relation to a relatively low basic price of housing.

In general, though, the cost of living differentials between Cleveland and its "competition" are small, and one of the largest differentials, housing prices, may have diminished substantially over the last few years.

SUMMARY AND IMPLICATIONS

This review has not attempted to rank Cleveland's competitive position in relation to other areas; we doubt that could be done validly on any single scale even if much more ample evidence was available. Rather, we have examined a number of local characteristics broadly in response to findings in earlier chapters. Our focus has been on the role of manufacturing. In Chapter II, we saw that the manufacturing sector declined in the Cleveland area during the 1970s. In Chapter III, we found that sector still to be of critical importance to the economic health of the metropolis overall. Here, we have asked in effect whether the various characteristics of Cleveland's environment are now so inhospitable to manufacturing that any further investment in that sector is improbable.

Clearly, the evidence we have collected does not support that conclusion. We have found that while the percentage growth of the sunbelt may have been phenomenal of late, it has not altered the basic geographic pattern of economic activity in the United States dramatically. Cleveland's location still offers important advantages with respect to distance from markets and suppliers. We have also found that while the overall wage gap between the Cleveland area and competitive locations remains substantial and has not been narrowing significantly, it should not rule out all prospects for investment in manufacturing.

Obviously, where sizable differences in labor costs persist, Cleveland can be expected to lose jobs it might otherwise have obtained. However, our data indicate that the wage gap is not uniform across industries: wages in some local industries are comparatively low. Other local industries should be able to grow in the Cleveland area despite high wages, i.e., industries that are not labor-intensive or place a higher value on other advantages of Cleveland's environment or location. These should include firms that sell or buy products with high transport costs to or from other manufacturing firms or require a great deal of fresh water or secure energy supplies. They might also include firms that have special needs for skilled labor available in the local market and those that are heavily dependent on a good existing network of customer-supplier relationships, easily accessible production know-how, and a broad array of supporting business services.

While we examined only a few characteristics, we also found that the Cleveland area offers a living environment with a mix of advantages and disadvantages. The mix casts some doubt on a simple hypothesis implicit in many accounts of growth in the sunbelt. Because of a general reduction in transportation costs and other factors, entrepreneurs have more freedom to locate their businesses in places that offer substantial amenities as a living environment. This much is true. The problem is that amenity is not always equated with climate; there has been little solid research on the comparative importance of other factors. If climate was the whole story, why did so many executives retain their residences in Cleveland's suburbs while they were helping their corporations establish new branch plants in the south during the 1970s? Surely, a social structure dominated by people with similar views and interests (i.e., other entrepreneurs), strong cultural institutions, and other advantages of the Cleveland environment belong somewhere in the definition of amenity.

Basically, the mix of conditions we have found suggests that any monolithic argument about locational advantages (i.e., the sunbelt is more attractive to everyone) is misleading. The view that different kinds of people and industries are attracted by different combinations of location factors seems a more realistic starting place for the analysis of prospects in the future. This view implies that "business climate surveys" cannot be expected to provide consistently reliable guidelines. One of the most frequently cited (Alexander Grant and Co., 1979) placed Ohio 45th among all states as a location for business in general. More recently, however, another rating of states that emphasized factors of concern to small business (Padda, 1981) placed Ohio in the second highest of five groups. Abend (1981) concludes: "All companies have different needs ... that's why studies of the so-called business climate don't mean much."

Looking only at the descriptive characteristics in this chapter, we conclude that metropolitan Cleveland should continue to be an attractive environment for a number of types of manufacturing enterprises as well as nonmanufacturing enterprises. These data, however, do not offer a sense of proportion. Are the industries that can work well in the Cleveland area insignificantly small in relation to others suffering serious declines? One way to address this question is to look beneath the surface trends presented in Chapter II, and to examine the actual performance of much more narrowly defined industries during the 1970s. This is the subject of our next two chapters.

PART C

TRENDS IN THE PERFORMANCE OF METROPOLITAN CLEVELAND INDUSTRIES

In Part B, we reviewed characteristics of metropolitan Cleveland's various industries and the roles they play in the local economy. Here we examine how they have changed over time. Again, we focus on the decade from 1967 to 1977 for the same reasons discussed in Chapter II—principally because it is the most recent period for which data are available to support comparisons of detailed (three- and four-digit) industries. Chapter V analyzes the performance of the area's manufacturing industries and Chapter VI analyzes performance among its nonmanufacturing industries.

There is no perfect single measure of "performance," however. In these chapters we rely consistently on three indicators, each of which tells us something different about the character of recent changes in local industries.[1]

- Change in a local industry's total employment.
- Change in a local industry's share of total employment in the same industry nationally.
- Change in a local industry's employment concentration ratio.

---

[1]It would of course be preferable to use other physical and financial measures related to industry output and profitability, in addition to measures related to employment, in assessing recent performance. Unfortunately, consistent data series on the former are not available. It should be understood that the data based on employment tell only part of the story, but they tell a very important part.

The first measure is straightforward. For example, Cleveland SMSA employment in wholesale trade in machinery, equipment, and supplies (SIC 508) increased from 11,860 in 1967 to 12,800 in 1977, an increase of 7.9 percent over the decade. This industry, therefore, made a clear contribution to the primary goal of economic development—job generation.

The industry's change in share of national employment, however, is a better measure of its competitive strength than its change in employment per se. For example, SIC 508 employment in metropolitan Cleveland represented 1.80 percent of all employment in the same group nationally in 1967, but only 1.34 percent in 1977: its share had declined by 26 percent, indicating that the industry was doing much better in the United States as a whole than it was locally. Another local industry that had the same 7.9 percent increase in jobs but also increased its national market share would obviously be a stronger bet for the future.

Actually, expecting a Cleveland industry to increase or even maintain its market share is too harsh a standard, given all of the growth that has been occurring elsewhere. A more reasonable expectation would be that its share decrease no more than that of all Cleveland SMSA industries on the average. That average was a decrease of 14 percent from 1967 to 1977; thus even by this standard the local performance of SIC 508 was not up to par.

The third measure—change in concentration ratio—is more complicated but no less important. In Chapter III we emphasized the importance of an industry's export or import orientation in its contribution to local growth or decline. There, we had an input-output framework enabling us to estimate export employment directly at the two-digit level. Similar data do not exist for the detailed industries we review in Chapters V and VI. The concentration ratio, however, is a crude proxy for the same thing that can be constructed with employment data alone.

The concentration ratio for a local industry is its share of total national employment in the same industry divided by the locality's share of total national population. In 1977, Cleveland SMSA residents represented 0.89 percent of total national population. If a particular local industry was just big enough to serve the SMSA population, we would expect it to have about the same 0.89 percent share of the national employment in that industry. In these circumstances its concentration ratio would be 1.00; 0.89 divided by 0.89. If the industry was a heavy exporter, however, we would expect a much higher concentration ratio; its share of national industry employment should be greater than the amount needed just to serve the local population. Similarly, if the SMSA has to import a large amount of a particular product, we would expect the local industry that produces that product to have a concentration ratio of less than 1.00.[2]

Concentration ratios in a metropolis, at least for major sectors, seldom change rapidly. A gain or loss in share of national employment is often accompanied by a gain or loss in share of national population. Thus it is a very good sign if a particular concentration ratio does increase noticeably in a short period of time. It is an indication that a foundation is being laid for yet more growth in the future. Similarly, any sharp drop in a concentration ratio is a serious blow to an area's future prospects.

Turning again to wholesaling in machinery, equipment, and supplies (SIC 508), we saw that its share of national employment in 1977 was 1.34 percent. Dividing this by 0.89 we find that its concentration ratio was 1.50. Thus it appeared export-oriented (50 percent more employees than needed to serve the local population alone). In 1967, however, its concentration ratio had been 1.71. The ratio had decreased by 13 percent over the decade; it would appear that the industry's export orientation was slipping.

There are two other measures available only for manufacturing industries, which we employ in Chapter V to analyze performance.

- Change in a local industry's value added per production worker hour.
- Change in a local industry's investment (new capital expenditures) per production worker hour.

There are some imperfections in the data available on these measures (which we will explain in Chapter V) but if used properly they add important dimensions to our understanding of local industrial change.

By our choice of measures (i.e., changing shares and concentration ratios) we are automatically building in comparisons of each industry's performance in metropolitan Cleveland against that of the nation as a whole. Comparisons with performance in other areas,

---

[2]The literature of regional economics commonly labels this measure "location quotient" rather than "concentration ratio." We chose the latter for this report because we believe it gives readers from a general audience a more direct sense of its meaning. It should also be stressed that this term is used in other ways in other fields; it should not be confused with the use that has wide currency in industrial organization, for example.

We also emphasize again that this measure is only a crude indicator of export-import orientation. In some cases, it could be quite inaccurate. For example, Houston probably has a high concentration ratio in air conditioning repair due more to the nature of local consumption compared to other areas than to significant exports. For other limitations see Isard (1960), pp. 125-126.

however, are needed as well. We are interested in learning about how well Cleveland industries are doing in relation to "the competition" and total U.S. performance averages out much variation between other competitors. On the other hand, given the large quantities of data to be examined, comparisons with too many other areas would make the story unintelligible.

We have chosen to present one other comparison each for the manufacturing and the nonmanufacturing sectors. For nonmanufacturing, we relate Cleveland SMSA data to comparable measures for the average of all SMSAs in the United States. Most nonmanufacturing industries are concentrated in metropolitan areas, thus we want to see how Cleveland area trucking, banking, business services, etc., are changing compared to those areas. Manufacturing, however, is no longer as concentrated in the SMSAs as it once was. The fastest manufacturing growth areas in the 1970s were in the sunbelt. The nine southern states as defined in Chapter II, therefore, offer more relevant comparisons for our purposes.

V. PERFORMANCE OF CLEVELAND MANUFACTURING INDUSTRIES

In Part B, we noted that even given its recent troubles, manufacturing remains by far metropolitan Cleveland's most critical economic sector. Sales of its products in external markets still bring in the bulk of the revenue needed to offset outflows of funds to pay for imports. In contrast, the service sector has grown significantly in the metropolis over the past two decades, but as late as 1980 its contribution to aggregate net exports remained comparatively small.

In this chapter, we examine the recent history of Cleveland's manufacturing sector. We first review how the area's manufacturing employment is divided among major industries. We then examine performance in each of these industries and their components, comparing the variables described in the last few pages.

COMPOSITION OF THE MANUFACTURING SECTOR

Table 5.1 provides 1977 employment data at the two-digit level for the Cleveland SCSA and SMSA. The SCSA had a total of almost 400,000 manufacturing employees; about 70 percent worked in the SMSA. Overall, the distributions in the two areas are similar. There are five to six very large industries, all producers of durable goods, and a host of smaller ones, for the most part producers of nondurables.

The analysis in the remainder of this chapter deals with the SMSA only, since comparable data on our performance measures at the three- and four-digit level exist for the SMSA but not for the SCSA. Thus we have organized the summary data in Table 5.1 in response to the structure of SMSA manufacturing. There the five largest industries account for 69 pecent of all employment classified by SIC: primary metals (SIC 33, 12 percent), fabricated metals (SIC 34, 18 percent), nonelectrical machinery (SIC 35, 18 percent), electrical machinery (SIC 36, 9 percent), and transportation equipment (SIC 37, 11 percent).[1]

---

[1]Clearly, if data had been available to support detailed analysis for the SCSA, the rubber industry in Akron would have placed SIC 30 (rubber and plastic products) in this class as well.

Table 5.1

MANUFACTURING EMPLOYMENT, CLEVELAND SCSA AND SMSA, 1977

Industry	Cleveland SCSA		Cleveland SMSA	
	Number (000s)	Percent	Number (000s)	Percent
TOTAL MANUFACTURING	398.9	--	265.4	--
Not Classified by SIC	17.2	--	23.2	--
TOTAL CLASSIFIED BY SIC	381.7	100.0	242.2	100.0
33 Primary Metals	50.3	13.2	29.2	12.1
34 Fabricated Metals	62.5	16.4	44.7	18.4
35 Nonelectrical Machinery	60.4	15.8	44.0	18.2
36 Electrical Machinery	26.0	6.8	21.7	9.0
37 Transportation Equipment	52.2	13.7	26.4	10.9
Other Manufacturing				
20 Food and Kindred Products	10.4	2.7	8.5	3.5
22 Textile Mill Products	2.1	.6	2.3	.9
23 Apparel & Other Textile Prod.	8.6	2.3	7.8	3.2
24 Lumber and Wood Products	1.3	.3	1.0	.4
25 Furniture and Fixtures	2.8	.7	2.4	1.0
26 Paper and Allied Products	6.8	1.8	5.0	2.1
27 Printing and Publishing	16.6	4.3	12.9	5.3
28 Chemicals and Allied Products	22.4	5.9	9.6	4.0
29 Petroleum and Coal Products	1.8	.5	1.8	.7
30 Rubber and Misc. Plastic Prod.	38.7	10.1	9.6	4.0
32 Stone, Clay & Glass Products	6.5	1.7	4.6	1.9
38 Instruments and Related Prod.	7.7	2.0	6.6	2.7
39 Misc. Manufacturing Industries	4.6	1.2	4.1	1.7
Total	130.3	34.1	76.2	31.4

SOURCE: Data files compiled by Rand from County Business Patterns records
(for Cleveland SCSA) and Census of Manufactures records (for Cleveland SMSA).
(See Appendix B.)

Concentration Ratios for Major Manufacturing Industries

In Fig. 5.1, we plot concentration ratios for the Cleveland SMSA's six major manufacturing industries (the five listed above plus "Other Manufacturing"). This is another way of reaching the conclusion we discussed in Chapter III, i.e., the largest two-digit manufacturing categories clearly mean the most to the metropolis in terms of export orientation. Large industries do not always have high concentration ratios—e.g., SMSA wholesale and retail trade employment is about seven times the size of employment in fabricated metals, yet its concentration ratio is only one-third as big—but within manufacturing, size seems to make a difference.

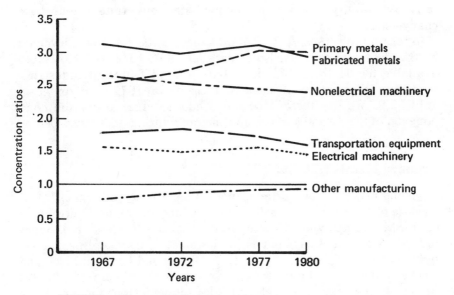

SOURCE: File compiled from Census of Manufactures records (see Appendix B).

Fig. 5.1—Concentration ratios for major Cleveland SMSA manufacturing industries, 1967-1980

Until recently, fabricated metals had been on top along this dimension, but during the 1970s its ratio declined moderately whereas that of primary metals increased and passed it by the end of the decade. It is noteworthy that all five of the major durable goods producers have high ratios while those for the "Other Manufacturing" category, are less than 1.0 throughout. Thus there is considerable diversity even among these major sectors. The concentration ratio for primary metals in 1980 (3.0) was twice that for the manufacturing sector on the average and more than three times the level for "Other Manufacturing."

Components of Major Sectors

The U.S. *Census of Manufactures* provides the only data that exist on several key performance indicators for manufacturing industries. Information is provided at different levels of detail for different geographical areas because of variations in industrial structures, e.g., data for a particular four-digit industry are likely to be available for SMSAs in which it is sizable but not for those where it is small. Similarly, availability changes for a single SMSA over time as industries change size.

In examining *Census of Manufactures* data for the Cleveland SMSA, we found that consistent data for 1967, 1972, and 1977 were available for 51 three-digit industries and 44 four-digit industries. Summary information on each of these as of 1977 is presented in Table 5.2. We use these data and others to characterize the components of Cleveland's six major manufacturing industries below.

Primary Metals (SIC 33)

Among major sectors, primary metals has the second highest average size of establishment (155 employees) and the highest percentage of all SMSA employment located in the City of Cleveland (55). About half of its total employment is in the blast furnace and basic steel industry; major firms are Republic and Jones and Laughlin. Iron and steel foundries are the next largest component (24 percent). Twelve percent of the sector's jobs are provided by nonferrous foundries, the Aluminum Company of America being the major employer.

Fabricated Metals (SIC 34)

This industry is made up of generally smaller establishments than in primary metals (average size 58 employees); 45 percent of its employees work in the city proper. The largest employer is the metal stampings group (in the 34X category in Table 5.2), which has been heavily oriented to supplying the automobile industry. Historically, Ford and General Motors have been its largest producers. Other large

Table 5.2

EMPLOYMENT AND EMPLOYMENT CHANGE IN CLEVELAND SMSA MANUFACTURING INDUSTRIES, 1967-77

SIC	Industry	1977 Employment		1967-77 Percent Change		
		Total Employ. (000s)	Concen- tration Ratio	Clev. SMSA Employ.	SMSA Share U.S. Employ.	SMSA Concen. Ratio
	Major Durable Goods Manufacturing					
33	PRIMARY METAL INDUSTRIES	29.2	2.96	−21.3	−9.5	6.3
331	Blast Fur. & Basic Stl. Prod.	14.1	3.00	−7.2	8.1	27.1
332	Iron & Steel Foundries	7.1	3.60	9.2	14.3	34.4
3341	Sec. Nonferrous Metals	1.2	7.17	9.1	−.7	16.7
335	Nonferrous Rolling & Drawing	2.1	1.33	−44.7	−39.3	−28.8
3351	Copper Rolling & Drawing	1.2	4.32	−33.3	−14.2	.7
335X	Other Nonfer. & Rol. & Draw.	.9	.70	−55.0	−52.4	−43.5
336	Nonferrous Foundries	3.5	4.81	−34.0	−27.9	−15.4
3361	Aluminum Foundries	2.7	5.84	−37.2	−45.6	−36.1
336X	Other Nonfer. Foundries	.8	3.03	−20.0	18.8	40.1
33X	Other Prim. Met. Industries	1.2	1.63	−76.9	−64.1	−57.9
34	FABRICATED METAL PRODUCTS	44.7	3.24	−1.3	−14.9	−.2
342	Cutlery, Hand Tools & Hdwe.	1.6	1.07	−59.0	−62.1	−55.3
343	Plumbing, Heat., Exc. Elec.	1.4	2.97	16.7	43.0	68.1
344	Fab. Struc. Metal Products	5.6	1.49	−18.8	−26.0	−12.8
3441	Fab. Structural Metal	1.0	1.14	−23.1	−16.7	−1.8
3443	Fab. Pl. Wk. (Boiler Shops)	.8	.73	−46.7	−58.4	−51.0
3444	Sheet Metal Work	2.2	3.21	37.5	21.0	42.1
344X	Other Fab. Structural Metal	1.6	1.43	−36.0	−40.9	−30.9
345	Screw Mach. Prod., Bolts, etc.	6.7	7.22	−36.2	−29.2	−16.7
3451	Screw Machine Products	2.4	6.19	−11.1	−.6	17.0
3452	Bolts, Nuts, Riv., & Wash.	4.3	7.97	−44.9	−39.2	−28.5
3471	Plating and Polishing	1.6	2.95	0.0	−10.0	5.9
349	Misc. Fab. Metal Products	6.7	2.71	−13.0	−41.2	−30.8
3494	Valves & Pipe Fittings	2.8	2.91	−39.1	−46.6	−37.2
349X	Other Misc. Fab. Met. Prod.	3.9	2.57	25.8	−31.2	−19.2
34X	Stampings & Other Fab. Metals	21.1	5.15	56.3	25.9	48.2
35	NONELECTRICAL MACHINERY	44.0	2.38	−15.2	−24.1	−10.8

Table 5.2 (Continued)

SIC	Industry	1977 Employment		1967-77 Percent Change		
		Total Employ. (000s)	Concentration Ratio	Clev. SMSA Employ.	SMSA Share U.S. Employ.	SMSA Concen. Ratio
	Major Durable Goods Manufacturing (Continued)					
353	Constr. & Related Machinery	10.4	3.52	5.1	-14.0	1.1
354	Metalworking Machinery	14.3	5.42	-21.4	-11.1	4.6
3542	Mach. Tools, Met. Form. Typ.	1.2	5.71	-33.3	-17.9	-3.4
3544	Spec. Dies, Tls., Jigs, Fix.	3.3	3.52	-10.8	-4.1	12.5
3545	Mach. Tool Accessories	4.1	8.56	-10.9	-.7	16.8
354X	Other Metalworking Machinery	5.7	5.62	-29.6	-17.6	-3.2
355	Special Industry Machinery	4.9	2.99	-16.9	-7.2	9.4
3559	Spec. Ind. Machinery, NEC	3.7	5.91	0.0	1.0	18.7
355X	Other Spec. Ind. Machinery	1.2	1.19	-45.5	-35.4	-23.8
356	General Industrial Machinery	3.8	1.37	-22.4	-30.9	-19.1
3564	Blowers and Fans	.5	2.02	66.7	25.0	47.2
3567	Ind. Furnaces & Ovens	.4	2.97	-20.0	-15.3	-.6
3569	Gen. Ind. Machinery, NEC	.8	1.57	-46.7	-63.5	-57.1
356X	Other Gen. Ind. Machinery	2.1	1.12	-19.2	-23.1	-9.0
358	Refrigeration & Service Mach.	1.0	.59	-28.6	-47.9	-38.9
35X	Other Mach., Exc. Electrical	9.6	1.42	-17.2	-31.7	-19.5
36	ELECTRICAL MACHINERY	21.7	1.42	-14.6	-7.0	9.7
361	Elec. Distributing Equip.	.7	.69	-77.4	-65.6	-59.3
362	Elec. Industrial Apparatus	7.3	4.15	-9.9	-6.1	10.4
3621	Motors and Generators	1.5	1.75	-51.6	-43.7	-33.7
3622	Industrial Controls	1.9	3.87	-5.0	-13.6	1.6
362X	Other Elec. Ind. Apparatus	3.9	9.55	30.0	22.7	44.2
363	Household Appliances	2.1	1.46	0.0	4.3	22.4
364	Elec. Light. & Wiring Equip.	4.7	3.22	-14.5	-18.6	-4.2
369	Misc. Elec. Equip. Supplies	4.2	3.12	31.3	-7.7	8.6
36X	Other Elec. & Electron. Equip.	2.7	.33	-20.6	-9.5	6.5
37	TRANSPORTATION EQUIPMENT	26.4	1.68	-33.2	-30.7	-18.5
371	Motor Vehicles & Equipment	20.8	2.68	-20.6	-33.0	-21.3
372	Aircraft and Parts	5.1	1.33	-60.5	-26.4	-13.8
37X	Other Transportation Equipment	.5	.12	25.0	-20.7	-7.5

Table 5.2 (Continued)

| SIC | Industry | 1977 Employment | | 1967-77 Percent Change | | |
		Total Employ. (000s)	Concentration Ratio	Clev. SMSA Employ.	SMSA Share U.S. Employ.	SMSA Concen. Ratio
	Other Manufacturing					
20	FOOD AND KINDRED PRODUCTS	8.5	.63	-26.7	-20.5	-6.0
201	Meat Products	.7	.26	-41.7	-41.5	-30.5
2011	Meat Packing Products	.4	.31	0.0	16.6	38.0
201X	Other Meat Products	.3	.20	-62.5	-67.9	-62.9
202	Dairy Products	.8	.59	-69.2	-53.7	-45.4
2026	Fluid Milk	.7	.85	-68.2	-43.8	-33.7
202X	Other Dairy Products	.1	.19	-75.0	-72.5	-66.7
203	Canned, Cured & Frozen Foods	1.6	.77	23.1	36.3	61.7
2086	Bottled & Canned Soft Drin.	1.2	1.19	0.0	8.1	27.3
209	Misc. Food & Kindred Prod.	.9	.70	-10.0	-15.7	-.1
2099	Food Preparations, NEC	.4	.63	0.0	-13.8	1.3
209X	Other Misc. Food, Kin. Prod.	.5	.76	-16.7	-15.9	-1.6
20X	Other Food & Kin. Products	3.3	.67	-23.3	-19.8	-5.0
22	TEXTILE MILL PRODUCTS	2.3	.29	-28.1	-23.7	-10.1
23	APPAREL & OTHER TEX. PRODUCTS	7.8	.66	5.4	7.2	25.9
233	Women's & Misses' Outerwear	2.3	.58	4.5	-4.4	11.2
23X	Other Appar., Other Tex. Prod.	5.5	.70	5.8	13.0	32.6
25	FURNITURE AND FIXTURES	2.4	.59	-33.3	-38.9	-28.1
251	Household Furniture	.9	.33	-25.0	-27.9	-36.7
254	Partitions and Fixtures	1.2	2.36	-40.0	-49.8	-41.0
2542	Metal Partitions & Fix.	1.0	4.03	-44.4	-55.0	-47.1
254X	Other Partitions & Fix.	.2	.77	0.0	-13.9	1.2
25X	Other Furniture & Fixtures	.3	.35	-25.0	-38.3	-27.1
26	PAPER AND ALLIED PRODUCTS	5.0	.90	8.7	10.5	30.7

Table 5.2 (Continued)

SIC	Industry	1977 Employment		1967-77 Percent Change		
		Total Employ. (000s)	Concentration Ratio	Clev. SMSA Employ.	SMSA Share U.S. Employ.	SMSA Concen. Ratio
	Other Manufacturing (Continued)					
265	Paperbd. Containers & Boxes	2.8	1.55	-6.7	0.0	17.6
2651	Folding Paperboard Boxes	.7	1.77	0.0	10.3	30.0
2653	Corrug. & Solid Fiber Bxs.	1.6	1.78	6.7	2.0	20.6
265X	Other Paperbd. Cont. & Bxs.	.5	.97	-37.5	-22.1	-8.8
26X	Other Paper & Allied Prod.	2.2	.59	37.5	36.1	60.8
27	PRINTING AND PUBLISHING	12.9	1.33	-27.5	-31.6	19.8
2711	Newspapers	4.1	1.32	-10.9	-14.4	.5
2721	Periodicals	1.1	1.77	-21.4	-11.1	4.3
273	Books	.3	.32	-76.9	-79.1	-75.6
278	Blankbooks & Bookbinding	.6	1.21	0.0	-4.3	12.4
2791	Typesetting	.3	1.24	0.0	-6.2	9.7
27X	Other Printing & Publishing	6.5	1.52	-32.3	-38.2	-27.2
28	CHEMICALS AND ALLIED PRODUCTS	9.6	1.23	-36.4	-39.2	-18.4
281	Industrial Inorganic Chem.	1.8	1.85	-61.7	-13.6	2.0
282	Plastics Materials & Synthe.	1.0	.72	-61.5	-57.8	-50.2
284	Soap, Clean., & Toilet Goods	.6	.61	-14.3	-25.6	-11.9
28X	Other Chem. & Allied Prod.	6.2	1.40	-12.7	-43.6	-33.4
29	PETROLEUM AND COAL PRODUCTS	1.8	1.39	50.0	44.8	70.1
30	RUBBER AND PLASTIC PRODUCTS	9.6	1.50	43.3	2.6	20.3
32	STONE, CLAY, & GLASS PRODUCTS	4.6	.85	-4.2	-7.9	8.9
3272	Concrete Products, NEC	.4	.73	0.0	-7.9	9.2
3273	Ready-Mixed Concrete	.8	1.03	14.3	-3.1	13.9
32X	Other Stone, Clay & Gls. Pr.	3.4	.82	-8.1	-9.2	6.0
38	INSTRUMENTS & RELATED PRODUCTS	6.6	1.33	73.7	22.5	44.6

Table 5.2 (Continued)

		1977 Employment		1967-77 Percent Change		
SIC	Industry	Total Employ. (000s)	Concen- tration Ratio	Clev. SMSA Employ.	SMSA Share U.S. Employ.	SMSA Concen- Ratio
		Other Manufacturing (Continued)				
382	Meas. & Control. Devices	5.3	2.99	76.7	-7.9	8.2
38X	Other Instr. & Relat. Prod.	1.3	.41	62.5	31.3	50.9
39	MISC. MANUFACTURING INDUSTRIES	4.1	1.05	-2.4	-6.3	10.5
395	Pens, Penc., Off., Art Supp.	.3	1.06	-57.1	-53.2	-45.3
399	Miscellaneous Manufactures	2.6	1.93	-7.1	-12.2	3.2
39X	Other Misc. Mfg. Industries	1.2	.53	71.4	63.2	90.6
TOTAL MANUFACTURING		265.4	1.79	-13.5	-14.7	37.5

SOURCE: Data file compiled by Rand from Census of Manufactures records (see Appendix B).

components include structural metal products (13 percent of total employment) and "screw machine products" (15 percent). The Eaton Corporation is the most notable firm in the latter group. The remainder of the industry is quite heterogeneous including the production of cutlery, handtools, hardware, plumbing and heating materials, valves and pipe fittings, and numerous other metal products.

Nonelectrical Machinery (SIC 35)

The nonelectrical machinery industry is about the same size as fabricated metals and has the same proportion of its employees working in the central city. Its average establishment size, however, is yet smaller: 39 employees. Its largest component (one-third of employment) is metalworking machinery; firms like Warner Swasey and Acme-Cleveland have helped to build a primary reputation for Cleveland in this field. Construction and related machinery is the second largest component with 24 percent of total employment. The "special industry machinery" group (11 percent) and the "general industry machinery" group (nine percent) come next. Machinery for the printing industry has been an important product of the former, whereas the latter includes heavy industrial machinery as well as office machines (included in SIC 356X on Table 5.2). Again, there is a large heterogeneous remainder, in this case made up of general machine shops and a host of other small firms.

Electrical Machinery (SIC 36)

The Cleveland SMSA's electrical machinery group is about half the size of the previous two industries we have discussed. More of its employees work in the suburbs (62 percent) and its typical plant size is larger (107 employees). One-third of its employees are in the electrical industrial apparatus group, including the production of motors, generators, and industrial control devices. Products of electrical lighting and wiring equipment account for 22 percent of its employment and producers of household appliances for another 10 percent. Once again, there is a large and diverse residual category.

Transportation Equipment (SIC 37)

This industry is dominated by large plants (256 employees per establishment on average). Eighty percent of its employment is in the motor vehicle category where Ford and Chevrolet are major firms. Most of the remaining employees are in the aircraft sector where TRW and Cleveland Pneumatic Co. are key producers.

Other Manufacturing

Other manufacturing industries together account for 31 percent of the SMSA's manufacturing employment. There are 12 two-digit industries in this group. Only seven of them have 5,000 employees or more (two percent of total manufacturing employment): printing and publishing (12,900 employees); rubber and plastic products (9,600); chemicals and allied products (9,600); food and kindred products (8,500); apparel and other textile products (7,800); instruments and related products (6,600); and paper and allied products (5,000).

Diversity in Cleveland Manufacturing

As noted in Chapter III, diversity is an attribute to be valued in any local economy. If a metropolis has all its eggs in a very few baskets it is particularly vulnerable when hard times hit its key producers. In a diversified economy, it is more likely that declines in some industries will be balanced out against gains in others.

Cleveland has always been thought of as one of the most diversified manufacturing centers in the nation. A glance at the number of listings on Table 5.2 should confirm that view. To gain a clearer understanding of Cleveland's position, however, we have developed a crude "diversity index" that permits quantitative comparisons of diversity in different metropolitan areas.

The SIC system lists 163 possible three-digit industry codes in manufacturing. A perfectly diversified manufacturing sector would have exactly 1/163 (0.6 percent) of its employment in each of these industries. The total U.S. economy (which should be more diversified than any of its component regions), however, has 0.6 percent or more of its employment in only 62. In our diversity index for a particular metropolis, we add up the number of three-digit industries with at least 0.6 percent of local manufacturing employment and divide by 62. If a metropolis had that level of representation in 31 industries, for example, its index value would be 0.5; i.e., it would be about half as diversified as the total U.S. manufacturing sector.

We have calculated the index values as of 1972 for the Cleveland SMSA, and other comparison SMSAs including the New York City SMSA, which has long been noted as perhaps America's most diversified metropolis.

The results show that several of these areas share high scores. The index value for both New York and St. Louis is 0.74. Cleveland comes next at 0.72. Anaheim and Houston do not fall far behind (0.69 to 0.71 range). The scores for Baltimore and Pittsburgh, however, are much lower (0.52 and 0.56, respectively).

Suppose we establish a similar index counting diversity of representation only in the major durable goods production industries (SICs 33 through 37) rather than, as above, the full range of manufacturing activities (again the U.S. count is set equal to 1.00). Here, Cleveland comes out far ahead of the rest with a score of 0.92. The scores for the other SMSAs are 0.79 for Anaheim, 0.71 for Detroit, 0.67 for St. Louis, 0.63 for Pittsburgh and Houston, 0.38 for New York and 0.33 for Baltimore.

While we have not calculated scores for all metropolitan areas, saying that Cleveland is one of America's most diversified manufacturing centers is a safe generalization. It may well be the nation's most diversified producer of major durables.

CHANGE IN EMPLOYMENT

In reviewing employment change since 1967, we first present data for total manufacturing and Cleveland's six major manufacturing industries. In each case, however, this tells only part of the story. Suppose, for example, that a particular major industry has been declining slightly since the late 1960s. That result could emerge in two quite different circumstances: (1) all of the detailed (three- and four-digit) subcomponents were decreasing at about the same rate; or (2) a sizable number of subcomponents were growing rapidly, but an even larger number were dropping sharply. To find out about the range of differences in performance we use the detailed groupings presented in Table 5.2. In all there are 84 nonoverlapping industries that account for all manufacturing employment. These include all four-digit sectors, those three-digit industries that have no identified four-digit subcomponents, and all two-digit industries without subcomponents.

Figure 5.2 shows changes in total manufacturing employment (expressed as an index, 1967 = 100) for the 1967-80 period in the

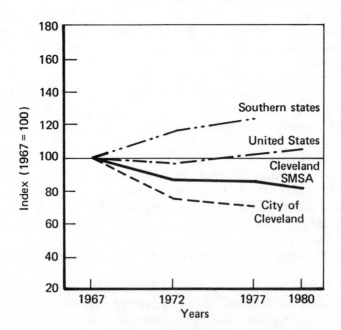

SOURCE: File compiled from Census of Manufactures
records (see Appendix B).

Fig. 5.2—Index of total manufacturing employment,
Cleveland, southern states, and United States,
1967-1980

Cleveland SMSA and other areas. Most of the graph simply depicts the same story we told in Chapter I in another way: the Cleveland SMSA manufacturing sector lost employment rapidly from 1967 to 1972 and then more gradually from 1972 to 1977; total U.S. manufacturing employment changed only modestly during the decade and the sector grew rapidly in the southern states throughout.

However, it adds two additional comparisons. First, it shows that manufacturing in the City of Cleveland followed the same general pattern as in the SMSA but its decline was more substantial. Second, where the needed data were available, it extends the lines through the 1980 recession year showing a more rapid decline for the Cleveland SMSA and a continued gradual increase for national manufacturing. By 1980, the Cleveland SMSA manufacturing sector supported only 81 percent of the jobs it had supported in 1967. Its share of total national manufacturing employment had dropped from 1.6 percent to 1.3 percent.

Growth and Decline in Major Industries

Graphs constructed similarly for Cleveland's six major industries appear in Fig. 5.3. In every case, rank comparisons between the areas are the same: the southern states exhibited the best performance, the national manufacturing sector came next, Cleveland SMSA employment fell behind the U.S. total, and manufacturing in the City of Cleveland suffered the most serious declines. But there are important differences in directions and rates of change among these industries.

Overall, fabricated metals and nonelectrical machinery had the best records. National employment in the former grew consistently over the period, although most rapidly during its first five years. In the Cleveland SMSA this industry's employment in 1977 was almost the same as it had been in 1967, although it was later hit hard by the 1980 downturn. The 1967-77 growth rate for the southern states was almost three times the national rate for the industry.

United States employment in nonelectrical machinery suffered a modest decline over 1967-72 but rebounded strongly thereafter. In the SMSA, the industry also showed strength after 1972, but not enough to regain its 1967 level. In the southern states, this industry experienced phenomenal growth; those states had 71 percent more nonelectrical machinery jobs in 1977 than they had a decade earlier.

Curves for electrical machinery were generally similar in shape but with less promising results. The 1967-72 decline for this industry in the United States was substantial; it did not regain its 1967 level

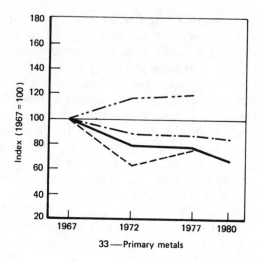

––– City of Cleveland
▬▬▬ Cleveland SMSA
–·– U.S.
–··– Southern states

33 — Primary metals

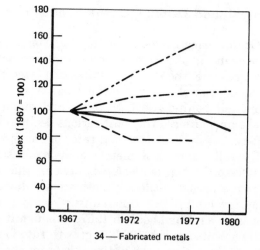

34 — Fabricated metals

SOURCE: File compiled from Census of Manufactures
records (see Appendix B).

Fig. 5.3—Index of employment in six major manufacturing
industries, Cleveland, southern states, and
United States, 1967-1980

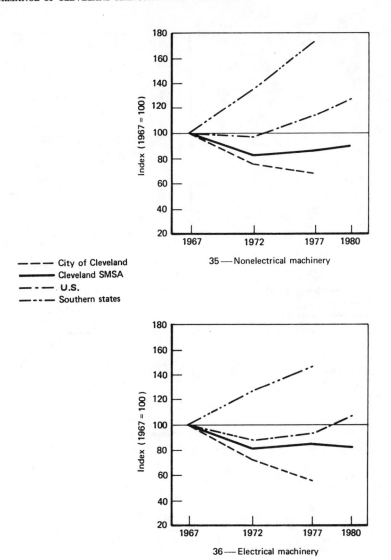

----- City of Cleveland
━━━ Cleveland SMSA
─ · ─ U.S.
─ ·· ─ Southern states

35 — Nonelectrical machinery

36 — Electrical machinery

SOURCE: File compiled from Census of Manufactures
records (see Appendix B).

Fig. 5.3—Continued

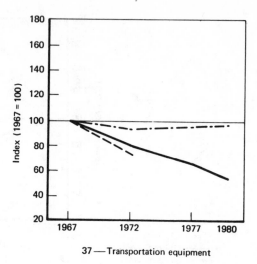

37 — Transportation equipment

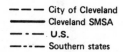

- - - City of Cleveland
—— Cleveland SMSA
—·— U.S.
—··— Southern states

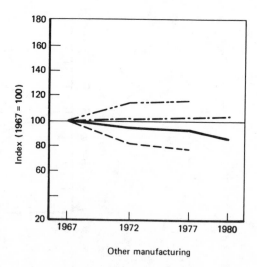

Other manufacturing

SOURCE: File compiled from Census of Manufactures
records (see Appendix B).

Fig. 5.3—Continued

until after 1977. The SMSA curve here is close to the U.S. curve through most of the period, but it dropped after 1977 while the industry was rebounding elsewhere. Electrical machinery employment also grew rapidly in the southern states, but not at the same pace as employment in the two industries noted above.

Among the six industries shown, "Other Manufacturing" exhibited the most gradual change over the period in all areas, thus the gaps between areas are less pronounced. The pattern, nonetheless, remained the same: the comparatively modest changes for the industry's employment in the United States as a whole and in the southern states were upward; in the Cleveland SMSA and the city, downward. An obvious implication is that the southern states are competing with Cleveland (and similar northern industrial centers) most aggressively in their traditional anchor industries (major durable goods production). The south is also winning in the battle for nondurables but the gap is not widening as rapidly.

The remaining two graphs confirm well publicized conclusions. The industries that have had the most serious problems in the 1970s—the only two with fewer employees in 1980 than they had in 1967—are primary metals (mostly steel production) and transportation equipment (mostly automotive production). Nationally, the decline in primary metals was considerably more pronounced than in transportation equipment. In the Cleveland SMSA, the reverse was true. Thus Cleveland's share of U.S. employment in automotive production has declined to a much greater extent than it has in steel.

In fact, the change in a local industry's share of national employment in the same industry is a more direct and thus important measure of its competitive strength than its rate of employment change. For example, the ratio of Cleveland SMSA employment in transportation equipment to national employment in that industry was .0215 in 1967 and .0149 in 1977; Cleveland's share had declined by 31 percent. Over the decade, changes in SMSA shares of national employment for the six major industries were (in rank order):

  Transportation equipment (− 31 percent)
  Nonelectrical machinery (− 24 percent)
  Fabricated metals (− 15 percent)
  Other manufacturing (− 13 percent)
  Primary metals (− 10 percent)
  Electrical machinery (− 7 percent)

As would be expected given the discussion above, changes in the ratio of Cleveland SMSA employment to southern states employment in counterpart industries show even more dramatic results. Again, in rank order:

Nonelectrical machinery (−51 percent)
Transportation equipment (−47 percent)
Electrical machinery (−42 percent)
Fabricated metals (−35 percent)
Primary metals (−34 percent)
Other manufacturing (−30 percent)

Changes in the Components of Major Industries

All of Cleveland's major manufacturing industries have lost employment since the late 1960s and in all cases Cleveland SMSA shares of national employment in the same industries have eroded. Trends expressed for these major industries, however, result from averaging out the performance of their many component industries. The outlook for metropolitan Cleveland's economy would be pessimistic indeed if all of the components have been performing in about the same way. But as Table 5.3 shows us, there has been substantial diversity in the performance of the 84 we have identified.

Between 1967 and 1977, 50 local industries lost a significant number of jobs; employment in half of them declined by 30 percent or more over the decade. But there were some impressive changes on the other side of the ledger: 14.1 percent of SMSA 1977 manufacturing employees were in 10 industries that had increased from five to 29 percent over the preceding decade, and another 22.1 percent worked in 11 industries that had grown by 30 percent or more.

We might have expected that the growing components would be concentrated in just a few sectors but considerable diversity is displayed in five of the six major industries. Industries growing by five percent or more accounted for 28 percent of 1977 employment in primary metals, 64 percent in fabricated metals, 25 percent in nonelectrical machinery, 37 percent in electrical machinery, and 41 percent of other manufacturing. Only in transportation equipment was the pattern consistently negative (98 percent of employment in industries that declined by five percent or more).

Table 5.4 summarizes the relationship between growth rates in these industries and changes in their shares of total employment in their U.S. counterparts. Typically, local industries that were growing were also increasing their share of national production whereas those that were declining in employment were also declining in share. For example, of the 11 local industries experiencing 1967-77 growth of 30 percent in employment, four also increased their national share by 30 percent or more, and another four increased their share by five to 29 percent. All of the 25 industries that suffered rapid declines in em-

Table 5.3

CHANGES IN EMPLOYMENT IN MAJOR CLEVELAND SMSA
MANUFACTURING INDUSTRIES, 1967-77

Change in Employment	Total Mfg.	33 Pri. Metals	34 Fab. Metals	35 Nonelect. Mach.	36 Elect. Mach.	37 Tnsp. Equip.	Other Mfg.
Number of Industries							
Rapid growth (+30% or more)	11	--	2	1	2	--	6
Moderate growth (+5% to +29%)	10	2	2	1	--	1	4
About same (-4% to +4%)	13	--	1	1	2	--	9
Moderate decline (-5% to -29%)	25	2	2	7	2	1	11
Rapid decline (-30% or more)	25	4	5	3	2	1	10
Total	84	8	12	13	8	3	40
Percent of Employment							
Rapid growth (+30% or more)	22.1	--	52.1	1.1	37.3	--	28.5
Moderate growth (+5% to +29%)	14.1	28.4	11.9	23.6	--	1.9	12.6
About same (-4% to +4%)	6.6	--	3.6	8.4	18.4	--	8.6
Moderate decline (-5% to -29%)	40.6	51.0	7.6	59.6	34.1	78.8	33.7
Rapid decline (-30% or more)	16.6	20.6	24.8	7.3	10.2	19.3	16.6
Total	100.0	100.0.	100.0	100.0	100.0	100.0	100.0

SOURCE: Data file compiled from Census of Manufactures records (see Appendix B).

ployment also declined in share over the decade. The pattern did not always fit, however. For example, five industries that grew locally over the decade declined in share; i.e., those industries grew yet faster in other parts of the nation. Two SMSA industries that lost employment increased in share; i.e., their national counterparts declined even more.

Certainly, this analysis illustrates that the level of detail one chooses in examining an economy can make a difference in the implications to be drawn. The fact that metropolitan Cleveland's manu-

Table 5.4

Changes in Employment and in Share of U.S. Industry Employment in Cleveland SMSA Manufacturing Industries, 1967-77

Change in Employment	Change in Cleveland SMSA Share of U.S. Industry					
	Total	Rapid Increase (+30% or More)	Moderate Increase (+5% to +29%)	About Same (-4% to +4%)	Moderate Decrease (-5% to -29%)	Rapid Decrease (-30% or More)
Number of Industries						
Rapid growth (+30% or more)	11	4	4	1	2	--
Moderate growth (+5% to +29%)	10	2	2	3	2	1
About same (-4% to +4%)	13	--	3	4	6	--
Moderate decline (-5% to -29%)	25	--	2	3	15	5
Rapid decline (-30% or more)	25	--	--	--	5	20
Total	84	6	11	11	30	26
Percent of Employment						
Rapid growth (+30% or more)	22.1	2.7	11.5	4.0	3.9	--
Moderate growth (+5% to +29%)	14.1	1.2	5.2	1.5	4.5	1.6
About same (-4% to +4%)	6.6	--	1.0	3.6	2.0	--
Moderate decline (-5% to -29%)	40.6	--	6.2	4.0	14.7	15.7
Rapid decline (-30% or more)	16.6	--	--	--	4.1	12.6
Total	100.0	3.9	23.9	13.1	29.2	29.9

SOURCE: Data file compiled from Census of Manufactures records (see Appendix B).

facturing sector suffered some serious losses in the 1970s stands out regardless of the choice, but analysis of change at the three- and four-digit levels shows signs of vitality not even hinted at when looking at trends for major industries alone.

Because of shifts in components, level of detail choices can alter perceptions of the future as well. For example, if we project the 1967-77 rates of decline for the six major sectors alone for another decade and add up the results, we find that total SIC-classified manufacturing employment in the SMSA drops from 242,200 in 1977 to 211,00 in 1987 (a 13 percent decline). If we follow the same procedure using the 84 component industries, the total drops only to 238,300 in 1987 (a 2 percent decline).

Table 5.5 lists each of the 84 industries in accord with the structure of Table 5.4 (showing both change in local employment and change in national share). An examination of these listings yields no simple explanations as to differences in the characteristics of industries that performed well and those that did not. Clearly, it was not the nature of the product manufactured (as indicated by SIC code) that made the difference. There were subcomponents of many two-digit SIC groups among both the winners and the losers during the 1970s. We will return to this question later in this section after we have reviewed the data on other aspects of their performance.

VALUE ADDED PER PRODUCTION WORKER HOUR

This measure, the dollar value added by manufacturing in an industry over a period divided by the total number of production worker hours devoted to the effort, is the one typically used by the federal government to represent productivity. It is not a measure of the productivity of the work force, however, but rather of the combined rate of output of workers and machinery in a given industry. A highly effective labor force working with outdated equipment, for example, could yield a comparatively low rate of value added per hour.

This is one of the most difficult measures the U.S. *Census of Manufactures* has to compile because of the complexity involved in firms' reporting of value added. Value added is the sum of profits plus the cost of all manufacturing inputs except those covering the raw materials and semifinished goods that go into a firm's product. A particular problem noted by the Census is the allocation of profit within multiplant firms. While such firms typically maintain the accounts needed to accurately report production hours and input costs for individual plants, it is doubtful that they allocate profits among their

Table 5.5

LISTING OF CLEVELAND SMSA MANUFACTURING INDUSTRIES BY CHANGE IN EMPLOYMENT AND CHANGE IN SHARE OF U.S. INDUSTRY EMPLOYMENT, 1967-77

Rapid Decrease in Share	*Moderate Decrease in Share*
Rapid Increase in Employment None	**Rapid Increase in Employment** 369 Misc. elec. equip. sup. 382 Measure./control. devices
Moderate Increase in Employment 349X Other misc. fab. metal	**Moderate Increase in Employment** 353 Const./related mach. 37X Other transport. equip.
About Same Employment None	**About Same Employment** 2099 Food preparations, NEC 254X Other parts. & fixtures 2791 Typesetting 3272 Concrete products, NEC 3471 Plating & polishing 3622 Industrial controls
Moderate Decrease in Employment 25X Other furn. & fixtures 28X Other chem. & allied prod. 358 Refrig. & service mach. 35X Other mach. except elec. 371 Motor vehicles & equip.	**Moderate Decrease in Employment** 20X Other food & rel. prod. 209X Other misc. food & rel. 22 Textile mill products 251 Household furniture 284 Soap, cleaners, & toilet 2711 Newspapers 2721 Periodicals 32X Other stone, clay, & glass 3441 Fab. structural metal 3567 Indust. furnaces & ovens 354X Other metalwork. mach. 356X Other gen. indust. mach. 364 Elec. light & wire equip. 36X Other elec. & electronics 399 Misc. manufactures
Rapid Decrease in Employment 201X Other meat products 2026 Fluid milk 202X Other dairy products 2542 Metal partitions & fix. 273 Books 27X Other print. & publishing 282 Plastics mater. & synth. 335X Other nonfer. roll. & draw 3361 Aluminum foundries 33X Other prim. metal indust. 342 Cutlery, hand tools, hdwr. 3443 Fab. plate work (boilers) 344X Other fab. struc. metal 3452 Bolts, nuts, rivets & wash. 3494 Valves & pipe fittings 355X Other spec. indust. mach. 3569 Gen. indust. mach., NEC 361 Elec. distributing equip. 3621 Motors & generators 395 Pens, pencils, off. & art	**Rapid Decrease in Employment** 265X Other paperbd containers 281 Indust. inorganic chem. 3351 Copper rolling & drawing 3542 Machine tools, metal form 372 Aircraft & parts

Table 5.5 (Continued)

About Same Share	*Rapid Increase in Share*

About Same Share

Rapid Increase in Employment
30   Rubber & misc. plastic

Moderate Increase in Employment
2653 Fiber boxes
3273 Ready-mixed concrete
3341 Sec. nonferrous metals

About Same Employment
233 Women & miss. outerwear
278 Blankbooks & bookbind.
363 Household appliances
3559 Spec. indust. machinery

Moderate Decrease in Employment
3451 Screw machine products
3544 Special dies, tools, etc.
3545 Machine tool accessories

Rapid Decrease in Employment
None

Moderate Increase in Share

Rapid Increase in Employment
34X Stampings/other fab. met.
3444 Sheet metal work
3564 Blowers and fans
362X Other elec. indus. appar.

Moderate Increase in Employment
23X Other apparel & other tex.
332 Iron & steel foundries

About Same Employment
2011 Meat packing products
2086 Bottled/can. soft drinks
2651 Folding paperboard boxes

Moderate Decrease in Employment
331 Blast furn./basic steel
336X Other nonferrous found.

Rapid Decrease in Employment
None

Rapid Increase in Share

Rapid Increase in Employment
26X Other paper & allied prod.
29   Petroleum & coal products
38X Other instruments & relat.
39X Other misc. manufacturing

Moderate Increase in Employment
203 Canned, cured, frozen food
343 Plumbing, heat exc. elect.

About Same Employment
None

Moderate Decrease in Employment
None

Rapid Decrease in Employment
None

SOURCE: Data files compiled by Rand from Census of Manufactures records (see Appendix B).
NOTE: Categories of change from 1967 to 1977 defined as follows: Rapid increase = +30% or more; moderate increase = +5% to +29%; about same = -4% to +4%; moderate decrease = -5% to -29%; rapid decrease = -30% or more.

plants reliably. Profits counted in at the firm's headquarters facility
are more likely to be overstated and those at branch plants understat-
ed. Since Cleveland is a headquarters location for so many firms, the
possibility of this type of error should be kept in mind in reviewing
the data presented below. Where large corporations are involved, we
suspect that Cleveland area values may be somewhat higher than
they should be and those for the southern states, on the average,
somewhat lower.

Value added per hour varies dramatically by industry. Among two-
digit SIC groups in metropolitan Cleveland in 1977, it ranged from a
low of $14 (rubber and plastic products) to a high of $43 (chemicals
and allied products). The average for SMSA manufacturing was $23.
Again, however, absolute values do not tell us much. To test the
strength of Cleveland industries along this dimension we must compare local experience with that in other areas.

In Fig. 5.4, we show total manufacturing value added per hour in
the City of Cleveland, the Cleveland SMSA, and the southern states
in 1967, 1972, and 1977 expressed as a percentage of the U.S. average
in each of those years. Rates in the City of Cleveland and its SMSA
were similar and both were well above the national average throughout the decade. This is not a surprising finding. Capital-intensive
manufacturing activity in large industrial complexes has traditionally yielded more per worker hour than in smaller centers and rural
areas. In 1972, for example, overall value added per hour in manufacturing exceeded the national average by eight percent in the Cleveland SMSA, eight percent in the Philadelphia SMSA, nine percent in
the New York and Baltimore SMSAs, and 15 percent in the Detroit
SMSA.

Cleveland's comparative advantage by this measure, however, has
deteriorated; the Cleveland SMSA rate was seven percent above the
national rate in 1967 but only three percent higher in 1977.

Manufacturing value added per hour in the southern states
remained at the same level in relation to the U.S. average from 1967
through 1977 (74 to 75 percent). Most surprising here is not the magnitude of the gap but the fact that it did not diminish in the 1970s. In
the first two decades after World War II, the scale of manufacturing
activity in the south remained small compared to the influence of
America's traditional industrial belt. Wages were low and plants
there tended to be more labor-intensive. With the shift in investment
toward the south more recently, one might have expected a notable
convergence in this measure, northern capital becoming proportionally older on average while the bulk of the new facilities (presumably
technologically superior and more capital-intensive) were located in
the sunbelt. Undoubtedly, there were new installations in the south

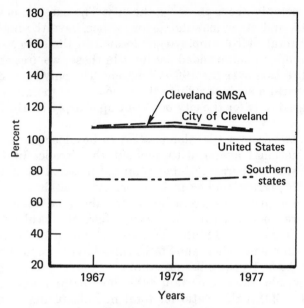

SOURCE: File compiled from Census of Manufactures
records (see Appendix B).

Fig. 5.4—Manufacturing value added per production
worker hour, Cleveland and southern states,
as a percent of United States, 1967-1977

fitting these specifications, but apparently their numbers have not
been sufficient to noticeably affect the average.

An alternative theory is that many plants built in the south in the
1970s were not much less labor-intensive than their predecessors. The
period was dominated by rising energy costs, and capital intensive
facilities are usually energy-intensive. Manufacturers may have
avoided some of the most efficient new technologies because of fears
about energy dependence.

Changes in Major Industries

Using the value added per hour yardstick, we find more divergence
in performance among the six major manufacturing industries than
we did looking at employment change.

First, we find that value added per hour in Cleveland's SMSA and
central city was not always closely related. In four industries SMSA

rates were notably above those for the city. The exceptions were primary metals and other manufacturing, which have the highest percentages of total SMSA employment located in the city. Most often, however, trends in value added per hour in these two areas moved in the same direction over the 1967-77 decade. The only clear exception was in electrical machinery where the ratio of local to national values decreased gradually for the city but went up sharply for the SMSA as a whole.

In all but two sectors, Cleveland SMSA value added per hour stayed above the national averages throughout the decade. In 1977, the SMSA rate was six percent higher than the national in other manufacturing, 25 percent higher in both primary metals and electrical machinery and just one percent higher in fabricated metals. The exceptions were nonelectrical machinery (where the local rate dipped below that for the United States for the first time in 1977), and transportation equipment (where the SMSA rates have remained below the national by 10 to 15 percent since 1967).

There were also some important differences in directions of change. Whereas the SMSA/U.S. ratio for total manufacturing value added per hour decreased slightly, it declined more steeply in nonelectrical machinery, transportation equipment, and other manufacturing. In fabricated metals there was virtually no change in the relationship, but in two sectors (primary metals and electrical machinery) the SMSA's position in relation to that of the United States improved significantly over the decade.

In each of these industries, value added per hour in the southern states remained well below levels in metropolitan Cleveland. In three cases, however, the rates were converging: fabricated metals and nonelectrical machinery (Cleveland's largest durable goods producers), and other manufacturing.

Changes in Component Industries

For each of the 84 detailed components of Cleveland's manufacturing sector, we have computed similar SMSA/U.S. ratios for 1967 and 1977, each relating value added per hour in the industry in the Cleveland SMSA to that in the same industry in the United States as a whole.

Table 5.6 shows that this approach uncovers the same sort of diversity it did when we reviewed employment changes: for 33 industries (37 percent of all employment) local value added per hour in 1977 was higher than U.S. averages by five percent or more; the rate in 36 local industries with 40 percent of all employment was below that of their national counterparts by five percent or more; in the remaining 15, SMSA and U.S. rates were about the same. Again, with the exception of transportation equipment, this diversity is displayed within all major industry groups.

Table 5.6

MAJOR CLEVELAND SMSA MANUFACTURING INDUSTRIES BY SMSA/U.S. RATIO, 1977 VALUE ADDED PER PRODUCTION WORKER HOUR

Ratio Cleveland SMSA to U.S. Industry 1977	Total Mfg.	33 Pri. Metals	34 Fab. Metals	35 Nonelect. Mach.	36 Elect. Mach.	37 Tnsp. Equip.	Other Mfg.
Number of Industries							
Much higher (+30% or more)	14	4	1	1	3	--	5
Moderately higher (+5% to +29%)	19	1	5	3	1	--	9
About same (-4% to +4%)	15	--	3	3	1	1	7
Moderately lower (-5% to -29%)	24	1	2	5	2	2	12
Much Lower (-30% or more)	12	2	1	1	1	--	7
Total	84	8	12	13	8	3	40
Percent of Employment							
Much higher (+30% or more)	18.9	78.4	3.6	2.7	46.1	--	13.0
Moderately higher (+5% to +29%)	18.2	9.3	23.3	31.1	9.7	--	20.0
About same (-4% to +4%)	23.0	--	65.5	29.8	21.7	1.9	10.5
Moderately lower (-5% to -29%)	30.0	4.1	5.8	14.6	19.3	98.1	42.7
Much lower (-30% or more)	9.9	8.2	1.8	21.8	3.2	--	13.8
Total	100.0	100.0	100.0	100.0	100.0	100.0	100.0

SOURCE: Data file compiled from Census of Manufactures records (see Appendix B).

Table 5.7 shows the relationship between the 1977 SMSA/U.S. ratios and changes in the ratios from 1967 to 1977. For example, there are seven industries in the upper lefthand cell next to the total column. These industries all had 1977 value added per hour rates 30

Table 5.7

CLEVELAND MANUFACTURING INDUSTRIES BY SMSA/U.S. RATIO, 1977 VALUE ADDED PER PRODUCTION WORKER HOUR, AND 1967-77 CHANGE IN RATIO

Ratio Cleveland SMSA to U.S. Industry, 1977	Change in Ratio Cleveland SMSA to U.S. Industry 1967-77					
	Total	Rapid Increase (+30% or More)	Moderate Increase (+5% to +29%)	About Same (-4% to +4%)	Moderate Decrease (-5% to -29%)	Rapid Decrease (-30% or More)
Number of Industries						
Much higher (+30% or more)	14	7	6	1	--	--
Moderately higher (+5% to +29%)	19	4	7	4	3	1
About same (-4% to +4%)	15	--	4	4	7	--
Moderately lower (-5% to -29%)	24	1	3	5	14	1
Much lower (-30% or more)	12	--	--	--	5	7
Total	84	12	20	14	29	9
Percent of Employment						
Much higher (+30% or more)	18.9	3.3	15.1	.5	--	--
Moderately higher (+5% to +29%)	18.2	2.7	7.8	3.6	3.1	1.0
About same (-4% to +4%)	23.0	--	5.3	5.1	12.6	--
Moderately lower (-5% to -29%)	30.0	.4	3.5	16.9	8.8	.4
Much lower (-30% or more)	9.9	--	--	--	2.9	7.0
Total	100.0	6.4	31.7	26.1	27.4	8.4

SOURCE: Data file compiled from Census of Manufactures records (see Appendix B).

percent or more above those of their national counterparts, and their SMSA/U.S. ratios had increased by 30 percent or more over the preceding decade; i.e., they yielded significantly more in value added per worker hour and the gap was widening.

In total, 32 industries (with 38 percent of total employment) were improving their rate of output significantly faster than their national conterparts, and in 38 (36 percent of employment) national productivity improvements were outpacing those locally.

CAPITAL INVESTMENT IN MANUFACTURING

The amount of new investment in Cleveland area manufacturing plants and equipment is obviously a critical measure in an assessment of future prospects. Even if a local industry had an outstanding record of performance in the 1970s according to all the measures we have reviewed so far, we would be justifiably dubious about its potential in the 1980s if it had experienced a dearth of investment over the preceding decade. In comparing investment rates, however, we cannot safely compare the data for one year (1967) to that of another (1977) and expect a reliable sense of the trend as we could with employment and value added. New capital expenditures are "lumpy." A firm may have made a substantial investment in rebuilding its factories in 1976 and spent virtually nothing on improving plant and equipment in 1977, for example. To gain a realistic understanding of changing investment patterns, then, we must compare averages over multiyear periods.

Unfortunately, annual data are available for only a limited number of industry aggregates from 1967 to 1977 (a number much smaller than the 84 groups we have dealt with earlier in this chapter). The data we have compiled are summarized in Table 5.8; all annual data were converted to constant 1977 dollars before averaging.

From 1973 through 1977, total new capital expenditures in Cleveland SMSA manufacturing industries averaged $513.8 million per year, the equivalent of $1.40 per worker hour. This represents a modest increase over the $1.35 average for the 1967-72 period. In the earlier period, Cleveland SMSA annual investment per worker hour had been exactly the same as the national rate. In the later period, it had dropped to 83 percent of the national average. Thus, while the investment rate had increased both locally and nationally, it had increased much more rapidly in the nation as a whole.

From the table, it is also clear that investment in the Cleveland SMSA in the 1970s remained strongest in those industries that have

Table 5.8

NEW CAPITAL EXPENDITURES BY CLEVELAND SMSA MANUFACTURING INDUSTRIES, 1967-77

(Constant 1977 dollars)

SIC	Industry	Ave. Annual Invest. Clev. SMSA 1973-77		Ave. Annual Invest. per Prod. Worker Hour	
		Total ($ mill.)	$ per Product. Worker Hour	Cleve. SMSA as % of U.S. Average	
				1967-72	1973-77
Major Durable Goods Manufacturing					
33	PRIMARY METAL INDUSTRIES	101.7	2.05	117	85
331	Blast furnace, basic steel	53.9	2.35	167	85
332	Iron & steel foundries	34.2	2.63	151	162
336	Nonferrous foundries	4.5	.68	62	58
34	FABRICATED METAL PRODUCTS	79.1	1.16	89	108
344	Fabricated structural prod.	6.5	.78	84	75
345	Screw mach. prod., bolts	10.2	.89	97	90
349	Misc. fab. metal products	9.2	.97	123	88
35	NONELECTRICAL MACHINERY	65.4	.99	106	70
353	Construction machinery	18.3	1.35	173	71
354	Metalworking machinery	17.7	.75	107	81
355	Spec. industry machinery	4.9	.75	208	73
356	General industrial mach.	11.1	1.80	85	138
36	ELECTRICAL MACHINERY	36.5	1.20	73	100
362	Elec. industrial appar.	17.7	1.73	74	172
364	Elec. light & wiring	4.9	.65	68	67
369	Misc. elec. equip. supp.	5.6	1.16	147	83
37	TRANSPORTATION EQUIPMENT	111.9	2.23	135	145
371	Motor vehicles & equipment	92.6	2.53	126	125
372	Aircraft and parts	7.5	.85	95	102
Total Major Durable		394.6	1.49	113	100

Table 5.8 (Continued)

SIC	Industry	Ave. Annual Invest. Clev. SMSA 1973-77		Ave. Annual Invest. per Prod. Worker Hour	
		Total ($ mill.)	$ per Product. Worker Hour	Cleve. SMSA as % of U.S. Average	
				1967-72	1973-77
Other Manufacturing					
20	FOOD AND KINDRED PRODUCTS	15.2	1.43	94	77
23	APPAREL & OTHER TEXTILE PROD.	4.6	.37	129	153
25	FURNITURE AND FIXTURES	1.9	.44	106	79
26	PAPER AND ALLIED PRODUCTS	9.2	1.34	51	45
265	Paperbd. containers, boxes	4.2	.97	87	77
27	PRINTING AND PUBLISHING	13.0	.86	79	68
28	CHEMICALS AND ALLIED PROD.	37.8	2.85	62	44
32	STONE, CLAY, GLASS PRODUCTS	8.5	1.12	72	58
38	INSTRUMENTS AND RELATED PROD.	4.0	.60	53	40
382	Measuring & control. device	3.2	.59	82	59
39	MISC. MANUFACTURING IND.	3.5	.52	85	67
Total Other Manufacturing		119.2	1.15	80	63
Total Manufacturing		513.8	1.40	100	83

SOURCE: Data file compiled from Census of Manufactures records (see Appendix B).

been the area's specialties traditionally—major durable goods manufacturing. Within the five major durable goods industries, investment per worker hour increased from a 1967-72 average of $1.44 to a 1973-77 average of $1.49—13 percent higher than the national average in the former period and equivalent to it in the latter. New capital investment in all other local industries combined amounted to $1.14 over 1967-72 and $1.15 over 1973-77—only 80 percent of the national average for these industries in the earlier period and only 63 percent of the national average in the latter.

Several local industries increased their investment rates (per worker hour) in relation to their U.S. counterparts comparing the two periods: iron and steel foundries; fabricated metals (portions not listed separately on the table); general industrial machinery; all of the components shown in the electrical machinery industry except the miscellaneous group; aircraft and parts; and apparel and other textile products. For most groups, however, investment rates deteriorated comparatively.

The numbers in Table 5.8 are difficult to interpret precisely for at least two reasons. First, data on new investment include expenditures for pollution control improvements and other facility changes that were not made solely to enhance production; we know that investments in pollution control were heavy over this period, but we cannot break them out separately. Second, by relating investment to production worker hours we have not controlled for the effects of productivity improvements that reduced the number of workers needed per unit of output. Nonetheless the conclusion that Cleveland area manufacturing investment slipped seriously in relation to the rest of the nation appears inescapable.

Is the pattern of investment ratios among industries as diverse as those we found for employment change and value added per hour? Because complete data were available for so few industries, we used information on 1977 investment values to respond to that question. Data were available for 60 nonoverlapping industry groups in the Cleveland SMSA.

Table 5.9 shows that in less than one quarter of these industries (14) did SMSA investment rates exceed the national rates in 1977. In 44 industries (covering 65 percent of total manufacturing employment), SMSA investment rates were at least five percent below those for the United States as a whole. Thus, we do not see diversity among industries here to the extent we have found it in our reviews of other variables.

RELATIONSHIPS BETWEEN VARIABLES

We have seen that Cleveland industries are not tightly clustered around the midpoint of any of the distributions we have discussed: employment change, change in share of U.S. employment, SMSA/U.S. ratio of value added per production worker hour, the change in that ratio, and, from Chapter IV, the SMSA/U.S. wage ratio, and the change in that ratio. We find that the diverse scores along each of these dimensions bear no strong interrelationships. For example, in-

Table 5.9

MAJOR CLEVELAND SMSA MANUFACTURING INDUSTRIES BY SMSA/U.S. INVESTMENT RATIO (1977 NEW CAPITAL EXPENDITURES PER $1,000 VALUE ADDED)

Ratio Cleveland SMSA to U.S. Industry	Total Mfg.	33 Pri. Metals	34 Fab. Metals	35 Nonelect. Mach.	36 Elect. Mach.	37 Tnsp. Equip.	Other Mfg.
Number of Industries							
Much higher (+30% or more)	9	--	1	2	3	1	2
Moderately higher (+5% to +29%)	5	--	2	--	--	--	3
About same (-4% to +4%)	2	--	1	1	--	--	--
Moderately lower (-5% to -29%)	16	1	3	5	1	--	6
Much lower (-30% or more)	28	5	3	4	2	--	14
Total	60	6	10	12	6	1	25
Percent of Employment							
Much higher (+30% or more)	17.4	--	1.8	15.0	49.3	100.0	1.7
Moderately higher (+5% to +29%)	8.0	--	14.5	--	--	--	14.8
About same (-4% to +4%)	9.7	--	50.8	7.5	--	--	--
Moderately lower (-5% to -29%)	18.3	24.3	12.1	35.9	21.7	--	15.8
Much lower (-30% or more)	46.6	75.7	20.8	41.6	29.0	--	67.7
Total	100.0	100.0	100.0	100.0	100.0	100.0	100.0

SOURCE: Data file compiled from Census of Manufactures records (see Appendix B).

dustries that increased market share most rapidly are not necessarily the same as those that had the lowest wages or experienced the most rapid improvements in value added per worker hour.

This conclusion is evidenced in the data on Table 5.10. There we show several characteristics of our 84 industries grouped by their 1967-77 change in share of national employment. For example, 3.9 percent of all 1977 SMSA employment was in manufacturing industries that increased their share of U.S. employment by 30 percent or more over the preceding decade. On the average, this group of industries had 40.6 employees per establishment in 1977; yielded value added per hour 74.8 percent as high as their national counterpart; and had an average wage 94.8 percent of that of their national counterpart.

Table 5.10

CHARACTERISTICS OF EIGHTY-FOUR CLEVELAND SMSA
INDUSTRIES BY GROWTH CATEGORY

Change in SMSA Share of U.S. Industry, 1967-77	Percent of Total Mfg. Employ.	Average Employ. per Estab.	SMSA/U.S. Value Added Ratio		SMSA/U.S. Wage Ratio	
			1977 Ratio	1967-77 Change	1977 Ratio	1967-77 Change
Rapid increase (+30% or more)	3.9	40.6	74.8	23.2	94.8	7.4
Moderate increase (+5% to +29%)	23.9	125.3	134.2	-11.3	119.7	-3.4
About same (-4% to +4%)	13.1	44.2	101.4	7.2	104.2	4.1
Moderate decrease (-5% to -29%)	29.2	63.3	105.8	-10.2	104.5	-.3
Rapid decline (-30% or more)	29.9	42.5	99.2	1.4	99.7	5.2
Total	100.0	57.2	104.7	-2.1	104.3	2.1

SOURCE: Data file compiled from Census of Manufactures records (see Appendix B).

As we look down the columns, we see more similarities than differences. There is no systematic increase or decrease in any of these characteristics as change-in-share moves from the "rapid increase" group down to the "rapid decrease" group.

As a further test, we ran a series of simple correlations, examining the relationship between the performance of the 84 local industries (again measured by 1967-77 change in share of national employment) and several of the other variables we have discussed. The results are shown in Table 5.11.

In an analysis of this kind, a correlation coefficient near 1.0 (either plus or minus) indicates that the two variables being tested are strongly related to each other. When one of them increases, the other changes (either increases or decreases) predictably. A correlation coefficient near zero indicates that there is a very weak relationship be-

Table 5.11

CORRELATION BETWEEN CHANGE IN CLEVELAND SMSA SHARE OF U.S. EMPLOYMENT IN EIGHTY-FOUR MANUFACTURING INDUSTRIES AND OTHER CHARACTERISTICS OF THOSE INDUSTRIES, 1967-77

	Correlation Coefficient
1. Employees per establishment, Cleveland SMSA, 1977.	0.127
2. Ratio, Cleveland SMSA to U.S. value, employees per establishment, 1977.	0.270^a
3. Value added per production worker hour, Cleveland SMSA, 1977.	-0.005
4. Ratio, Cleveland SMSA to U.S. value, value added per production worker hour. 1977 ratio Percent change in ratio, 1967-77	0.092 -0.046
5. Average wage per production worker hour, Cleveland SMSA, 1977.	0.140
6. Ratio, Cleveland SMSA to U.S. value, average wage per production worker hour. 1977 ratio Percent change in ratio, 1967-77	0.180^a 0.184^a

SOURCE: Rand analysis of data files compiled from Census of Manufactures records (see Appendix B).

^{a}Significant at the 10 percent critical level.

tween the two variables. Looking over Table 5.11, we see that for our 84 industries, none of the variables listed were strongly correlated with change-in-share.

These results do not mean that further statistical analysis will not be helpful in understanding factors affecting industry growth. This has been only a crude test using data that were readily available; not a formal analysis with sound foundations in economic theory. Although beyond the scope of our initial study, the latter can certainly be recommended in future economic monitoring.

The test does tell us, however, that some surface hypotheses do not hold up, e.g., that local growth cannot occur in industries that have comparatively high wages. It also hints that the causes of industry growth and decline in the Cleveland area are quite complex. Barriers and opportunities unique to individual narrowly defined industries may have important effects. Special studies of such factors are warranted in industries that are particularly important to the metropolitan economy.

SOME IMPLICATIONS

Our analysis clearly confirms that serious problems emerged in Cleveland's manufacturing sector in the 1970s: large losses of employment in a number of Cleveland's historically most important industries; slow growth in value added per hour even compared to a sluggish national rate; and new capital investment proportionally below the national average.

The causes of many recent difficulties are powerful adjustments in the national and international economy whose effects have often been amplified in the local environment. We have reported trends only through 1977 for most variables; in some industries (particularly automotive production) problems have deepened seriously since then.

Nonetheless, looking below the surface, we have found substantial diversity in the performance of local manufacturers. There is nothing in our data at this level to suggest that Cleveland manufacturing activity is likely to collapse. A broad array of strengths has been uncovered that gives community leaders something to work with.

One policy implication is that sound economic development strategies must be sensitive to what is going on *within* major sectors. In this chapter we showed that along the major sectors, nonelectrical machinery has performed reasonably well, in the aggregate, since 1972. The analysis in Chapter III also brought out additional information emphasizing the importance of this industry to the metropolitan economy. But while some of its components have done quite well of late, others have deteriorated. The aggregate performance of the primary metals group, in contrast, has been weak. Yet, some of its components have also exhibited strengths. Cleveland has important location advantages for elements of primary metals production that are hard to match in the south. Clearly, a strategy that "writes off" primary metals as a whole and concentrates only on nonelectrical machinery would be overly simplistic.

Our listing of the 84 industries in various performance categories forms a starting point for a more realistic economic development strategy. At both ends of the spectrum, there are likely to be industries that do not warrant interventions, i.e., those that have been performing well and will probably continue to do so without extra help, and those with such severe problems that local actions cannot avert further declines. But there will be other industries where modest interventions might gain large payoffs. Constructing these lists has been a first step toward finding those payoffs.

VI. PERFORMANCE OF CLEVELAND NONMANUFACTURING INDUSTRIES

In Chapter I, we found that nonmanufacturing employment grew substantially in metropolitan Cleveland during the 1970s; a sharp contrast to the disturbing aggregate trend in local manufacturing. The most notable increase occurred in the service sector (average annual employment growth rate of 4.0 percent from 1967 to 1977); growth in wholesale and retail trade was less rapid (2.2 percent) and in other nonmanufacturing sectors, even less so (0.4 percent on average).

The good news was tempered, however, when we compared the performance of Cleveland nonmanufacturing industries to those of other areas. While local growth rates exceeded those in several other metropolitan areas in the northeast, they fell slightly below those for the Great Lakes states on the average and substantially below those for the nation as a whole and particularly those for the sunbelt.

We have also found, however, that aggregate trends in major sectors can be misleading. Performance among Cleveland's many manufacturing industries has been much more diverse than was suggested by summary data for major sectors. Is this also true for nonmanufacturing industries?

Answering that question is one of the purposes of this chapter. Another is to learn whether some nonmanufacturing industries (at a more detailed level than analyzed in Chapter III) are becoming more "export oriented" and thus capable of generating new growth. We noted earlier that nonmanufacturing has traditionally been seen as a follower rather than a leader; a complex of activities that serves local needs and thus is likely to grow or decline in proportion to local business and consumer demand. More recently it has been recognized that all do not necessarily behave in this way (see, for example, Gruenstein and Guerra, 1981, Pascal and Gurwitz, forthcoming). Some particularly in the service sector, can and do serve external markets as well.

The growth of the service sector, in fact, has been so impressive over the past decade that some observers have seen it replacing manufacturing as the dominant force in our economy. We are, of course, interested in testing the reasonableness of this view in this chapter, as our data permit.

APPROACH

Detailed information on productivity and investment do not exist for local nonmanufacturing industries; therefore, our analysis has been confined to variables derived from counts of employment and establishments. As we review performance in each sector, we begin by discussing structure: comparative size and export-import orientation of detailed component industries. Our focus, however, is on change. At the greatest level of detail the data permit, we examine the three variables noted in the introduction to Part C: (1) change in absolute levels of employment in the metropolis; (2) change in local industry shares of employment in the same industry nationally; (3) and change in concentration ratios. Our data source is the most complete available for these purposes: the *County Business Patterns* series compiled by the U.S. Department of Commerce. We measure change over the 1967-77 period, for the same reasons noted earlier.

Actually, the trade and service sectors in most metropolitan areas are somewhat export-oriented; a part of each metropolis's reason for existence is to serve its rural hinterland. It is important then to compare each industry's concentration ratio in metropolitan Cleveland with the average for the same industry in all SMSAs nationally. We are most interested in local industries whose ratios fall significantly above or below that average.

Also, as in the last chapter, we examine trends for the four-county Cleveland SMSA, rather than the seven-county SCSA, because consistent data at a sufficient level of detail are not available for the latter. Table 6.1 shows the 1977 employment totals by major nonmanufacturing sector for both areas. With 494,700 employees, the SMSA accounts for 70 percent of the SCSA total. Percentage distributions of employees across major sectors in the two areas are very nearly the same.

The account structure for Table 6.1, as well as all other tables in this chapter, is consistent with the SIC system with two important exceptions. First, we divided the subcomponents of the SIC-defined service sector into two categories according to their primary work orientation: "business related services" and "other services." Second, we assigned all employment in the SIC's various "administrative and auxiliary" accounts to our business related service category. The administrative and auxiliary accounts include central administrative offices and auxiliary establishments such as warehouses, research laboratories, and maintenance facilities. In the SIC system, employment in such establishments is counted with the industry they serve; e.g., employees working in the headquarters office of a manufacturing firm are counted in the manufacturing total, employees in the ware-

Table 6.1

NONMANUFACTURING EMPLOYMENT, CLEVELAND
SCSA AND SMSA, 1977

Sector	Cleveland SCSA		Cleveland SMSA	
	Number (000s)	Percent	Number (000s)	Percent
Mining	2.1	.3	1.0	.2
Contract construction	44.1	6.3	28.9	5.9
Transportation, communication and utilities	62.3	8.8	43.0	8.7
Wholesale trade	80.2	11.4	54.5	11.0
Retail trade	191.5	27.1	126.2	25.5
Finance, insurance, real estate	56.5	8.0	44.0	8.9
Business related services	111.2	15.8	82.7	16.7
Other services	156.9	22.2	113.9	23.0
Not classifiable	.7	.1	.5	.1
Total nonmanufacturing	705.5	100.0	494.7	100.0

SOURCE: Data file compiled by Rand from County Business Patterns records (see Appendix B).

house of a major department store chain are counted with retail trade. Here, all such employees are counted as a part of the total for business related services.

The business related service group is of special interest in our analysis, since its growth in particular has been seen as an alternative to Cleveland's traditional reliance on the manufacturing sector.

MINING AND CONSTRUCTION

Direct mining activity has never played an important role in the economy of the four-county SMSA. Although the industry's total employment grew by more than a third from 1967 to reach its 1,000 total in 1977, that total represented less than 0.2 percent of all SMSA employment (Tables 6.2 and 6.3).

Table 6.2

COMPOSITION OF MINING, CONSTRUCTION, TRANSPORTATION, COMMUNICATION, AND UTILITIES SECTORS, CLEVELAND SMSA, 1977

SIC	Sector/Industry	No. of Estab.	No. of Employ. (000s)	Employ. per Estab.	Concen. Ratio
	Mining				
10	MINING	37	1.0	28.4	.16
	Contract Construction				
15	GENERAL BUILDING CONTRACTORS	743	6.9	9.3	.80
151	General building contractors	446	5.7	12.9	.87
153	Operative builders	79	.8	10.8	.88
16	HEAVY CONSTRUCTION CONTRACTORS	172	5.5	32.0	.87
162	Heavy construction, exc. highway	117	4.8	40.8	.99
17	SPECIAL TRADE CONTRACTORS	2,068	16.5	8.0	1.00
171	Plumb., heat., air conditioning	424	3.6	8.4	.96
172	Paint., paper hanging, decor.	244	1.0	4.0	1.02
173	Electrical work	201	2.6	13.0	.89
174	Masonry, stonework, plastering	296	2.4	8.2	.91
1741	Masonry and other stonework	182	1.2	6.7	1.08
1742	Plastering, drywall, insula.	96	1.2	12.5	.89
175	Carpentering and flooring	205	.9	4.3	.70
176	Roofing and sheet metal work	167	1.5	9.2	1.22
177	Concrete work	181	1.2	6.5	1.32
179	Misc. Spec. trade contractors	315	3.3	10.3	1.24
1799	Spec. trade contractors, NEC	127	.9	7.1	.96
TOTAL	CONTRACT CONSTRUCTION	2,983	28.9	9.7	.91
	Transportation, Communication, Utilities				
41	LOCAL/INTERURBAN TRANSIT	51	2.2	42.4	.94
412	Taxicabs	10	.8	81.0	1.25
413	Intercity highway transportation	4	.7	187.5	2.36

Table 6.2 (Continued)

SIC	Sector/Industry	No. of Estab.	No. of Employ. (000s)	Employ. per Estab.	Concen. Ratio
Transportation, Communication, Utilities (Continued)					
42	TRUCKING AND WAREHOUSING	535	16.1	30.2	1.59
421	Truck., local and long distance	480	14.7	30.6	1.59
422	Public warehousing	44	1.1	24.2	1.67
4225	General warehousing & storage	27	.8	30.5	2.77
44	WATER TRANSPORTATION	43	1.9	44.1	1.15
446	Water transportation service	24	1.4	56.7	1.42
4463	Marine cargo handling	12	1.3	107.4	1.82
45	TRANSPORTATION BY AIR	46	2.6	56.3	.84
451	Certificated air transportation	36	2.4	66.7	.89
47	TRANSPORTATION SERVICES	179	1.3	7.3	.95
472	Arrangement of transportation	144	4.7	32.8	.98
48	COMMUNICATION	165	12.5	75.8	1.23
49	ELECTRIC, GAS AND SANITARY SERV.	52	6.4	122.2	1.08
491	Electric services	8	4.1	515.6	1.44
492	Gas production and distribution	8	2.0	248.1	1.82
TOTAL TRANSP. COMMUNICATION UTILITIES		1,074	43.0	40.0	1.24

SOURCE: Data file compiled by Rand from County Business Patterns records (see Appendix B).

The construction industry is quite a different matter; it was significant regionally with 28,900 employees in 1977. The largest number (16,500) worked for special trade contractors—plumbing, heating and air conditioning, electrical work and masonry, stonework, and plastering being the most sizable components (Table 6.2). High concentration ratios in concrete work (1.32), roofing and sheet metal work (1.22), and miscellaneous contractors (1.24), however, indicate that the region is more specialized in these areas. The dearth of general construction activity in the SMSA in the late 1970s is indicated by the low concentration ratio for general construction contractors (0.80).

Construction was the only nonmanufacturing sector that suffered an absolute loss of employment (three percent) from 1967 to 1977. Since the industry was growing nationally, the SMSA's share of U.S. construction employment dropped more noticeably (by 21 percent). The industry's concentration ratio also declined (by seven percent) indicating a drop in the number of SMSA construction workers per capita.

Table 6.3

EMPLOYMENT CHANGE IN THE MINING, CONSTRUCTION, TRANSPORTATION, COMMUNICATION, AND UTILITIES SECTORS, CLEVELAND SMSA, 1967-77

SIC	Sector/Industry	1977 Concentration Ratio		1967-77 Percent Change		
		Clev. SMSA	All U.S. SMSAs	Clev. SMSA Employ.	Clev. Share U.S. Employ.	Clev. Concen. Ratio
	Mining					
10	Mining	.16	.51	36.9	0.0	17.9
	Contract Construction					
15	General building contractors	.80	1.03	-17.5	-24.5	-11.2
16	Heavy construction contractors	.87	1.02	49.7	16.7	37.3
17	Special trade contractors	1.00	.52	-8.6	-26.5	-13.9
	Total Contract Construction	.91	1.08	-3.2	-20.6	-6.6
	Transportation, Communication, Utilities					
41	Local/interurban transit	.94	1.17	-58.4	-43.2	-33.1
42	Trucking and warehousing	1.59	1.11	25.5	8.5	27.5
44	Water transportation	1.15	1.20	-38.6	-40.4	-29.9
45	Transportation by air	.84	1.30	24.7	1.4	19.1
47	Transportation services	.95	1.28	40.3	-16.0	-1.2
48	Communication	1.23	1.12	8.8	-8.4	7.7
49	Electric, gas & sanitary serv.	1.08	1.05	9.6	1.1	18.9
	Total Trans., commun., utilities	1.24	1.14	3.5	-7.6	8.8

SOURCE: Data file compiled by Rand from County Business Patterns records (see Appendix B).

Among the components, general contractors declined most rapidly (by 18 percent in contrast to nine percent for special trade contractors). A significant increase in the smaller, heavy construction group (50 percent) partially offset the losses of the other two components. This group also had a surprisingly low concentration ratio (0.87), but it was catching up rapidly in the 1970s.

In the aggregate, construction must be considered as a deficit industry for Cleveland. It is the only major nonmanufacturing sector in the SMSA with a concentration ratio less than 1.00 (0.91). The ratio for construction in the average U.S. metropolis is 1.08. Per 1,000 population, the typical metropolis has 19 percent more construction workers than the Cleveland SMSA.

TRANSPORTATION, COMMUNICATION, AND UTILITIES

Comparatively, this sector is one of the Cleveland area's continuing strengths. With a total 1977 workforce of 43,000 employees, it was larger than all but two of the area's two-digit manufacturing industries. However, there have been substantial differences in performance among its components.

By far the largest and strongest component is trucking and warehousing (trucking firms account for 91 percent of this component's 16,100 employees—Table 6.2). This is clearly one of metropolitan Cleveland's specialties, with a local concentration ratio of 1.59 in contrast to the 1.11 average for all national SMSAs. It was also among the fastest growing, increasing in employment by 25.5 percent from 1967 to 1977. Considering the rapid expansion of goods production and goods movement in the southern and western states over that period, it is yet more impressive that the Cleveland SMSA increased its share of national employment in trucking and warehousing (by nine percent) and its concentration ratio for that industry (by 28 percent).

The next largest components are communications (12,500 employees) and other utilities (electric, gas and sanitary services—6,400). Both are also Cleveland specialties with concentration ratios clearly above those for the typical SMSA. They had a much smaller 1967-77 growth rate than trucking, however (nine and 10 percent, respectively). Cleveland SMSA concentration ratios for both of these industries increased over that decade but due to rapid growth in other parts of the United States, their shares of national employment did not. Metropolitan Cleveland's share of U.S. employment in communications declined by eight percent and its share in the other utilities stayed about even.

The rest of the sector is composed of four smaller transportation related industries (ranging from 1,300 to 2,600 employees): local and interurban transit, water transportation, transportation by air, and transportation services (firms that make arrangements for freight or passenger transportation, handle freight forwarding, etc.). Cleveland does not have comparative strength in any of these four; 1977 concentration ratios fell well below those for the typical U.S. metropolis in each case.

In one of these industries, however, Cleveland appears to be catching up. SMSA employment in air transportation increased by 25 percent from 1967 to 1977; the local share of U.S. employment in this industry increased slightly (by one percent) and its concentration ratio jumped appreciably (by 19 percent). Cleveland SMSA employment in transportation services also rose dramatically over the period (by 40 percent), but this industry grew even more rapidly elsewhere in the nation and thus Cleveland's share declined.

The other two fell much further behind. Local and interurban transit lost 58 percent of its 1967 employment by 1977; water transportation lost 39 percent. Concentration ratios and shares of national employment in both of these industries also suffered serious declines.

WHOLESALE AND RETAIL TRADE

The trade sectors together had a workforce of 180,700 in 1977 in the Cleveland SMSA (Tables 6.4 and 6.5). On the average during the 1970s, both experienced significant increases in employment and modest increases in concentration ratios, although their shares of national employment declined. Again, however, there was considerable diversity in the performance of their components.

Historically, wholesale trade has been a strong export-oriented industry in the SMSA. With 54,500 employees in 1977, the local concentration ratio for wholesaling was 1.43 compared to only 1.13 in metropolitan America on the average. Per 1,000 population, the Cleveland SMSA had 28 workers in the wholesale trade; the typical metropolis, 24.

Within this industry, Cleveland's forte is clearly durable goods, as would be expected given the composition of its manufacturing sector. The SMSA's 1977 concentration ratio was 1.73 for durable goods wholesalers on average in contrast to 1.00 for wholesale trade in nondurables; 70 percent of all local employees in wholesaling work for

Table 6.4

COMPOSITION OF THE WHOLESALE AND RETAIL TRADE SECTORS, CLEVELAND SMSA, 1977

SIC	Sector/Industry	No. of Estab.	No. of Employ. (000s)	Employ. per Estab.	Concen. Ratio
	Wholesale Trade				
50	WHOLESALE TRADE-DURABLE GOODS	2,788	38.3	13.7	1.73
501	Motor vehicle & auto equipment	338	6.2	18.4	1.67
5012	Auto. & other motor vehicles	45	1.2	26.7	1.25
5013	Auto. parts & supplies	255	4.7	18.5	1.98
502	Furniture & home furnishings	128	1.1	8.7	1.28
503	Lumber & construction materials	162	2.2	13.4	1.35
5031	Lumber, plywood & millwork	63	1.1	17.3	1.25
5039	Construction materials, NEC	96	1.1	11.1	1.48
504	Sporting goods, toys, & hobby	50	.9	18.2	1.34
505	Metals & minerals, exc. petrol.	277	4.0	14.5	3.54
5051	Metals service center & office	252	4.0	15.8	3.70
506	Electrical goods	336	4.4	13.1	1.84
5063	Electrical apparatus & equip.	167	1.8	10.6	1.48
5064	Elec. appliances, TV, & radio	42	1.3	30.9	2.44
5065	Elec. parts & equipment	125	1.4	10.9	2.10
507	Hardware, plumb., heat., equip.	249	4.0	16.1	2.36
5072	Hardware	108	2.4	22.5	3.60
5074	Plumb., hydronic heat. suppl.	73	1.0	13.8	1.59
508	Mach., equipment & supplies	1,052	12.8	12.2	1.50
5081	Commercial mach. & equipment	145	2.9	19.8	1.40
5082	Construction & mining mach.	42	.8	19.2	1.17
5084	Industrial mach. & equipment	381	3.1	8.1	1.96
5085	Industrial supplies	247	3.0	12.0	2.30
5086	Prof. equipment & supplies	106	1.9	18.2	1.99
509	Miscellaneous durable goods	179	2.6	14.4	1.78
5093	Scrap & waste materials	95	1.7	18.3	2.27
51	WHOLESALE TRADE-NONDURABLE GOODS	1,036	16.2	15.7	1.00
511	Paper & paper products	143	2.0	13.7	1.51
5112	Stationery supplies	74	.8	11.4	1.50
512	Drugs, proprietaries, sundr.	34	1.0	28.5	1.28
513	Apparel, piece goods, notions	81	.9	10.8	.74
514	Groceries & related products	277	5.3	19.2	1.03
5141	Groceries, general line	19	1.0	50.6	.90
5147	Meats & meat products	46	1.2	26.3	1.64
5149	Groceries & related prod., NEC	95	1.4	14.7	1.03
516	Chemicals & allied products	145	2.5	17.5	3.21
517	Petroleum & petroleum products	72	.9	12.2	.55
518	Beer, wine, distilled beverages	38	1.3	35.3	1.26
5181	Beer and ale	18	.8	44.7	1.32

Table 6.4 (Continued)

SIC	Sector/Industry	No. of Estab.	No. of Employ. (000s)	Employ. per Estab.	Concen. Ratio
Wholesale Trade (Continued)					
519	Miscellaneous nondurable goods	235	2.4	10.2	.76
TOTAL	WHOLESALE TRADE	3,824	54.5	14.3	1.43
Retail Trade					
52	BUILDING MATERIALS & GARDEN SUPPL.	307	2.4	7.9	.60
521	Lumber & other building mater.	80	1.3	16.6	.62
525	Hardware stores	112	.8	6.8	.74
53	GENERAL MERCHANDISE STORES	230	24.1	105.0	1.46
531	Department stores	79	20.0	253.8	1.56
533	Variety stores	64	1.6	24.6	.78
539	Misc. general mdse. stores	86	2.5	29.6	1.41
54	FOOD STORES	1,508	21.9	14.5	1.24
541	Grocery stores	936	18.4	19.7	1.23
546	Retail bakeries	217	1.6	7.3	1.37
55	AUTO. DEALERS & SERVICE STATIONS	1,732	15.9	9.2	1.02
551	New and used car dealers	178	6.8	38.0	.82
553	Auto. & home supply stores	219	1.5	6.7	.82
554	Gasoline service stations	1,213	7.0	5.8	1.21
56	APPAREL & ACCESSORY STORES	977	7.6	7.7	1.01
561	Men's, boys' clothing, furnish.	204	1.8	8.9	1.43
562	Women's ready-to-wear stores	268	2.9	10.8	1.04
566	Shoe stores	289	1.5	5.3	1.16
57	FURNITURE & HOME FURNISHINGS STORES	705	4.5	6.4	1.01
571	Furn. & home furnishings stores	429	3.0	7.0	1.09
5712	Furniture stores	232	2.0	8.5	1.04
573	Radio, television & music stores	208	1.0	4.8	.90
58	EATING AND DRINKING PLACES	2,747	35.7	13.0	1.08
581	Eating & drinking places	2,744	35.6	13.0	1.08
5812	Eating places	1,735	31.0	17.9	1.08
5813	Drinking places	914	3.8	4.2	1.32

Table 6.4 (Continued)

SIC	Sector/Industry	No. of Estab.	No. of Employ. (000s)	Employ. per Estab.	Concen. Ratio
	Retail Trade (Continued)				
59	MISCELLANEOUS RETAIL	1,916	13.9	7.2	.94
591	Drug stores & proprietary stor.	357	4.4	12.2	1.08
594	Misc. shopping goods stores	681	4.3	6.3	1.11
5944	Jewelry stores	146	1.0	6.5	.98
5949	Sewing, needlewk., piece stor.	80	.8	9.7	1.43
596	Nonstore retailers	142	2.2	15.7	.94
5962	Merchandising mach. oper.	57	1.3	22.5	2.08
599	Retail stores, NEC	478	1.8	3.8	.97
5992	Florists	146	.8	5.2	.98
5999	Misc. retail stores, NEC	286	1.0	3.4	1.02
	TOTAL RETAIL TRADE	10,122	126.2	12.5	1.13

SOURCE: Data file compiled by Rand from County Business Patterns records (see Appendix B).

establishments that handle durable goods. The largest components are machinery, equipment and supplies (12,800 employees), motor vehicles and automobile equipment (6,200), electrical goods (4,400), hardware, plumbing and heating equipment, and metals and minerals (both 4,000). The largest concentrations of employment among wholesalers of nondurable goods are in groceries and related products (5,300 employees), chemicals and allied products (2,500), and paper and paper products (2,000).

The best 1967-77 performance in local wholesale trade was recorded by the hardware, plumbing and heating equipment group. It generated a 69 percent increase in jobs and substantially increased its share of national employment and its concentration ratio. Wholesalers of motor vehicles and automobile equipment also recorded solid gains in employment (25 percent increase) and increased their export orientation (concentration ratio) but suffered a modest decline in their share of the U.S. market. The largest wholesaling component (machinery, equipment, and supplies) did not fare as well. It experienced a modest gain in employment (eight percent), but both its share of U.S. employment and its concentration ratio declined substantially. The remaining components (electrical goods and other wholesale trade) experienced modest absolute losses in employment and sizable declines in market shares and concentration ratios.

Metropolitan Cleveland's retail sector is somewhat more export-oriented than the typical U.S. metropolis but the gap is not large

Table 6.5

EMPLOYMENT CHANGE IN THE WHOLESALE AND RETAIL TRADE SECTORS, CLEVELAND SMSA, 1967-77

		1977 Concentration Ratio		1967-77 Percent Change		
SIC	Sector/Industry	Clev. SMSA	All U.S. SMSAs	Clev. SMSA Employ.	Clev. Share U.S. Employ.	Clev. Concen. Ratio
Wholesale Trade						
501	Motor vehicles & auto. equip.	1.67	NA	25.2	−6.9	9.4
506	Electrical goods	1.84	NA	−.4	−11.9	3.7
507	Hardware, Plumb. & heat. equip.	2.36	NA	69.3	37.5	61.7
508	Machinery, equip. & supplies	1.50	NA	7.9	−25.7	−12.6
50X	Other wholesale trade	1.24	NA	−6.1	−17.3	−2.7
	Total Wholesale Trade	1.43	1.13	3.9	−14.2	.9
Retail Trade						
52	Building mater. & garden supp.	.60	.91	−23.6	−27.4	−14.7
53	General merchandise stores	1.46	1.13	−8.1	−7.9	8.3
54	Food stores	1.24	1.03	20.0	−10.6	5.3
55	Auto. dealers & service sta.	1.02	.99	21.9	1.1	19.0
56	Apparel & accessory stores	1.01	1.09	12.9	−6.3	10.2
57	Furniture & home furn. stores	1.01	1.06	23.8	−4.3	12.5
58	Eating & drinking places	1.08	1.08	38.1	−22.6	−8.9
59	Miscellaneous retail	.94	1.08	45.9	−1.2	16.3
	Total Retail Trade	1.13	1.07	18.6	−9.9	6.0

SOURCE: Data file compiled by Rand from County Business Patterns records (see Appendix B).

(concentration ratio of 1.13 vs. 1.07). The essential role of Cleveland retailers, unlike its wholesalers, remains serving the local market.

The internal structure of Cleveland retailing is not unlike that in many metropolitan areas. Its largest component employer is eating and drinking places (28 percent of total sector employment), followed by general merchandise stores (19 percent), food stores (17 percent), and auto dealers and service stations (13 percent).

The sector did grow by 19,800 jobs (19 percent) from 1967 to 1977 bringing its 1977 SMSA employment total to 126,200, and it increased its export orientation slightly (an increase of six percent in its concentration ratio). However, retail employment was growing even faster in other parts of the United States; the Cleveland SMSA share of the national total declined by 10 percent.

Most of its components followed the same basic pattern—growth in employment but decline in national share—yet some important differences should be noted. First, on the positive side, "miscellaneous retailing" (drug stores, jewelry stores, florists, etc.) in Cleveland almost kept up with the phenomenal expansion of this component nationally from 1967 to 1977. The SMSA's share of U.S. employment in this group declined slightly (by 1.2 percent), but even so, the number of local jobs had increased by 46 percent. Actually the best performance of any Cleveland retailing component over the decade was recorded by automobile dealers and service stations. Although its absolute employment growth rate (22 percent) was not the highest among the several components, it was the only one to increase its share of the national market, even if by a small amount (1.1 percent).

On the negative side, both general merchandise stores and building materials and garden suppliers suffered absolute employment losses from 1967 to 1977. The decline in the former was not due to local problems, however. General merchandise stores lost employment in much of the country during the 1970s. In fact the decline in the Cleveland SMSA's share of national jobs in general merchandising (eight percent) was smaller than the decline in its share of retail trade in the aggregate. The loss in building materials and garden suppliers, in contrast, does represent a local problem, no doubt related to the decline of the construction industry we noted earlier. This one component of retailing had the lowest 1977 concentration ratio, and by far the largest declines in local jobs, in share of national jobs, and in concentration ratio.

FINANCE, INSURANCE, AND REAL ESTATE

This sector had a total of 44,000 employees in 1977. Its largest components were banking (11,100 employees), insurance carriers (10,500), real estate (9,600), and other credit agencies (6,400, for the most part in savings and loan associations) (Table 6.6).

The sector is yet to become one of Cleveland's competitive strengths. Its overall concentration ratio in 1977 was 1.11, lower than that for local retail trade for example and quite a bit below the 1.19

average for finance, insurance, and real estate in all U.S. metropolises (Table 6.7). Within the sector, however, Cleveland does have some impressive specialties: e.g., savings and loan associations (concentration ratio of 2.27), health insurance carriers (2.10), title insurance carriers (2.75), and real estate agents and managers (1.63).

There was little diversity in 1967-77 performance within this sector, at least as far as employment change is concerned. All of the larger components (i.e., all except SIC 66 and 67) followed the same pattern we noted for retail trade: sizable increases in local employment but increases smaller than those experienced in the same industries nationally. Employment growth rates averaged 23 percent, ranging from five percent (security and commodity brokers) to 26 percent (other credit agencies). Losses in national shares averaged 13 percent and ranged from eight percent (insurance carriers) to 21 percent (security and commodity brokers).

Only two of the larger components increased their export orientation over the decade: other credit agencies (four percent increase in concentration ratio) and insurance carriers (eight percent increase).

Even though it is too small to have an important impact on total employment, the spectacular performance of the "holding and other investment office" group (which also includes the offices of religious, educational, and other trusts) deserves mentioning. Its 1977 employment totaled 1,200, having increased almost eightfold over the preceding decade. Its concentration ratio increased by 241 percent and its share of U.S. employment in the same group by 190 percent.

BUSINESS RELATED SERVICES

Business related services, with 82,700 local employees in 1977, is dominated by two components. First is the business service group (30,400 employees) which includes such activities as: management consultants and public relations firms (9,700 jobs), personnel supply services (6,400), building maintenance and operations (4,800), and detective and other protective services (4,100). The second is manufacturing administrative and auxiliary (A&A) establishments (for the most part, corporate headquarters offices and R&D facilities) with 25,600 employees. The third largest component is the category we have created by combining administrative and auxiliary establishments for all sectors other than manufacturing (14,900 employees). (See Table 6.6.)

Table 6.6

COMPOSITION OF THE FINANCE, INSURANCE, REAL ESTATE, AND SERVICE SECTORS, CLEVELAND SMSA, 1977

SIC	Sector/Industry	No. of Estàb.	No. of Employ. (000s)	Employ. per Estab.	Concen. Ratio
	Finance, Insurance and Real Estate				
60	BANKING	346	11.1	32.2	.97
61	OTHER CREDIT AGENCIES	737	6.4	8.7	1.49
612	Savings & loan associations	238	3.8	15.9	2.27
614	Personal credit institutions	442	1.9	4.4	1.14
62	SECURITY/COMMODITY BROKERS	91	1.7	19.1	1.04
621	Security brokers & dealers	56	1.6	28.5	1.15
63	INSURANCE CARRIERS	337	10.5	31.2	1.06
631	Life insurance	160	3.5	21.9	.77
632	Medical serv. & health ins.	17	2.0	118.4	2.10
6324	Hospital & med. serv. places	8	1.9	237.6	2.55
633	Fire, marine, & casualty ins.	59	3.7	62.1	1.05
636	Title insurance	26	1.0	37.1	2.75
64	INSURANCE AGENTS, BROKERS	704	3.2	4.5	.93
65	REAL ESTATE	1,572	9.6	6.1	1.26
651	Real estate oper. & lessors	1,039	4.4	4.3	1.16
653	Real estate agents & managers	437	4.3	9.9	1.63
66	COMBINED REAL ESTATE, INS., ETC.	22	.1	4.0	.34
67	HOLDING & OTHER INVEST. OFFICES	111	1.2	10.7	1.02
TOTAL	FINANCE, INSURANCE AND REAL ESTATE	3,930	44.0	11.2	1.11
	Business Related Services				
73	BUSINESS SERVICES	1,627	30.4	18.7	1.49
731	Advertising	148	1.6	10.7	1.49
7311	Advertising agencies	120	1.3	10.9	1.77
732	Credit reporting & collecting	59	.8	14.4	1.56
733	Mail, reprod., stenographic	151	1.1	7.1	1.29
734	Services to buildings	233	4.8	20.6	1.33
7349	Bldg. maint. services, NEC	179	4.3	24.3	1.37

Table 6.6 (Continued)

SIC	Sector/industry	No. of Estab.	No. of Employ. (000s)	Employ. per Estab.	Concen. Ratio
Business Related Services (Continued)					
736	Personnel supply services	162	6.4	39.4	1.75
7361	Employment agencies	107	1.9	17.7	2.81
7362	Temporary help supply serv.	49	4.5	91.9	1.73
737	Computer & data proc. serv.	100	1.7	16.8	.95
7374	Data processing services	50	1.2	24.4	1.06
739	Misc. business services	741	13.9	18.8	1.58
7392	Management & public rela.	257	9.7	37.9	2.01
7393	Detective & protective serv.	88	4.1	46.7	1.73
7394	Equipment rental & leasing	84	.9	11.0	1.23
7399	Business services, NEC	263	3.8	14.3	1.81
81	LEGAL SERVICES	807	4.4	5.4	1.26
89	MISCELLANEOUS SERVICES	682	7.4	10.9	1.25
891	Eng. & architectural services	296	3.5	11.7	1.06
893	Account., audit., bookkeeping	335	3.6	10.8	1.74
AM	MANUFACTURING ADM. & AUXILIARY	172	25.6	149.1	2.42
AO	OTHER ADMIN. AND AUXILIARY	267	14.9	55.7	1.32
149/	Mining admin. & auxiliary	10	.7	75.0	1.06
179/	Contract const., admin. & aux.	6	.6	104.7	4.46
497/	Transp., admin. & aux.	20	.2	12.0	.25
519/	Wholesale trade, admin. & aux.	69	4.8	70.0	2.19
599/	Retail trade, admin. & aux.	119	7.6	64.2	1.50
679/	Finance, admin. & aux.	--	--	--	--
899/	Services, admin. & aux.	43	.8	18.0	.55
TOTAL	BUSINESS RELATED SERVICES	3,555	82.7	23.3	1.60
Other Services					
70	HOTELS AND OTHER LODGINGS	187	7.7	41.2	.95
701	Hotels, motels, tourist centers	158	7.5	47.7	.99
72	PERSONAL SERVICES	1,489	9.4	6.3	1.17
721	Laundry, clean., garment serv.	416	3.7	8.8	1.16
7216	Dry clean. plants, exc. rug	198	1.3	6.8	1.17

Table 6.6 (Continued)

SIC	Sector/Industry	No. of Estab.	No. of Employ. (000s)	Employ. per Estab.	Concen. Ratio
	Other Services (Continued)				
723	Beauty shops	603	3.0	5.0	1.22
726	Funeral serv. & crematories	142	.9	6.1	1.38
729	Misc. personal services	108	1.2	11.0	1.08
75	AUTO. AND RELATED SERVICES	851	5.6	6.6	1.33
751	Auto. rentals, without drivers	84	1.0	11.5	1.42
753	Auto. repair shops	550	2.8	5.1	1.04
7531	Top & body repair shops	185	.8	4.5	1.07
7538	General auto. repair shops	202	1.1	5.4	.97
754	Auto. services, exc. repair	106	1.3	12.3	2.46
7542	Car washes	77	1.1	13.8	2.67
76	MISCELLANEOUS REPAIR SERVICES	494	3.2	6.4	1.41
762	Electrical repair shops	164	.9	5.8	1.31
769	Miscellaneous repair shops	249	2.0	7.9	1.55
7699	Repair services, NEC	189	1.1	6.0	1.33
78	MOTION PICTURES	92	1.0	11.4	.66
783	Motion picture theaters	67	.9	14.1	.98
79	AMUSEMENT AND RECREATION	412	6.2	15.0	1.20
792	Producers, orch., entertain.	36	1.2	32.3	1.94
7922	Theatrical produc. & serv.	18	.9	49.4	3.25
793	Bowling, billiard estab.	85	1.4	17.0	1.53
799	Misc. amusement, recrea. serv.	221	2.8	12.5	.93
7997	Membership sports, clubs	68	1.7	25.7	1.38
80	HEALTH SERVICES	2,672	48.9	18.3	1.27
801	Offices of physicians	1,280	4.9	3.8	.91
802	Offices of dentists	764	2.7	3.5	1.11
805	Nursing & personal care fac.	103	6.7	36.2	.96
806	Hospitals	47	32.1	682.9	1.59
807	Medical & dental laboratories	109	.9	8.2	1.12
808	Outpatient care facilities	57	.8	13.9	.71
82	EDUCATION SERVICES	249	11.3	45.4	1.29
821	Elementary & secondary schools	126	3.4	27.2	1.31
822	Colleges & universities	19	6.4	334.5	1.24
824	Correspondence & voca. schools	32	1.0	31.1	2.44
829	Educational services, NEC	65	1.3	20.0	1.86

Table 6.6 (Continued)

SIC	Sector/Industry	No. of Estab.	No. of Employ. (000s)	Employ. per Estab.	Concen. Ratio
Other Services (Continued)					
84	MUSEUMS, ZOOS, ETC.	10	.6	60.3	3.01
86	MEMBERSHIP ORGANIZATIONS	1,170	10.9	9.4	1.13
863	Labor organizations	302	3.4	11.1	2.23
864	Civic and social associations	255	1.9	7.6	.82
866	Religious organizations	446	4.3	9.7	1.02
TOTAL OTHER SERVICES		8,095	113.9	11.5	1.22

SOURCE: Data file compiled by Rand from County Business Patterns records (see Appendix B).

Among all nonmanufacturing sectors, business related services is by far the greatest asset for metropolitan Cleveland's economy. First, it has the strongest export orientation, with an aggregate concentration ratio of 1.60 (wholesale trade comes second with 1.43). All of its components have concentration ratios significantly above those for their counterparts in metropolitan America on the average (Table 6.7). Manufacturing A&A stands out with a concentration ratio of 2.42 in Cleveland vs. 1.26 in the typical U.S. metropolis.

Second, its employment has grown most rapidly, increasing by 43 percent from 1967 to 1977 (wholesale trade was again second, registering a 25 percent increase over that decade). The highest growth rate among its components was for the other A&A group (72 percent), followed by legal services (68 percent), business services (55 percent), and then manufacturing A&A (31 percent).

As rapid as the growth of these components was in metropolitan Cleveland, it was even more rapid in other parts of the nation. The Cleveland SMSA share of national employment in business and legal services and nonmanufacturing A&A decreased noticeably over the 1967-77 period (declines ranging from 13 to 22 percent). Seen more broadly, then, the performance of manufacturing A&A was the strongest. Cleveland's share of manufacturing A&A jobs decreased

Table 6.7

EMPLOYMENT CHANGE IN THE FINANCE, INSURANCE, REAL ESTATE, AND SERVICE SECTORS, CLEVELAND SMSA, 1967-77

SIC	Sector/Industry	1977 Concentration Ratio		1967-77 Percent Change		
		Clev. SMSA	All U.S. SMSAs	Clev. SMSA Employ.	Clev. Share U.S. Employ.	Clev. Concen. Ratio
Finance, Insurance and Real Estate						
60	Banking	.97	1.09	23.7	-19.6	-5.5
61	Other credit agencies	1.49	1.16	25.9	-11.4	4.2
62	Security/commodity brokers	1.04	1.33	4.6	-20.7	-6.7
63	Insurance carriers	1.06	1.27	10.6	-7.8	8.4
64	Insurance agents, brokers	.93	1.15	23.1	-20.4	-6.3
65	Real estate	1.26	1.22	22.6	-14.5	.6
66	Combined real est., ins., etc.	.34	.94	2.3	15.4	35.6
67	Holding & other invest. off.	1.02	1.26	797.0	190.3	240.9
Total Finance, Ins. and Real Estate		1.11	1.19	22.6	-13.3	2.0
Business Related Services						
73	Business services	1.49	1.28	55.0	-14.3	.8
81	Legal services	1.24	1.17	67.5	-13.2	2.1
89	Miscellaneous services	1.25	1.22	13.5	-14.6	.4
AM	Manufacturing adm. and aux.	2.42	1.26	30.6	-8.2	8.0
AO	Other admin. and auxiliary	1.32	1.16	72.2	-22.0	-8.3
Total Business Related Services		1.60	1.00	43.3	-17.0	-2.3
Other Services						
70	Hotels and other lodgings	.95	1.02	39.2	6.3	25.1
72	Personal services	1.17	1.12	-24.1	-13.3	1.9
75	Auto. and related services	1.33	1.15	11.3	-20.8	-6.9
76	Miscellaneous repair services	1.41	1.13	-.1	-26.5	-13.5
78	Motion pictures	.66	1.18	-17.1	-22.7	-9.0
79	Amusement and recreation	1.20	1.13	33.0	-10.9	4.7
80	Health services	1.27	1.10	59.5	-13.1	2.2
82	Education services	1.29	1.18	14.2	-12.3	3.1
84	Museums, zoos, etc.	3.01	1.29	52.3	1.1	18.9
86	Membership organizations	1.13	1.13	-18.0	-27.5	-14.7
Total Other Services		1.22	1.11	31.8	-13.6	1.6

SOURCE: Data file compiled by Rand from County Business Patterns records (see Appendix B).

less (by eight percent). Also, Cleveland's manufacturing A&A experienced the largest increase in its concentration ratio over the decade (eight percent) in contrast to two percent or less for the others.

OTHER SERVICES

This final nonmanufacturing sector perhaps exhibits the most diversity in recent performance. In total, it provided 113,900 jobs in 1977; its concentration ratio shows that it is also more export-oriented in Cleveland than in the typical U.S. metropolis. On the average, like a number of the other sectors we have discussed, it had a healthy 1967-77 employment growth (32 percent) and a modest increase in concentration ratio but a decline in national share (by 14 percent).

Almost half of its 1977 employment (48,900) was in the health services component. It has six other components with 5,000 employees or more: education services (11,300), membership organizations (10,900), personal services (9,400), hotels and other lodging places (7,700), amusement and recreation (6,200), and automobile and related services (5,600).

In the health group, roughly two-thirds of all jobs are provided by Cleveland's hospitals. Nursing and personal care facilities account for another 14 percent and physicians offices for 10 percent. Concentration ratios for most of its elements hover around 1.00; it is hospital employment (concentration ratio of 1.59) that boosts the overall ratio to 1.27 in metropolitan Cleveland, well above the 1.10 national SMSA average. Hospitals therefore appear to be one of the area's important export-oriented industries.

Health services was not only the largest component of the other services sector, it was also the fastest growing with a 1967-77 increase of 60 percent in employment. It also maintained a relatively stable concentration ratio over the period. Health services employment, however, skyrocketed in almost all parts of the country; even with its substantial growth locally, metropolitan Cleveland's share of national employment in the industry declined by 13 percent.

The recent performance of the remaining six major components in this sector was mixed. Four increased employment locally from 1967 to 1977, but two declined. The largest increase was recorded by hotels and lodgings (39 percent). This is the only major component for which the Cleveland SMSA also increased its share of national employment over the decade (by six percent). It is important to note, though, that this was also the only one that as late as 1977 was less export-oriented in Cleveland than in the typical SMSA nationally. Cleveland's concentration ratio was 0.95; that for the typical SMSA, 1.02. Cleveland's hotel industry, therefore, was not yet fulfilling its potential, but it was catching up rapidly.

Amusement and recreation services had the next highest growth rate over the decade (33 percent). This group includes a broad array of activities ranging from high culture (theaters and Cleveland's famed orchestra) to the not so high (bowling alleys and billiard parlors). It recorded an increase in concentration ratio (five percent) and, although its share of national employment declined, its loss rate (11 percent) was less serious than most in this sector.

The other two components that grew over the 1967-77 decade were education services (private schools and colleges only—government paid employees are not included in this data series) and automobile and related services. The former increased employment by 14 percent and the latter by 11 percent. Education services increased its export orientation (by three percent), but the auto service group slipped behind in this regard (by seven percent). Cleveland's share of national employment in these industries declined, by 12 and 21 percent, respectively.

The two "losers" in this sector were membership organizations (decline of 18 percent in employment over the decade) and personal services (decline of 24 percent). The latter, however, represents a less serious problem for Cleveland. The personal services group includes such diverse establishments as laundries, beauty shops, and funeral homes, activities that together lost employment nationally during the 1970s. The 1967-77 decline in Cleveland's share of national employment in this group (13 percent) was less severe than for membership organizations (28 percent), a component that was growing nationally.

The membership organization group includes all types of nonprofit associations: business, professional, labor, civic, political, religious, and social. Cleveland's concentration ratio for this group (1.13) was the same as that for the typical SMSA in 1977, but it had declined by 15 percent since 1967. The implication is that in relation to the rest of the United States, employment by such organizations in Cleveland declined on a per capita basis.

COMPARATIVE PERFORMANCE OF COMPONENT INDUSTRIES

The preceding pages make it clear that in Cleveland's nonmanufacturing sector, as in its manufacturing sector, there was considerable diversity in industry performance in the 1970s. Some components declined seriously whereas others remained relatively stable and yet others expanded.

In Table 6.8, we compare the extent of this diversity among the 84 component manufacturing industries we discussed in Chapter II against that found among the 47 nonmanufacturing components examined in this chapter. In the top part of the table, we look at the distribution of components and employment in each sector by 1967-77 percentage increases in employment. For example, the two percentages on the top line tell us that 22.1 percent of all manufacturing employment, but 41.5 percent of all nonmanufacturing employment in 1977, was in component industries that had grown by 30 percent or more over the preceding decade.

Table 6.8

Diversity in Employment Change, Components of Cleveland Manufacturing and Nonmanufacturing Sectors, 1967-77

Change	Manufacturing		Nonmanufacturing	
	No. of Components	% of Employ.	No. of Components	% of Employ.
Change in Employment, Cleveland SMSA				
Rapid growth (+30% or more)	11	22.1	15	41.5
Moderate growth (+5% to +29%)	10	14.1	18	35.4
About same (-4% to +4%)	13	6.6	4	1.9
Moderate decline (-5% to -29%)	25	40.6	8	20.3
Rapid decline (-30% or more)	25	16.6	2	.9
Total	84	100.0	47	100.0
Change in Cleveland SMSA Share of U.S. Employment				
Rapid increase (+30% or more)	6	3.9	2	1.1
Moderate increase (+5% to +29%)	11	23.9	4	6.1
About same (-4% to +4%)	11	13.1	7	9.3
Moderate decrease (-5% to -29%)	30	29.2	32	82.7
Rapid decrease (-30% or more)	26	29.9	2	.8
Total	84	100.0	47	100.0

SOURCE: Rand analysis of data files compiled from Census of Manufactures and County Business Patterns records (see Appendix B).

It is evident that using this yardstick (percentage change in employment) nonmanufacturing industries come out ahead: 77 percent of their employees were in industries that grew by five percent or more vs. only 36 percent for manufacturing. But how relevant is the yardstick? A competitively weak local industry may have increased employment simply because it was swept along in the tide of a ubiquitous national increase in demand for its product. Conversely, a strong local branch of a declining national industry may have been much more successful by achieving an employment loss rate proportionally smaller than the average. In other words, the change in a Cleveland industry's share of national employment in the same industry is a better measure of competitive strength.

Looking at things this way (bottom half of Table 6.8), a quite different picture emerges. During the 1970s it appears that Cleveland's manufacturing sector exhibited more strength than its nonmanufacturing sector; 28 percent of local manufacturing employment was in industries that increased their national share by five percent or more over the 1967-77 decade vs. only seven percent of all local nonmanufacturing employment.

Expecting a Cleveland industry to increase or even hold its share of U.S. employment, however, is an unreasonable standard. A local industry may in fact be competing effectively even if its national share is going down, i.e., if it is expanding its output and employment aggressively in Cleveland but other entrepreneurs in Houston, San Diego, etc., happen to be achieving even faster growth due to a more supportive general environment in those areas. A more reasonable guide to local economic health may be the change in industry concentration ratios. If a Cleveland industry has maintained a stable concentration ratio, the relationship between per capita employment locally and nationally has not changed. It is reasonable to conclude that it is "holding its own."[1] If the industry has experienced a sizable increase in its concentration ratio, regardless of its change in share, it can be seen as a strong competitor. It has increased its export orientation (or if the ratio was much below 1.00 to begin with, it has reduced the need for imports).

In Table 6.9, we have grouped 43 of the 47 nonmanufacturing components according to this measure.[2] At the top, we identify those that had an increasing concentration ratio from 1967 to 1977; in the middle, those with a fairly stable ratio; and at the bottom, those

---

[1]Remembering, of course, that complete information on changes in dollar flows and other conditions might point out problems we cannot discern looking at employment data alone.

[2]We excluded the four smallest (having 1,000 employees or less in 1977).

whose ratio declined. We further divide each of these categories into two subgroups. In the lefthand column, we identify industries that can be considered Cleveland specialties; they were more export-oriented than their counterparts in the typical U.S. metropolis. On the right are those that were comparatively import-oriented.

Note that the eight at the top whose concentration ratios increased the most are the only ones that had increased their share of the U.S. market. But using change in concentration ratio as the yardstick we see that there are a number of others whose performance is noteworthy. To summarize:

- 17 component industries (with 39 percent of all nonmanufacturing employment) had increasing concentration ratios:
  - nine of them (with 28 percent of employment) were strong Cleveland specialties and were getting stronger;
  - eight (11 percent of employment) were proportionally small in Cleveland compared to the typical metropolis, but were catching up.
- 12 industries (35 percent of nonmanufacturing employment) maintained relative stability, "holding their own" in relation to their national counterparts. All but one of these had an export orientation in 1977 stronger than that in the average metropolis.
- 14 industries (27 percent of employment) were having serious problems. A significant decline in concentration ratio implies a significant deterioration of competitive position:
  - five of them (11 percent of employment) were export-oriented but were losing ground;
  - nine (16 percent of employment) were weak in Cleveland to begin with and were getting weaker.

Components that have been traditionally strong in Cleveland (lefthand column on Table 6.9) accounted for 73 percent of all local nonmanufacturing employment, but they accounted for 85 percent of employment in categories that had either stabilized or improved their competitive position in the 1970s. Among those that were suffering serious declines, 59 percent of their employees were in components that were traditionally weak in Cleveland (i.e., had concentration ratios below those in the typical U.S. metropolis). There is no evidence here of any important shift in the basic functions of metropolitan Cleveland's nonmanufacturing sector.

Table 6.9

CHANGE IN CONCENTRATION RATIOS, CLEVELAND SMSA NONMANUFACTURING INDUSTRIES, 1967-77

Concentration Ratio Higher Than Average for U.S. SMSAs, 1977		Concentration Ratio Same or Lower Than Average for U.S. SMSAs, 1977	
Increasing concentration ratio (+5 percent or more)		**Increasing concentration ratio** (+5 percent or more)	
^{a}507 Hardwr., plumb. & heat. equip.	+61.7	^{a}67 Holding & other invest. off.	+240.9
^{a}42 Trucking & warehousing	+27.5	^{a}16 Heavy constr. contractors	+ 37.3
^{a}55 Auto dealers & serv. stations	+19.0	^{a}70 Hotels & other lodgings	+ 25.1
^{a}49 Electric., gas & sanit. serv.	+18.9	^{a}45 Transportation by air	+ 19.1
501 Motor vehicles & auto. equip.	+ 9.4	59 Misc. retail trade	+ 16.3
53 General merchandise stores	+ 8.3	57 Furniture & home furn. sto.	+ 12.5
AM Manufacturing, admin. & aux.	+ 8.0	56 Apparel & accessory stores	+ 10.2
48 Communications	+ 7.7	63 Insurance carriers	+ 8.4
54 Food stores	+ 5.3		
Stable concentration ratio (-5 to +5 percent)		**Stable concentration ratio** (-5 to +5 percent)	
79 Amusement & recreation	+ 4.7	47 Transportation services	- 1.2
61 Other credit agencies	+ 4.2		
506 Electrical goods	+ 3.7		
82 Education services	+ 3.1		
80 Health services	+ 2.2		
81 Legal services	+ 2.1		
72 Personal services	+ 1.9		
73 Business services	+ .8		
65 Real estate	+ .6		
89 Miscellaneous services	+ .4		
50X Other wholesale trade	- 2.7		
Declining concentration ratio (-5 percent or more)		**Declining concentration ratio** (-5 percent or more)	
75 Auto. and related services	- 6.9	60 Banking	- 5.5
AO Other admin. & auxiliary	- 8.3	64 Insurance agents, brokers	- 6.3
508 Machinery, equip. & supplies	-12.6	62 Security/commodity brokers	- 6.7
76 Misc. repair services	-13.5	58 Eating & drinking places	- 8.9
17 Special trade contractors	-13.9	15 General building contractors	-11.2
		52 Bldg. materials & gard. sup.	-14.7
		86 Membership organizations	-14.7
		44 Water transportation	-29.9
		41 Local/interurban transit	-33.1

SOURCE: Rand analysis of data file compiled from County Business Patterns records (see Appendix B).

^{a}Increased share of employment in U.S. counterpart industry, 1967-77.

THE ROLE OF SERVICES IN CLEVELAND'S ECONOMIC BASE

In the popular press as well as technical literature, there has been much discussion of late about America's shift from a production economy to a service economy. There is no doubt about the facts; the service sector indeed is growing rapidly as a proportion of all economic activity and manufacturing is declining. There is also no doubt that local service industries are often export-oriented and thus capable of bringing in new income to pay for needed imports. Trends and opportunities have been examined for the national economy (e.g., Birch, 1981), other metropolitan areas (Gruenstein and Guerra, 1981), and for Cleveland (Knight, 1980).

There is very little basis, however, for estimating exactly how far the trend can go. Can it go all the way? Can we envision a future for Cleveland in which all or almost all production operations have drifted away and a metropolitan population of three million or more is supported entirely by nonmanufacturing enterprise?

In our judgment, this scenario is implausible. In fact, the evidence we have reviewed suggests that the health of metropolitan Cleveland's service sector and its other nonmanufacturing sectors remains tied to the continuation of strong local manufacturing activity.

Support for this view is found in the composition of nonmanufacturing activity in the SMSA. The data in this chapter have shown that many of Cleveland's strongest nonmanufacturing industries are those directly dependent on the local production of goods: e.g., trucking, warehousing, and durable goods wholesaling.

Second, it is important to keep relative proportions in mind. In 1977, employment in the Cleveland SMSA manufacturing sector totaled 242,200. Business related service employment was about one-third as large; 82,700 employees, 25,600 of whom worked in manufacturing administrative and auxiliary establishments. If the business related services category could continue to grow at the same rate it did from 1967 to 1977, it would take 30 years before it would provide 240,000 jobs.

Third, we find that the competitive strength of metropolitan Cleveland's business related service sector is not that much greater than that of its manufacturing sector; a large difference would be expected if advanced services were really "taking over." We have noted above that change in a local industry's share of employment in its national counterpart is a more solid measure of competitive strength than its employment growth rate per se. Cleveland SMSA shares (in percent) in the relevant industries changed as follows from 1967 to 1977.

Manufacturing (excluding A&A) .... − 14.9

Business services .... − 14.3

Legal services .... − 13.2

Miscellaneous services (accountants, engineers) ...... − 14.6

Manufacturing A&A .... − 8.2

Other A&A .... − 22.0

Manufacturing administrative and auxiliary establishments (dominantly corporate headquarters offices and related facilities) had by far the best record among these components (smallest decline in share, and as shown on Table 6.7, largest increase in concentration ratio). Two important studies of job generation nationally have demonstrated that the geographical splitting of manufacturing headquarters and production operations became commonplace in the 1970s (Birch, 1979, and Schmenner, 1980). Large corporations headquartered primarily in the northeast have expanded their productive capacity for the most part in other locations, but they have not shifted central office employment proportionately.

This is good news for Cleveland, but once again, there are limits. Numerous interviews conducted in the progress of our study suggest that when Cleveland-based manufacturing firms establish new plants in the south or the west, there is a more than negligible shift in office activity if not a proportionate one. In some cases, some central office workers move from Cleveland to the new location, and they may well be accompanied by a few staff members from other Cleveland firms that serve the corporation; e.g., lawyers and accountants. In other cases, particularly in rapidly expanding corporations, there may be no direct outmigration of Cleveland employees, but a significant share of the corporation's total increase in management and related service capacity winds up in an office building in the sunbelt rather than in Cleveland. Clearly, when a firm with headquarters in Cleveland reaches a point that virtually all of its productive capacity is located elsewhere, Cleveland has more reason to worry about the long-term stability of the headquarters location when the next change in top management occurs.

The service sector (particularly business related services) has made an important contribution to metropolitan Cleveland's economy over the past decade and the opportunity appears to exist for it to become an even more critical sector locally in the 1980s. Efforts by the community to create an environment that will facilitate its expansion are certainly warranted. Nonetheless, the evidence we have compiled suggests that the retention, and where possible, expansion of production activity in Cleveland must remain one of the key objectives of economic development policy; evidence further suggests that this objective may be as important to the nonmanufacturing sector as it is to the manufacturing sector itself.

PART D

PROSPECTS AND PROBLEMS OF THREE CLEVELAND INDUSTRIES

INTRODUCTION: THE PURPOSE OF CASE STUDIES

Analyses of historical data and the manipulation of structural models like those presented in Part B of this report are essential elements of any attempt to devise a strategy for economic development of a region. However, actual, tactical decisions about community actions require a deeper understanding of more detailed institutions and conditions in particular sectors or industries than available statistical data can convey. At some point the process of policymaking for economic development comes down to "go" or "no go" decisions about specific proposals aimed at helping specific sectors. At that decision point, the data must be augmented with nonstatistical information that gives the decisionmaker a "feel" for the prospects and problems of individual sectors.

Over the course of years many such decisions will be made and the prospects and problems of individual sectors will change. Consequently, decisionmakers would be well served by a constant stream of case studies of specific industries. The three case studies presented here are intended to start that flow. We have not examined all the industries that are important to Cleveland nor have we developed all of the information about those industries that might prove useful to decisionmakers. Instead, because one must start somewhere, we chose three industries that were important to Cleveland in some predetermined ways. After a brief initial investigation of national and local conditions in that industry, we identified a fairly specific question or set of questions to answer. Once our focus had been narrowed sufficiently, we reviewed the literature on the industry and conducted a number of interviews with industry leaders in Cleveland with the aim of answering the specific questions.

CHOOSING INDUSTRIES

Our choice of industries was determined by the following considerations:

- Each industry must be "important" to Cleveland in more than one way, and
- The chosen industries must be important to Cleveland in different ways.

An industry's importance to Cleveland was determined by how high it ranked among (roughly) all two-digit industries on the following nine criteria:

General Importance
- Total employment in Cleveland
- Percentage growth rate in Cleveland

Prospects for Growth
- National growth rate

Contribution to General Regional Economic Growth
- Income multiplier
- Cleveland's relative share of U.S. employment

Contribution to Metropolitan Welfare
- Average wages
- Percentage of sectoral employees in the central city
- Percentage sectoral employees who are black
- Percentage sectoral employees who are under twenty-five years of age.

These criteria do not perfectly measure all of the factors that determine an industry's importance to the Cleveland economy. They do, however, reflect as large a number of dimensions of importance as available data can measure. The "general importance" criteria indicate the absolute size of different industries and identify those industries that, while small now, are an important source of dynamism in the economy. "National growth rate" is a key indicator of industrial potential, but it is far from a perfectly complete or reliable predictor of future growth or of Cleveland's potential for capturing a substantial share of that growth. In fact, a major objective of our case studies is to inform our expectations about industrial growth potential. The multiplier[1] and the relative share of U.S. sectoral employment[2] are commonly accepted, simple measures of the degree to which different industries stimulate local growth.

Different sectors differ in the degree to which they contribute to general metropolitan well being or to the solution of metropolitan problems. Observers differ in the entries they would include in the list of urban problems and in the rankings they would assign to those problems; however, structural unemployment among minority group members and youths and the relative decline of the central city would probably rank high on most people's list of problems to be solved. Sectors that contribute to the solution of these problems are important to the metropolitan economy. Average industry wages is included in this list of indicators because high wages could help solve the fiscal problems of the Cleveland metropolitan area.

We used data on these indicators to rank all two-digit SIC industries in Cleveland on each criterion. We then identified the industries in the top five by each criterion. Since there were 14 such industries, some further narrowing had to be done. Two of the service sectors—health and medical services and hotels—ranked high on three criteria and were of general policy interest to the community as well, and, hence, were selected for case studies. Among the manufacturing sectors, two—motor vehicles and primary metals—ranked in the top five on three criteria. Neither of these was selected. Because these case studies are envisioned as the first phase of a continuing agenda of analysis, it makes the most sense to investigate the consuming sectors among Cleveland's "anchor" industries (i.e., nonelectrical machinery and motor vehicles) before the producer industries (i.e., primary and fabricated metals). Because another study of the motor vehicle industry in Cleveland was already under way when we began our work, the choice among the anchor industries was further narrowed to nonelectrical machinery.

---

[1]A multiplier measures how much total regional income is generated by a one dollar increase in business for a given sector.

[2]This is computed as the industry's share of local employment divided by the industry's share of national employment. The multiplier, essentially, measures the proportion of an industry's inputs that are purchased locally and, therefore, stimulate local growth, while the relative share indicates the degree to which the industry exports its products and, hence, brings income into the metropolitan area.

SPECIFIC QUESTIONS

Because we did not intend to analyze every aspect of each of these industries thoroughly, we devoted some initial effort to identifying a narrow focus of analysis that would be both possible to do and useful. Early discussions in Cleveland indicated that a fairly well defined question associated with each industry was the "right" one for inclusion in a baseline analysis of the metropolitan economy.

The first step in narrowing the focus of study was to define the industry under investigation more narrowly. Each of the broad sectors —nonelectrical machinery, hotels, and medical and health services— is composed of many subsectors (three- and four-digit SICs) of varying relevance to economic development issues. Within the nonelectrical machinery sector we focused on machine tools (SIC 354) mostly because this industry is heavily concentrated in Cleveland and because it is undergoing rapid change worldwide. Public and private policy discussions directed our general attention to hotels specifically toward the downtown luxury segment of that industry. Our overall purpose of analyzing prospects for economic growth coupled with the assertion that exports stimulate growth suggested a focus on the subsector of the medical and health services industry that serves nonresidents of the Cleveland SMSA—the major teaching and research hospitals. This is the part of the medical and health services sector that "exports" services.

Once we had focused on these subsectors, specific questions to answer came immediately to mind. Machine tool manufacture has been a traditional source of strength to the Cleveland economy, but that industry is changing rapidly in market structure and technology. The obvious questions were, "will Cleveland be able to maintain its traditional share of this rapidly changing market, and what, if anything, can the community do to keep its competitive position?"

Public discussions dictated the key question about hotels: "why hasn't Cleveland been able to attract a large, signature, luxury hotel for its downtown, and what would it take to attract one?"

Analysts and managers of medical and health services have all been asking themselves the same general question over the last six months, "how will the major changes in health care financing and regulation proposed by the Reagan administration affect my institution, and what can I do to take advantage of or protect myself from those changes?" Discussions of the potential contribution of the health and medical services industry to economic growth in Cleveland must deal with the same question. Because the "market" for these services has suddenly become much more uncertain than it was before November 4, 1980, our analysis of this industry is, essentially, an exploration of that uncertainty. In other words, we asked, "does expansion of the export segment of the health services sector still look like a good idea given recent changes in federal policy?"

We now turn to a report of each case study and its findings. This chapter will conclude with a brief summary and tying together of the conclusions.

VII. THE MACHINE TOOL INDUSTRY IN CLEVELAND: EROSION OF A BASIC STRENGTH?

INTRODUCTION

Nonelectrical machine production, especially of machine tools, has been a basic strength and support of Cleveland's industrial economy. Cleveland is a major center of the U.S. machine tool industry. The strength of this industrial sector, however, may be weakening due to the decline of industry in northeastern and north central metropolitan areas, industrial relocation to the sunbelt, and the general decline of the U.S. competitive position in this industry.

In this case study we identify the role of the machine tool industry in Cleveland and describe the U.S. machine tool industry and its potential for growth. This analysis is based on U.S. and international trade data as well as literature from trade journals and the popular press. Then, we assess whether Cleveland's machine tool industry can take advantage of growth opportunities by identifying both strengths and weaknesses in the local industry. Finally, we suggest a number of potential community actions that might encourage growth. The analysis for the last two topics is based on material provided by local industry representatives and community leaders in personal interviews, a telephone survey, and general literature.[1]

We conclude that the U.S. machine tool industry has great potential for growth over the next decade, but only if the industry can take advantage of favorable business conditions by investing substantial resources in new production capital and technologies. Cleveland's historic strengths, skilled labor, and diversity and density of local customers will not assure that Cleveland's machine tool industry will maintain its traditionally large market share. Potential threats to the machine tool industry in Cleveland may include high labor costs, apparent shortages of workers with certain skills, technological conservatism, dispersion or decline of local customers, and obsolescence of existing plants. However, community actions might be designed to combat some of these problems. Actions that might be considered include increasing vocational training programs, encouraging long-term financing, and assisting small businesses. Our purpose in this chapter

---

[1]Participation in personal interviews or our telephone survey was conducted under proprietary agreements; thus, names of specific firms or persons will not be used.

is not to flesh out these proposals but to indicate potential problems and suggest that some solutions can be devised.

THE MACHINE TOOL INDUSTRY IN CLEVELAND'S ECONOMY

The Cleveland SMSA is a major center of machine tool production (SIC 354). In fact, as illustrated in Fig. 7.1, while one percent of the U.S. population reside in Cleveland and Cleveland firms employ 265,400 (1.4 percent) of the country's manufacturing workers, Cleveland employs 14,300 (4.8 percent) of all U.S. electrical machine workers. In other words, machine tool manufacturing is 3.4 times as concentrated in Cleveland as manufacturing in general. We conclude that Cleveland is a major center of this industry in the United States. In addition, a majority (61 percent) of machine tool employment is concentrated in the central city, lending strength to the industrial base of inner city Cleveland (see *County Business Patterns*). In addition, nonelectrical machinery has historically been a major export of

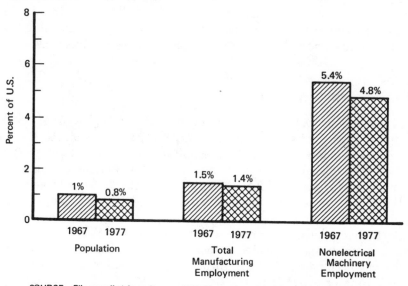

SOURCE: File compiled from Census of Manufactures records (see Appendix B).

Fig. 7.1—Cleveland SMSA shares of U.S. population manufacturing employment and nonelectrical machinery employment, 1967-1977

the Cleveland area and a source of economic stability in recent years (see Chapter III). It therefore appears that this industry is a major contributor to the well-being of the greater Cleveland economy.

Two particularly important components of SIC 354 are the industries manufacturing metal cutting (SIC 3541) and metal forming (SIC 3542) equipment. Ohio is the second largest producer of machine tools in the fifty states (after Illinois) and Cleveland is the second largest producer of machine tools of cities in the United States (NMTBA, 1980-81, pp. 67, 68; Greater Cleveland Growth Association, n.d., p. 3). Thus, the performance of the U.S. machine tool industry should be a leading indicator of the expected prosperity of the Cleveland economy.

THE U.S. MACHINE TOOL INDUSTRY AND ITS POTENTIAL

In the last decade, the United States has changed from a net exporter of machine tools to a net importer (see Fig. 7.2). In addition the U.S. market share of international machine tool production has dwindled from a high of 34 percent to the current level of 18 percent (Ashburn, 1981, p. 93). This dramatic shift in the U.S. market position can be explained by the historic structure of the U.S. industry, by increased foreign competition and innovation, and by the machine tool industry's historic vulnerability to downswings in the business cycle.

Historic Structure

The machine tool industry has evolved into a highly fragmented industry of product specialists. In 1972, 1,277 firms employed a total of 76,600 persons. Only 10 firms employed more than 1,000 people. Since 1972, 63 percent of all firms in the industry have had fewer than 20 employees (NMTBA, 1980-81, pp. 62, 69). The few large firms that exist—Warner and Swasey, Cincinnati-Milacron, Acme-Cleveland, and Cross and Trecker—do not maintain a market dominance.

Each firm tends to produce a few highly specialized items over which it maintains a production monopoly. Historically, machine tool firms have competed, if at all, through product differentiation rather than through price (Fawcett, 1976).

Business Cycles

Because of the nature of machine tools as long lasting capital equipment, their demand has been highly cyclical. In downswings demand

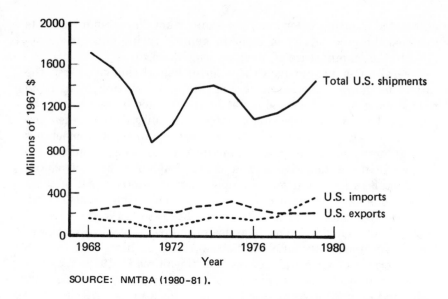

Fig. 7.2—U.S. shipments of machine tools

drops rapidly resulting in labor layoffs, lowered capacity, and slips in necessary capital replacement. In boomtimes, capacity and labor are cautiously added and equipment slowly replaced or added, resulting in delivery backlogs. The downswing in the U.S. economy in the mid-1970s resulted in backlogs of up to two years during the ensuing upswings and helped foreign producers increase their share of the U.S. market (Mayfield, 1979, p. 50).

Innovation

The last decade has seen a jump in the rate of technological changes in both machine tool products and the methods of production (Sutton, 1980). The development of automated controls, microcomputers, new materials, and completely new technologies such as lasers precipitated a technological revolution in machine tools. Once a piece of metal had to be loaded and unloaded by manual labor from several machines to complete a simple tool. Now a machining center (a single machine) can perform all these functions with higher precision and less waste material. With numerical controls, computer assisted numerical control, and robotics, this process can be almost completely automated reducing labor inputs to a minimum. These improvements increase the productivity of labor in manufacturing and can be applied to the manufacture of machine tools themselves.

Several forces have driven these technological changes. First, the cost of metals has increased, forcing the metal cutting industry to reduce the amount of wasted metal scrap produced by its products by pushing the limits of precision cutting. Some substitution to less expensive metals or plastics has taken place requiring new machines with different tolerances. Second, engineering for weight and size reduction in the automotive and aerospace industries has introduced new metals, alloys, and more complex part geometries. All of these innovations have required new capabilities for machine tools. Third, the drive to reduce production line costs has resulted in the development of automated systems. The use of numerical control machines has grown from .5 percent of all metalworking machines used in 1968 to 3.7 percent of all metalworking machines used in 1978. This is a phenomenal increase considering that the average life of capital is 20 years and only 30 percent of all machine tools in use are under 10 years old (NMTBA, 1980-81, pp. 248-249).

The latest wave of innovation involves designing complete new factory systems. Adding a single highly productive machine to an assembly line can cause backups and shortages in other parts of the plant. Machine tool firms are beginning to market their products by providing the management inputs needed to custom design complete factory systems as opposed to selling a single piece of equipment.

Current U.S. Position and Foreign Competition

The height of U.S. international market dominance was in 1967. Since then, serious inroads have been made into international and U.S. markets by foreign products, especially from Japan (Ashburn, 1981, pp. 93-97). In the early and mid-1970s the U.S. domestic demand shrank with the downswing of the business cycle. U.S. machine tool manufacturers responded by laying off workers and not investing in new capital or R&D during a period of rapid technological change. Although U.S. manufacturers did introduce more sophisticated numerical control machines at this time, these machines suffered from poor reliability of control systems as compared with foreign products.

As this was occurring, other nations had distinctly different reactions. For instance, with backing from the Japanese government and concerted R&D efforts, Japanese manufacturers perfected their numerical control products. Furthermore, a conscious government/

industry policy was adopted to increase Japan's market share by investing in expanded plant for the Japanese machine tool industry and taking full advantage of the innovative technology available. The result was that by 1975 the Japanese were ready to export less-expensive, higher-quality machine tools to the United States.[2]

The upswing in the market in the late 1970s saw the U.S. manufacturers unable to meet the high domestic demand. Reduced capacity resulted in severe backlogs. Japanese and other foreign producers were able to offer firms advanced tools with 90 day deliveries. Having no other choice, consumers began ordering from foreign producers and found the products very satisfactory. Japan's exports to the United States increased from 37,765 units with a value of $99 million in 1977 to 72,169 units with a value of $321 million in 1979 (NMTBA, 1980-81, p. 195). U.S. producers, a disjointed group, have only just begun to respond to the situation. Initially satisfied with the high demand and backlogs, only recently have they realized that 24 percent of the U.S. market is now supplied by imports.[3] It remains to be seen whether the response will be sufficient to slow down the U.S. loss of domestic market share, much less to recoup its former world market position.

Prospects

The prospects for increases in U.S. and world demand for machine tools are excellent. Domestic demand could be fueled by increases in defense orders, retooling by the U.S. auto industry, strong aerospace demand, or hoped-for general increases in business investments induced by investment tax credits and other government policies.

The U.S. producers' market outlook is clouded despite the potential for growth. If U.S. firms are to recapture lost market share, capital for expansion and technological upgrading must be available to them well before the next investment boom begins. The U.S. machine tool industry must increase productivity and innovation very quickly or face another episode of lost market shares similar to that of the 1970s.

CLEVELAND'S STRENGTHS

Cleveland became a major machine tool center because of its closeness to the auto industry, closeness to supplies of metals, concentrated

---

[2]"Japan's 20-Firm Joint FMS Plan" (1981); "Toolmakers Rush into the U.S." (1980); "Japan: FANUC Edges Closer to a Robot Run Plant" (1980).
[3]"Foreign Competition Stirs U.S. Toolmakers" (1980).

and diverse local industry demand, inexpensive transportation, and skilled labor. It remains a dominant producer for many of the same reasons. For larger machine tool firms that produce generic products, Cleveland is located at the center of industrial demand in the United States and also has good access to materials suppliers (see Chapter IV). These larger firms have a substantial investment in fully amortized plants that keeps them in Cleveland. Small machine tool firms have not traditionally had national reputations. They compete through service and highly customized work. This requires a strong local base upon which to establish close customer relations. Cleveland has provided a dense and diverse set of local customers. Any movement of industry, thus customers, out of Cleveland would be debilitating to the small machine tool firms.

In addition, the location of firms, especially small ones, is dependent on the location of skilled machinists. In the past, Cleveland attracted, kept, and produced skilled machinists through job opportunities offered by its diverse industrial base and the strong apprenticeship programs offered by individual firms. Relocation of any firm requires finding a group of comparatively skilled machinists at equivalent or lower pay rates in another location.

POTENTIAL THREATS

Continued growth of the industry in Cleveland requires that Cleveland based firms both compete successfully in national and world markets and continue to perceive potential benefits to location in Cleveland. Several factors or economic trends threaten continued growth, including high labor costs, simultaneous "deskilling" of production, technological conservatism, and general dispersion of economic activity away from Cleveland. It is also possible that shortages of certain types of skilled labor exacerbate these problems.

Labor Costs

Industry representatives consistently claimed that the wage rates for machinists in the northeast and midwest including Cleveland were high compared to equivalently skilled labor in the sunbelt. However, analysis of data on wages by industry indicates that average wages for SIC 354 in Cleveland were just about equal to the national average. This is in stark contrast with the average for all manufacturing wages in Cleveland, which are about 20 percent above the national average. One explanation of this divergence between the views of industry representatives and the statistical data relates to the differences in wages paid by large and small firms. The Cleveland machine tool industry is dominated by very small shops, and, consequently, relatively low wages paid by these firms dominate the average statistics. Wages paid by the larger firms may, indeed, be higher in Cleveland than elsewhere. Larger firms might be willing to pay higher wages if that was the only way to employ labor with the right production skills. However, the most recent automated, computer-assisted systems reduce the need for some skilled labor inputs and change the mix of skills required. These systems have been applied successfully to the production of generic assembly machine tools. As "deskilled" and "reskilled" production is disseminated within the machine tool industry, firms will be able to locate away from traditional centers of skilled workers. Of course, these new production techniques do not apply to customized tooling jobs, and some proportion of production will always be dependent on skilled labor input. Highly skilled machinists and tool and die makers may become more valued as a small, but essential, input to certain jobs. Nevertheless, most industry representatives felt that local high labor costs, a local shortage of some skills (e.g., electronic technicians), and the availability of deskilled production processes make relocation to other cities a promising option for reducing costs and increasing productivity.

Industrial Conservatism

Much machine tool manufacturing in Cleveland takes place in tiny firms. One or two machinists may operate one or two machines in a garage. Because the owner-operators of these firms tend to be older and tend to depend on skills that were developed early in the post-World War II period, they are unlikely to adopt new production techniques, or try to develop new markets, or attempt to produce new designs. To the extent that these numerous smaller firms constitute a major component of Cleveland's machine tool industry, the limited potential of this relatively conservative subsector may constrain future development.

Economic Dispersion

More long-term in nature is the threat of continued dispersion of economic activity away from Cleveland and the midwest. As mentioned in the previous section, both large and small firms are somewhat dependent on local or regional demand. Small firms, especially,

rely on strong consumer service interaction to sell customized products. As local and regional manufacturing declines, small machine
tool firms may be pressed to locate nearer to their customers in new
markets. Larger firms, while less dependent on local demand, still
prefer to locate in areas with strong regional supply and demand sectors.

Obsolescence of Plant

Much of the machine tool industry's plant in Cleveland is old. Some
of the biggest factory buildings date back to the 1920s or earlier. In
the next several years, with continued rapid technological advance,
some of the larger factories may become obsolete. Faced with this
condition more firms will consider the prospects of relocation to areas
that offer greater net benefits.

All of the above factors might combine to encourage movement of
the machine tool industry from Cleveland. The "deskilling" of production enables firms to consider relocation seriously when faced with
high labor costs, reduced demand, and obsolete plants, especially if
other areas of the country can offer more positive investment conditions. This situation is exacerbated by the possible near-term shortages of skilled machinists in the Cleveland area.

Shortage of Machinists

The problem, as presented to us by various industry and trades
people and vocational educators (not a perfectly disinterested sample),
is that the average age of skilled machinists in the Cleveland area is
around 55. Within the next few years these machinists will be retiring. In fact, some 2,000 machinists in the Cleveland area retire each
year.[4] This would not be serious except for the fact that enrollment in
vocational programs has fallen, machine tool shops have begun to
discontinue apprenticeship programs, vocational programs have not
kept up with industry demands, and the general high school
education has deteriorated. In short, many conclude that the retiring
machinists are not being replaced with a younger generation of
skilled workers.

The situation is in fact more complicated than it first seems. The
machine tool industry employs several types of skilled workers: semi-
skilled operatives to run specific machines, electronics and computer

---

4"Trades Association Fund Aids East Tech Machine Shop" (1980).

technicians, and high skilled master machinists and tool and die makers. The first group can be easily trained and are flexible in the varying jobs they do. They can move freely between machining firms. The "deskilling" of production largely affects the jobs in this category. We found that many firms will train qualified people to become operatives. The second group requires more specialized training and is less easily recruited in Cleveland. Demand will strengthen for these technicians as more firms adopt automated or computer-assisted machine tools. Training can take two or more years and most firms do not have apprenticeship or other on-the-job programs for these occupations. The master craftsman requires years of training, including on-job time in each of the other job categories. This group of craftsmen is in shortest supply. Major firms we talked with do not have apprenticeship programs for this training. According to spokesmen, at the most only a handful of small firms still can and do provide the one-on-one training needed to produce a master craftsman. The demand for these craftsmen may lessen due to computer-assisted tooling, but a core demand will always be present.

Several solutions have been proposed to the problem of the skilled machinist shortage depending on which job category one is talking about. General machinists or operatives can be produced by improving general vocational education programs. Vocational programs could be improved through better job placement, new equipment, and stronger industry input into curriculum development. Several new programs have been formed in the Cleveland area to meet these needs. Training for computer and electrical technicians requires some post-secondary level training and must be provided by a vocational-technical school or junior college with proper equipment. Strong support from industry for both types of programs can be garnered if training can be customized to the needs of specific firms or if firms can have some input into the curricula. The master craftsman category is less easily filled. On-the-job training is both essential and costly. We found no educational programs in the Cleveland area that addressed the shortage of master craftsmen.

Programs designed to solve problems of labor shortage are easy to imagine. The difficulty is deciding which problems are most in need of solution. We heard too many different, often conflicting diagnoses of the labor component of the machine tool industry's difficulties to be able to conclude which problems are worst or which solutions best.

COMMUNITY ACTIONS

These potential threats to the growth and well-being of the machine tool industry in Cleveland are neither necessarily inevitable nor unavoidable. Community actions might avert some negative repercussions of these threats. We have not analyzed existing programs, the financial capabilities of Cleveland, or the specific needs of firms to a depth that would allow us to recommend specific community actions. We can, however, suggest possible areas of intervention that might be helped by community programs.

- *Vocational and technical training*—All local firms might benefit by improvements in the vocational and technical training programs provided by the community. If properly conducted these programs can also provide employment opportunities for Cleveland's unskilled unemployed. Several Cleveland area programs designed to increase industry input and job placement in existing vocational education systems are already leading the way in this area. Improved training can lead to more productive workers, improving Cleveland's competitive position in the national market, and help overcome the "disadvantage" of relatively high wages. The problem is that we do not know which kinds of training or education would best complement Cleveland's strengths or compensate for Cleveland's weaknesses. Candidates for support may range from basic "vocational literacy" programs in junior high schools to Ph.D. programs in metallurgical and mechanical engineering.

- *Long-term financing and planning*—Favorable long-term financing guarantees, such as those available to Japanese firms, could improve the capability of the industry to weather downswings without resorting to layoffs, slower innovation, and lower investment in new capital. The financial structure of machine tool firms is also a problem that may be subject to amelioration. A slowdown in orders could be seen as a blessing for a firm in an industry undergoing rapid technological change. Recessionary periods can be used as a time to retool physical and human capital in preparation for the next upswing, which always seems to come. In fact, during the last business cycle, some firms in other parts of the country began to take this course. To do this, however, firms need steady financial support from their creditors over the downswing. If further analysis of this approach indicates that it would pay off, local banks might discover a way to both help Cleveland retain a traditional strength and make a profit.

- *Stimuli to creativity*—To keep competitive with foreign producers, Cleveland firms must continue to innovate and to improve precision or customized products. Community action that increases funds for R&D or encourages investment in innovative capital might be beneficial. Proposals for an industrywide pool for R&D or technology dissemination center are common. Cleveland may want to consider a local institute of this nature, or if a national R&D center materializes, Cleveland may wish to compete vigorously to be the site.

- *Assistance to smaller firms*—The small (sometimes tiny) machine tool firms are both the base of the tool industry in Cleveland as well as the most severely affected by possible economic adversity and a general aging process. They are less likely to have funds for R&D, labor training, or investment, especially in downswings. Any community actions should be especially concerned with the needs of these smaller shops.

CONCLUSIONS

It was shown that the machine tool industry is an important sector of Cleveland economy and can be used as an indicator of the well-being of the local economy as a whole. The U.S. machine tool industry has potential for growth in the next decade, but foreign competition is much more a factor than ever before. Cleveland's industry could also grow if certain historic strengths are maintained and possible threats are averted. Labor costs, possible shortages of some kinds of skilled labor, general dispersion of economic activity, obsolescence of plant, and technological conservatism might be weakening the past assets of the Cleveland economy. A number of community actions by public and industry groups might help prevent this from occurring. We cannot recommend a detailed plan of action. We conclude, however, that well thought out proposals based on more precise diagnoses of some of the problems we point out should be given serious attention by community leaders.

VIII. THE GROWTH POTENTIAL OF THE HOTEL INDUSTRY IN DOWNTOWN CLEVELAND

The focus of this research is on the potential for hotel[1] development in downtown Cleveland for two related reasons. First, hotels in the central city appear to be an important ingredient for the area's economic development.[2] Second, a desire from the business community and the local government to obtain a new hotel for downtown Cleveland was discovered in the course of conducting this study; this case study, therefore, is especially timely. One conclusion of this study is that there is a public and private commitment for the development in downtown Cleveland of a sizable, luxury, nationally known hotel, but current activity levels in downtown Cleveland are not sufficient for its guaranteed success.

The information in this chapter is based on a review of the applicable literature and on interviews with national and local hotel executives, members of trade associations, hotel consulting firms, and officials and residents of Cleveland. The chapter is organized into four sections: a discussion of what hotels contribute to Cleveland's economy, a review of national principles for hotel development, an assessment of the hotel situation in Cleveland, and a statement of conclusions drawn from our analysis.

WHAT HOTELS CONTRIBUTE TO CLEVELAND

Hotels benefit Cleveland with both jobs and money. In 1977, hotels in the SMSA employed about 8,000 people (which is less than one percent of the total SMSA work force), an increase of 40 percent from a decade before. The hotels in Cleveland have kept pace with their parent sector—the service industry—which has experienced about the same percentage of growth during the decade.

Hotels employ both managerial and unskilled labor;[3] some commonly accepted ratios are between 0.85 and 1.25 unskilled jobs

---

[1]Today, few distinguishing characteristics separate a "hotel" from a "motel"; we will use the former term for consistency throughout this chapter.

[2]Horwath (1970).

[3]Hotels have other employees, such as engineers and physical plant personnel, who are not included in this discussion.

per hotel room,[4] and one managerial position for every 10 rooms. Even so, hotels may not have a significant impact on problems associated with structural unemployment because this industry is notorious for its high level of personnel turnover among unskilled workers: a hotel needing 1,000 unskilled workers may employ as many as 1,500 to 2,500 different individuals in any given year.[5]

Hotels contribute dollars to Cleveland's economy. A statistic often used to assess the monetary effect is the multiplier, which measures the impact on a local economy of every dollar spent in a particular industry. National data from 1972 show a multiplier of $2.50 for every $1.00 spent by a hotel guest in Cleveland. Other analysts estimate a multiplier of $2.79 for every dollar spent by a convention delegate, and $3.10 for each dollar spent by a commercial or business traveler.[6]

Two ways that hotels benefit the local economy deserve special mention. First, there are increased revenues for the city from taxes, including property, sales, and bed taxes.[7] Second, hotels create benefits for other existing businesses, such as restaurants or florists that do well when the hotel business grows.

PRINCIPLES OF HOTEL DEVELOPMENT

The basic principles determining the growth of the hotel industry can be summarized as a set of generalized standards or "rules of thumb" that hotel developers take into account when considering the likely success or failure of proposed development. These principles, briefly stated, are:

- Hotels are not a lead industry;
- Supply and demand must be properly balanced;
- The right consumer mix is necessary; and
- Community commitment is essential.

Each of these is discussed below.

Perhaps the most important facet of hotel development is that hotels are not a lead industry. That is to say, hotels are dependent on an

---

[4]Lawson (1976).

[5]American Hotel and Motel Association (1973).

[6]We wish to caution the reader not to treat these figures as certain, because a multiplier depends on the estimated values of certain variables. The multiplier for any industry usually falls between two and four. The recent data were provided by the Convention and Visitors Bureau of Greater Cleveland.

[7]A recent study indicates that hotels contribute more per job to local tax bases than any other industry. See Gurwitz (forthcoming).

existing base of support; they do not, in and of themselves, create their own demand for services.[8] The key element for the hotel developer is the presence of activity centers that generate demand for hotel usage. Most developers believe that the sequence of events leading to the right environment for hotel development can be illustrated as follows:[9]

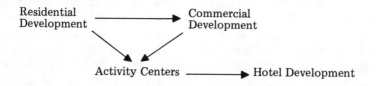

This model basically begins with residential development, after which commercial enterprises will follow. These two factors, taken together, will produce "life and activity in the streets," which is, almost without exception, a necessary precondition for successful hotel development.

The hotel developer is seeking a proper supply-demand balance. Getting into the hotel business is a very expensive undertaking: it now costs about $100,000 per room to build a luxury hotel, which means a 400-room hotel requires a $40 million investment.[10] As a result, the developer needs to be convinced of profitability before investing, and will usually do so by monitoring a potential location and assessing the demand with a feasibility study. One useful measure of the supply-demand balance is occupancy rate. A hotel operating between 55 and 60 percent occupancy is generally breaking even; 70 percent occupancy is the level at which profits are usually made.[11] If most hotels in a location are already operating at or below the breakeven point, that location will not be attractive to new developers.

Hotels need to have a mix of guests, and the developer often seeks an "ideal" consumer mix of 50 percent commercial or business customers, 25 percent tourists, and 25 percent convention travelers.[12]

---

[8]The exceptions to this are mentioned below.

[9]This "causal model" has not been specifically articulated in the literature in the fashion depicted here. The literature does make explicit the need for activity centers, such as described by Gray and Liguori (1980), and Peters (1978). We are grateful to Stephen W. Brener, Executive Vice President, Helmsley-Spear Hospitality Services, Inc., New York, for suggesting the model.

[10]This figure was projected from 1978 estimates. See "No Vacancy Means Big Profit for U.S. Hotels" (1978).

[11]Laventhol and Horwath (1980).

[12]The market mix is discussed in Coffman (1975). The figures in the text are those considered "ideal" by the American Hotel and Motel Association.

This reflects a basic fact about the hotel business: except under unusual circumstances, a single-function hotel cannot survive. The exceptions are few, but they would include a hotel well known as a resort such as the Greenbriar in West Virginia or hotels in certain areas known as convention cities such as Las Vegas or New Orleans. A multi-functional hotel is better able to survive cyclical and seasonal peaks and troughs in different segments of the travel industry.

Last, the hotel developer is looking for evidence of community commitment. Financial and economic conditions of the past decade or two have forced this principle onto the hotel industry to the point where many developers are seeking a public-private partnership to build or manage hotels.[13] Public involvement is essential for two reasons. First, hotels, like any other downtown development, require numerous permits and licenses. A project that lacks active support will almost certainly be blocked. Second, and perhaps more important, hotel projects have become such an integral part of public development projects that hotel developers have come to expect some amount of financial support from the public sector (e.g., land acquisition or special tax treatment). The developer wants solid evidence of support from the local government, corporate world, and financial community.

HOTEL SITUATION IN CLEVELAND

Currently there are 54 hotels in the greater Cleveland area. The downtown area has four large hotels: The Bond Court Hotel, the Holiday Inn, the Hollenden House, and Stouffer's Inn on the Square. Together, they contain 1,900 rooms, 195 suites, and a variety of food and beverage and meeting facilities.[14] In contrast, there are some 3,000 rooms in downtown Detroit, 2,400 in Pittsburgh, and 2,300 in Cincinnati.[15] Occupancy rates for the downtown Cleveland hotels average 55 percent—just about the breakeven point.

None of these downtown hotels is owned by a major national hotel chain. The large hotel chains such as Sheraton-ITT, Marriott, and Hilton have not overlooked Cleveland. Rather, they have chosen to locate in the suburban areas of Cleveland. Proximity to the major modes of travel—the airport and the interstate highway system—and to corporate headquarters, businesses, and factories (the majority of

---

[13]Green (1979).

[14]Convention and Visitors Bureau of Greater Cleveland (n.d.).

[15]Metropolitan Detroit Convention and Visitors Bureau (1981), Pittsburgh Convention and Visitors Bureau (n.d.), Cincinnati Convention and Visitors Bureau (n.d.).

which are located in suburban areas) make these modern suburban hotels attractive to travelers and business meeting planners. In addition, the large number of commuter-type flights operating through Cleveland's airport provide additional business for these hotels.[16] Occupancy rates for the suburban hotels range near 70 percent. These hotels, which contain complete entertainment and meeting facilities, are strong competition for their downtown counterparts.

Downtown Cleveland as an Environment for Hotel Development

In addition to locational advantage, the suburban hotel trade has prospered in part because of the current downtown environment. After dark, the streets of downtown Cleveland are usually devoid of people and activity. With the exception of entertainment activities, such as Browns' football games and a few theaters and restaurants, there is no central activity or place to draw people to the downtown area. This problem is exacerbated by the lack of accessible and convenient downtown transportation. Taxicabs, which are usually the most convenient form of downtown evening transportation, appear to be in short supply and are not readily available.[17] Moreover, people do not live downtown. With the exception of two relatively new apartment buildings in the downtown area, there is no evidence of the return of the middle class to the central city in Cleveland. As a result, the accompanying growth of services, stores, and entertainment facilities has not materialized. In short, downtown Cleveland at night is still not a very inviting environment for either native or visitor.

Despite these drawbacks, certain aspects of downtown Cleveland might attract the interest of hotel developers. First, Cleveland has the fifth largest convention center in the United States; the center has been undergoing a modernization program over the past few years. The convention center's central location and extensive facilities could serve to attract meetings and trade shows to Cleveland, but in the fall of 1981 it was operating at only 32 percent of its capacity. This low rate arises not only from the age and structural problems of the building, but allegedly also from the lack of hotel rooms in nearby locations. (See Bornino, 1981).

---

[16]Cleveland's accessibility via commuter flights has negatively affected its hotels because travelers can come in, conduct their business, and leave Cleveland all in the same day. Hotels in other strategically located cities are also facing this problem; see Stein (1971).

[17]One observer has concluded: "Cleveland's taxi service . . . [is] arguably the worst in America." See Harris (1981), p. 288.

Perhaps more important, the proposed downtown development activities of the Tower City Complex, SOHIO, and the Playhouse Square Foundation, to mention but a few, indicate that the downtown area is about to undergo a major revitalization that would bring some life and activity to its streets and presumably generate a demand for hotel space. The Tower City Complex located on the equivalent of 34 acres near Public Square will contain an office building, shops, a department store, some residences, the imaginative renovation of the underground arcade surrounding Union Terminal, and possibly a hotel. The proposed SOHIO headquarters office complex located directly on Public Square is a multimillion dollar project in which one million square feet of new space is to be constructed for offices and other uses. The Playhouse Square project will renovate three large old theaters for presentations of local, regional, and national acting companies and other theatrical events. In addition to providing a focus of theatrical entertainment that, it is hoped, will bring people to Cleveland, the theater complex will eventually serve as the vehicle for renovating the entire Playhouse Square area consisting of several large city blocks. Additional building and expansion activities include the Medical Mutual office tower and the consolidation of Ohio Bell in a new location.

These projects, coupled with the other ongoing and proposed major investment projects in downtown Cleveland, offer great potential for the area's economic development. They will induce more people to come downtown and will produce more amenities for the central business district. When these projects will create the requisite "life and activity in the streets" so important to hotel developers is unknown.

Prospects for Development

There is both a public and private commitment to obtain a luxury "signature" hotel of 400 to 800 rooms in downtown Cleveland to enhance downtown Cleveland's image, provide rooms for conventions, and meet anticipated increased demand. Several possible sites have been mentioned, which are illustrated on the following map (Fig. 8.1). The most frequently mentioned location is on the west side of the mall across from the convention center, where an old structure, the Vulcan Building, currently stands. Other possible sites for a hotel have been mentioned in connection with or located within the Tower City Complex, the SOHIO project, the Playhouse Square project, and the Gateway project along the lake-front. Thus far, the city has unsuccessfully negotiated with the Hyatt Corporation to build a hotel in the mall

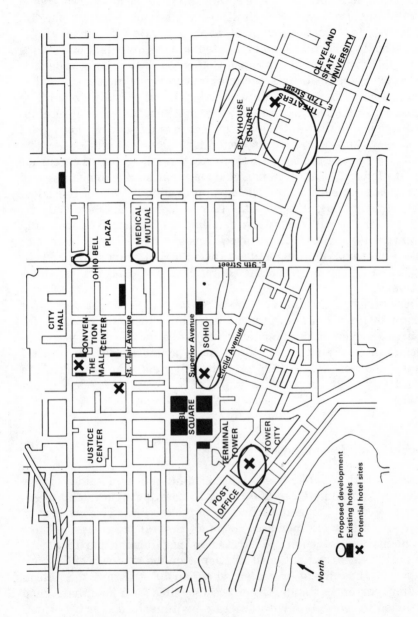

Fig. 8.1—Downtown Cleveland

area. The Marriott Corporation recently conducted an informal feasibility study and informed Cleveland officials that until several of the proposed development projects become a reality and a special "vitality" is created within the city, it is not interested in locating a major hotel in downtown Cleveland.

CONCLUSIONS

Having reviewed some of the basic principles of hotel development and having taken a brief look at current conditions in Cleveland, these two sections are now juxtaposed to assess the growth potential for hotels in downtown Cleveland. The findings are summarized in Table 8.1.

Table 8.1

GROWTH POTENTIAL FOR HOTELS IN DOWNTOWN CLEVELAND

Basic Principles	Cleveland Situation
Environment	Plans exist
Supply–demand	Potential demand
Consumer mix	Acceptable
Commitment	Yes, but needs coordination

The activity centers necessary for successful hotel development are not yet present in the Cleveland downtown environment. The amount of "life and activity in the streets" after 5:00 p.m. or on weekends remains generally minimal. Plans do exist that offer promise for enlivening downtown Cleveland, but plans, in and of themselves, have not been sufficient. It is our opinion that current plans offer a great potential for revitalizing the city center, but hotel developers are waiting to see the plans move closer to actual implementation before committing themselves.

Furthermore, current plans may have to be supplemented to support successful hotel development. Another lesson from general principles, known as the "10-minute rule," states that people will spend 10 minutes traveling between a hotel and a major activity center by car or taxi or by walking. That is equivalent to 2½ city blocks. Given Cleveland's poor taxi system, careful attention needs to be paid to improved transportation or hotel site selection, or both. For example, if a hotel were to be built on the Vulcan Building site, guests would in all likelihood not come from Playhouse Square unless efficient transportation were available.

Developers looking at the current supply-demand balance would probably not be inclined to commit themselves to a downtown hotel. The critical factor for the developer is profitability—which, it should be recalled, usually requires a 70 percent occupancy rate. Yet existing hotels are operating in the 50 percent occupancy range. Claims that the convention center is underutilized because of an insufficient number of available hotel rooms may be valid, as may well be the claims that current and proposed building activity will create a need for more, newer, or nicer rooms. However, the developer is not likely to undertake a risky venture until the supply-demand balance improves or shows definite promise of improving.

The current consumer mix of 40 percent commercial, 40 percent convention, and 20 percent tourism for hotels in the metropolitan area is fairly close to the ideal mix of 50, 25, and 25 percent. However, the downtown tourist market is quite slack. Several private and public officials in Cleveland commented on the desirability of a large "convention hotel," but the caveat should be issued again that a single-function hotel can rarely survive. To make downtown Cleveland attractive to hotel developers, efforts to balance the consumer mix should proceed in several areas. More specifically, convention business should not be sought to the exclusion of other hotel business, and the need for a more appealing downtown environment should not be overlooked.

Clevelanders should keep in mind the experience of two other cities—Dallas and Detroit—as they plan for new hotel developments. In Dallas, hotels are presently in financial difficulty because of overbuilding that occurred during an uncoordinated hotel building boom. In Detroit, the investors in the landmark Renaissance Center have lost about $100 million because of inadequate demand.

We draw two lessons. The first is that successful downtown hotel development requires sound planning and coordination—coordination not only among those who are negotiating with hotel developers, but also between plans for hotels and plans for other downtown development projects. In the past few years, Cleveland's economic development and city planning offices have not been strong enough to handle such functions adequately. The city's recent initiatives to expand the staffs of these units and their authority for these purposes are important steps in the right direction. They should make it easier for the city to mobilize the serious commitment from the local government and corporate and financial communities that prospective hotel developers are looking for. As they proceed, however, community leaders should regard the attraction of a first class hotel as but one element in an integrated overall development program for downtown.

Second, success also depends on good timing in relation to market conditions. Clearly, when the supply-demand balance looks sufficiently promising for a new hotel, delays by the city could result in lost opportunities. On the other hand, all-out efforts to attract hotel investment before there is adequate evidence of improving market conditions could require subsidies and other inducements that would not appear reasonable later on. In the short term, expediting other downtown development projects—increasing the general activity levels in the center city that will improve market demand—may well be the most important element in a strategy to secure a new hotel.

IX. HEALTH CARE IN CLEVELAND: AN UNCERTAIN FUTURE FOR THE "EXPORT" SEGMENT

INTRODUCTION

The choice of the health care services industry for a case study was guided by several considerations. First, the health care sector is a major part of the national economy and has experienced tremendous growth in the past two decades. Second, the health care sector is an important part of Cleveland's economic base. Third, Cleveland's medical community serves patients from the region, from the nation, and even from other countries; that is, Cleveland "exports" health care services. Finally, many observers of the Cleveland economy have been looking to continued growth of the "export segment" of this industry as a stimulus to general regional economic development.

This case study focuses on Cleveland's role as an exporter of health care services. This accords with a basic presupposition of the overall study: that exports, by bringing income into the region, are the main stimulus to local economic growth. The objective of this chapter is to assess the export segment of the health services industry as a potential source of general economic development.

To investigate this question, we undertook several tasks, including: (1) compiling descriptive materials about national trends in health and health care; (2) gathering information about the health facilities, manpower, and research capabilities that make up the health care industry in Cleveland; (3) conducting semi-structured telephone interviews with a number of experts and leaders in Cleveland's medical community; (4) interviewing selected leaders in person on a site visit to Cleveland; and (5) on the basis of these data, drawing out the prospects for and consequences of inducing growth in health care exports.[1]

The next section of this chapter gives a brief overview of important

---

[1]This chapter summarizes our findings and the perceptions of leaders in Cleveland's medical care sector as they pertain to the metropolitan area's role as a regional and national center for the delivery of medical care. National data given here were taken from information contained in U.S. Department of Health, Education, and Welfare (1980); Freeland and Schendler (1981); various publications of the Bureau of the Census. Expenditure and employment information for the national health sector can also be found in the quarterly *Health Care Financing Trends* (HCFA, 1979) and in selected articles appearing in the quarterly *Health Care Financing Review*, both published by the Health Care Financing Administration of the Department of Health and Human Services.

national trends in the health industry and discusses changes in health policy that render continuation of those trends uncertain. We then turn to a short description of Cleveland's health care sector, followed by a discussion of some of the general problems facing the health services industry and of how expansion of the export sector would affect those problems. This discussion leads to the general conclusion that, while Cleveland does have a number of valuable strengths in this field, the medical and health industry should probably *not* be expected to make a major independent contribution to regional economic development. Community attention to this industry should focus, first of all, on the very real problems of providing high quality health care to Clevelanders at a reasonable price.

We can, however, highlight two types of community actions that could help maintain and build upon Cleveland's existing strengths as a center for medical services. First, with reductions in federal funding for medical care and medical research and training, communities that wish to retain a competitive edge in this field will have to increase their own local support for these activities. Second, as medical care becomes more capital-intensive, the few metropolitan areas that, like Cleveland, have traditional strengths in both medical services and a wide variety of industrial technologies could be in a very good competitive position. Proposals that build on and exploit this combination of strengths should be given serious consideration.

NATIONAL TRENDS IN THE HEALTH SECTOR

The health care industry is one of the bigger and faster growing segments of the national economy. Within the past 20 years, and especially within the past 10 years, health care has become a very significant part of the nation's economy. During the 1960s health care expenditures grew from 5.4 percent to 7.6 percent of Gross National Product (GNP) and by 1980 exceeded nine percent of GNP. Price rises in the last decade accounted for about one-half of the growth in health care expenditures. Increased use per person accounted for an additional one-third, and the remaining one-sixth can be attributed to population growth and aging.

Much of the price rise took place because of the ways we pay for health care in this country (Fig. 9.1). Less than 10 percent of hospital expenditures are directly out-of-pocket payments from patients; federal governmental payors alone—largely the entitlement programs such as Medicare (for the elderly and disabled) and Medicaid (for the

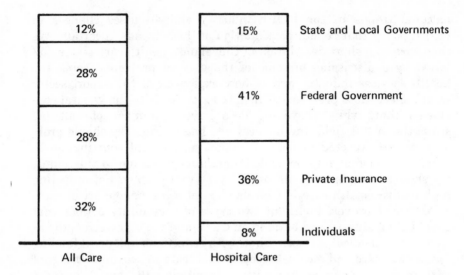

SOURCE: Freeland and Schendler (1981).

Fig. 9.1—How we pay for health care

poor)—cover over 40 percent of the bill and state and local government another 15 percent. The remainder is paid by private insurance.

These mechanisms for financing health care mean that individuals have been shielded from the true cost of their consumption of medical services. They have been freer to demand more and more care. As demand has expanded, the use of additional labor and nonlabor inputs in the health sector has increased as well. The flow of additional resources, coupled with the higher-than-average rise in wages and prices needed to attract new resources, has led to medical care price increases that are higher than price increases in other segments of the economy.[2] For example, from 1970 to 1979, the *yearly* rise in the price of a hospital room was 11 percent as compared with an average annual seven percent rise in the Consumer Price Index.

To date, attempts to deal with the alarming upward spiral of health

---

[2]The factors affecting the growth of health expenditures and the increases in medical prices have received considerable attention in the literature. The reader may wish to consult the following works and collections: Phelps and Newhouse (1972); Newhouse et al. (1974); Newhouse (1977, 1978); Fuchs (1974); Weeks and Berman (1977); Enthoven (1978); Altman and Blendon (1979); and Zook et al. (1980).

care costs, especially those associated with hospital care, have been chiefly regulatory. Regulation has been used to control capital investment and expansion through health planning and certificate-of-need requirements. Monitoring the costs and quality of care delivered through public sector programs (largely Medicaid and Medicare) is the principal concern of Professional Standards Review Organizations (PSROs). Drugs, pharmaceuticals, medical devices, and the like have been heavily regulated for years. The success of these regulatory efforts, especially in dealing with the virtually unchecked rise in the costs of care, have been at best only mixed. Some regulatory or quasi-regulatory efforts, however, have had positive effects in other ways, such as PSROs' efforts at improving the quality of medical care delivered through publicly funded programs.[3]

Some critics believe that regulation has not been (and cannot be) successful in controlling costs because it does not address the underlying market failure caused by high levels of insurance coverage. Others contend that regulation has actually contributed to rising costs. These latter critics believe that, similar to the experience in other industries, regulatory bodies and systems have tended to act in the interest of the industry they are intended to regulate, by favoring existing institutions or facilities, blocking entry by competitors, or hindering development of lower-cost substitutes for hospital care. They also argue that the growing size of the regulatory structure itself may be a major factor in increasing health sector costs.

Thus, during the past decade the country experienced enormous expansion of the health sector (including more services to the poor and elderly), a nearly unchecked rise in prices of health care, and a large increase in regulation in an effort to deal with the cost increases. Most observers of the health scene now contend that these characteristics of the health sector are likely to change. To summarize the arguments: The nation cannot afford the current rate of increase in the costs of health care. Public financing of many types of services—not just health—is being cut back as a reflection of changed social and political preferences. Finally, regulation and planning have fallen out of favor as solutions to spiraling costs.

Many of these observers anticipate at least three major changes in the health sector during the 1980s, and the evidence that these changes will take place is mounting. First, we will see substantial efforts directed at reducing the outlays on Medicaid and Medicare. We

---

[3]The literature on regulation in the health sector is easily as extensive as that on costs. The reader is referred to the following publications and collections for an introduction to some of these issues: Peltzman (1973); Salkever and Bice (1976); Seidman (1977); Bice (1980); Levin (1980); Lohr et al. (1981); Altman and Sapolsky (1981); Milbank Memorial Fund Quarterly (1981); and Temin (1980).

will see, as well, considerable diminution of regulation in this sector. Third, deregulation will be coupled with a movement toward greater "competition" and use of "incentive systems" in the medical marketplace.

The overall consequences of these changes are unpredictable, but to the degree they represent a turning away from the priorities and conditions of the past, they may have dampening effects on the provision of health care in the nation. Were that to be the ultimate outcome, the prospects for growth and expansion of the health care industry in Cleveland are considerably less sanguine today than they might have been ten years ago.

CLEVELAND'S HEALTH CARE SECTOR

Health Care Services in General

This section describes[4] the health care industry in Cleveland. Because we are interested in whether this industry will contribute to Cleveland's growth, we wished to determine the extent to which Cleveland is a national center for medical services, a north central regional center, or a center for northeastern Ohio. Because we have no direct measure of the value of Cleveland's health services exports, we rely on a number of objective measures of facilities and manpower in Cleveland and some comparison sites: Boston, Baltimore, Detroit, and Pittsburgh. The first two of these are widely recognized as national or international health service centers. Detroit and Pittsburgh were selected because they are industrial towns of the midwest or northeast with characteristics similar to Cleveland's.

These statistical descriptions of the local health care industry in general will be followed by some discussion of Cleveland's specific strengths as a health service center. Cleveland may be preeminent in the provision of certain services, and this preeminence might contribute to economic growth.

One obvious measure of the importance of the health services industry in the Cleveland economy is the fact that it employs about 6.6 percent of the salaried workers in the SMSA, a larger proportion than the nonelectrical machinery (5.7 percent) or construction (4.4 percent)

---

[4]General sources of data include the following: American Hospital Association (1981); American Medical Association (1980); U.S. Department of Health, Education, and Welfare (1980); U.S. Department of Commerce, Bureau of the Census (1980a, 1980b).

industries. Over 50 percent of the health sector employment is concentrated in the central city. (Note that employment here refers to wage and salary earners, and thus would exclude self-employed physicians, dentists, and the like. Hence, more people are actually involved in the delivery of health care or in medical research and teaching than the 6.6 percent figure might suggest.)

Despite the health sector's importance in Cleveland, as a percentage of total private employment it is smaller in this SMSA than in the other SMSAs. Considering the percentage of salaried workers who are in the health sector, for instance, comparable figures for Boston and Baltimore are 9.3 and 7.7 percent and for Detroit and Pittsburgh, 7.5 percent.

Tables 9.1 and 9.2 give basic data on hospital facilities in the Cleveland SMSA as of 1978-79. At that time, Cleveland had approximately 5.2 beds in general short-stay hospitals per 1,000 persons (Table 9.1). The national average in the late 1970s was about 4.6 community hospital beds per 1,000 persons. A figure of 4.0 beds per 1,000 population was established under the National Guidelines for Health Planning in 1978 as one that will provide adequate access to care and yet not provoke higher health care costs through excess capacity. In compari-

Table 9.1

AVAILABILITY OF HOSPITAL BEDS BY
SELECTED SMSA, 1978-79

SMSA	Hospital Beds^a per 1000 Persons	Occupancy Rate (Percent)
Cleveland	5.2	79
Baltimore	4.2	82
Boston	4.2	83
Detroit	4.2	82
Pittsburgh	5.3	80

SOURCE: American Hospital Association (1980).

^{a}General, short-term private and non-federal hospitals.

Table 9.2

LEVELS OF COMPLEXITY OF HOSPITAL FACILITIES
BY SELECTED SMSA, 1979

SMSA	Percentage of Hospitals Classified as Having[a]		
	Basic Services Only[b]	Moderately Complex Services[c]	Very Complex to Community-Oriented Services[d]
Cleveland	10	30	60
Baltimore	0	4	96
Boston	2	16	82
Detroit	8	29	63
Pittsburgh	9	6	85

SOURCE: American Hospital Association (1980).

[a]Classification scheme adapted from Berry (1972).

[b]Operating and delivery rooms.

[c]Basic services plus postoperative recovery rooms, staffed pharmacies, blood banks, etc.

[d]Moderately complex services plus community-oriented services, intensive care, megavolt radiation, etc.

son with other selected SMSAs, Cleveland appears to have more beds per person than all but Pittsburgh. The average occupancy rate for hospital beds in Cleveland was about 79 percent in 1979, a figure that is slightly lower than those for the comparison sites.

As an indicator of the regional or national role of Cleveland's health care industry, the distribution of types of hospital may be more important than the number of beds per capita (Table 9.2). When Cleveland hospitals are categorized on a continuum that ranged from "basic services only" to "very complex services" (adapted from Berry, 1973), they appear (taken together) to be less oriented toward the very complex institutions than are hospitals in the comparison SMSAs.

The Cleveland SMSA has a physician-to-population ratio (22.2 per 10,000 persons) that is lower than that of Boston or Baltimore but higher than that of Detroit and Pittsburgh (see Table 9.3). The national figure at the end of the 1970s was about 18.0 per 10,000 persons. The percentage of the Cleveland SMSA's active physician community engaged in medical research, teaching, or administration—nine percent—is also closer to the figure for Detroit and Pittsburgh than it is to that for the other two comparison SMSAs. The national figure is about nine percent.

The above data reflect only the most basic descriptors of the health care industry in Cleveland. They by no means exhaust the types of data one would need to collect in any thorough examination of the comparative advantages and disadvantages of Cleveland in producing health care services for an export market, and they must be interpreted with caution. By and large, however, the Cleveland SMSA can be viewed as being much like any metropolitan area in its complement of health care services. It is neither markedly high nor marked-

Table 9.3

NUMBER OF PHYSICIANS PER 10,000 PERSONS
AND TYPE OF PHYSICIAN ACTIVITY,
BY SELECTED SMSA

SMSA	Number of Active Physicians per 10,000 Population	Percentage of Active Physicians in		
		Office-Based Practice	Hospital-Based Practice	Other Professional Activity[a]
Cleveland	22.2	58	.33	9
Baltimore	26.8	48	36	16
Boston	27.9	52	33	15
Detroit	15.9	60	33	7
Pittsburgh	18.4	60	30	9

SOURCE: American Medical Association (1980); U.S. Department of Commerce, Bureau of the Census (1980b).

[a]Includes teaching, research, and administration.

ly low in per-population levels of the fundamental inputs into health care delivery. From this simple point of view, Cleveland does not stand out as a national center for health services. In this respect, it apparently is more like Detroit and Pittsburgh than like Boston and Baltimore.

This conclusion does not mean that Cleveland exports no health services. By any measure of the specific medical resources available in Cleveland, the SMSA clearly has a viable export sector. Relative to the entire health care industry in Cleveland, however, it is not large.

During the 1970s, about 15 percent of inpatients in hospitals in the Cleveland SMSA came from outside Cleveland and its environs.[5] However, the proportion of health expenditures in the area that can be attributed to the export of medical services is undoubtedly greater than that. Another rough indicator is the estimated proportion of total employment in the health sector devoted to exports in 1978 reported in Chapter III: 24 percent. That chapter, however, noted that this figure was probably an overestimate. Furthermore, for the several institutions in Cleveland that are engaged in this export market, the proportions of patients and money coming from inside or outside the local area obviously vary from the overall average. In general, the export subsector can be characterized as a relatively small, but highly prestigious and visible, part of Cleveland's economy.

The medical community in Cleveland has for years been regarded as highly qualified. It has included a number of physicians and health professionals widely viewed as pioneers in medical care delivery and financing. Examples include, respectively, researchers and surgeons responsible for developing transplantation and dialysis methods for treating end-stage kidney failure and hospital leaders instrumental in establishing one of the first Blue Cross health insurance plans in the country.

The base of general and specialty hospitals (numbering around 40) in the SMSA is quite solid. Among the more well known, of course, are the University hospitals associated with Case Western Reserve University, whose School of Medicine is of national repute, and the Cleveland Clinic. The Clinic is internationally acclaimed for high quality patient care, historically including open heart surgery and treatment of kidney failure, and now extending to many complex procedures and serious diseases. Both the University Hospitals system and the Clinic have good patient referral networks from sources in the region and state, and indeed from colleagues and institutions around the nation and the world.

---

[5]For data relating to hospital use and other aspects of the Cleveland SMSA health care sector, see, e.g., James A. Hamilton Associates (1976) or Midwest Research Institute (1981).

The Cleveland health community has a broad array of programs and services of a regional and national character, and numerous activities in basic and applied medical research are carried out at the medical institutions in the area. Of the many that might be cited, the following are representative of the breadth of biomedical problems and patient populations served:

- the regional burn center at county Metropolitan General Hospital;
- centers for genetics, care for critically ill, and pediatric emergency care at Case Western Reserve University School of Medicine and University hospitals;
- departments of the Cleveland Clinic that concentrate on artificial organs, hypertension, or immunology; and
- the research program on ion beam technology of the Lewis Research Center (National Aeronautics and Space Administration).

In short, in a variety of specialties in medical care and research, Cleveland ranks with leading medical centers of the country. The export segment of the health care industry is, therefore, an important asset of the regional economy and can perhaps play a supportive role in stimulating local economic development. As the information presented earlier indicates, however, this industry should probably not be thought of as a mainstay of the regional economy. Medical services does not come close to rivaling the key durable goods manufacturing industries as a source of export earnings.

The Role of the Health Services Industry in Economic Development

Even though the health services industry should not be expected to "turn Cleveland around" economically, projects aimed at developing the export segment of this industry can perhaps make a valuable contribution to the economic development of the region. Three specific characteristics of this industry enhance its potential contribution to an economic development strategy. First, as indicated in the introduction to these case studies, the medical and health services industry as a whole exerts a relatively high multiplier effect on the local economy. Growth of this industry generates more general economic stimulus than growth of most other industries. Second, the institutions that specialize most in serving patients from outside of the metropolitan area—most notably the Cleveland Clinic and the University-affiliated hospitals—are located in the central city. Growth of these institutions could play a role in planned development of Cleveland's Euclid Corridor. Third, even though the medical and health care industry as a whole does not employ large proportions of minority group members, the central-city hospital segment probably does. Growth of this segment might contribute to the short-run solution of structural unemployment problems in the region. Over the longer term, however, expansion will be on the frontiers of medical technology, meaning that the overall trend in job openings will be toward the higher skilled and away from the lower skilled. Further, medical care activities of the future are likely to be less labor-intensive than they are today.

The export segment of the health care industry may well make a contribution to Cleveland's economic development. Nevertheless, policies aimed at stimulating the growth of this industry should not be adopted lightly. The provision of health services in Cleveland, as in the United States as a whole, is fraught with a number of very complex and very troublesome problems, some of which might be exacerbated by attempts to enhance the local growth of the more complex and sophisticated elements of the industry. Most of the experts in the health services community in Cleveland with whom we spoke labeled rising health care costs as the most important problem they face today. Attempts to stimulate exports may accelerate increases in health care costs. The reasons for the rapid rate of increase in health care costs nationwide are subject to considerable debate among health analysts. One argument, though, is that once a new and expensive technology is introduced at one hospital in a region, other regional hospitals feel that they must also purchase the new equipment to remain competitive. The result is underutilized equipment and higher average patient care costs throughout the metropolitan area.[6]

If, for instance, the Cleveland Clinic or one of the University hospitals wishes to attract new patients from outside the SMSA, it is likely to do so at least partly by enhancing amenities in its facilities and partly by investing in advanced technologies that involve both costly hardware and highly skilled labor that may be in relatively short

---

[6]The debate in health economics and health policy circles over the role of technology in aggravating the increase in health care costs in the 1970s is quite complex and by no means resolved. Certain new technologies may substitute for existing therapies and lead to reductions in the costs of care. Some experts argue, however, that much of the impetus for higher costs came from vastly increased investments in large, very expensive technologies (the computerized axial tomography (CAT) scanner being the typical example). Others claim that "little ticket" technologies, low in unit cost but extremely high in volume, are the main culprit. All agree, nonetheless, that the acquisition and increased use of ever-more sophisticated and expensive medical hardware and procedures play some role in fostering continued price rises in health care. For further discussion of this issue, see (for instance) Moloney and Rogers (1979); Russell (1978); or the papers edited by Altman and Blendon (1979).

supply. Additional demand for the new or higher quality products and services may also be observed among local residents. This is particularly true for local patients with extensive insurance coverage, because the insured pay only a small fraction of the cost of hospital services. Other hospitals serving primarily local residents, say Lutheran Medical Center or Garfield Heights Hospital, might then feel pressure to acquire the new technologies or amenities to compete for local patients.[7]

Indeed, anything that further pushes up the cost of medical care in Cleveland will exacerbate a problem that is recognized by many local leaders in the medical community as the most significant problem in the health care sector. Medical costs appear to have risen more rapidly in Cleveland than on average. During the last decade, medical prices in Cleveland rose 101 percent. In contrast, the increase for the United States as a whole was 99 percent, for Baltimore, 97 percent, and for Boston, 86 percent. Cleveland's price increases, however, were below those of our comparison industrial centers (U.S. Department of Commerce, Bureau of the Census, selected years). Further increases in medical care costs would have a feedback effect on developmental prospects of other industries by raising the price of health insurance and, hence, labor costs. Consequently, in considering actions aimed at expanding the tertiary-care segment of the industry as a means of promoting exports and economic growth, community leaders should pay careful attention to the adverse and unintended consequences of increased health care costs.

Development of the export segment of the industry could have adverse side effects on the nonexport segment in a number of other ways as well. Resources to provide care for the poor, the near-poor, and the elderly will be severely strained as the costs of care continue to rise and as public financing for medical care falls. This may, in turn, foster the emergence—some might say the re-emergence—of two classes of medical care: one level of care for the privately insured who can continue to demand the best that Cleveland can offer, and another level of care for those dependent on Medicaid, Medicare, or charity. Hence, financial constraints in the face of rising costs of care may prevent

---

[7]Upward pressures on health care costs stemming from such investment activities may seem undesirable. In theory, however, there should be no objection to the costs of care rising to cover these new acquisitions, as long as individuals judge that the benefits of new products and services are equal to the cost of producing them. In practice, because insured consumers pay only a small portion of the cost of medical care, they are not fully aware of those costs. Thus, they will seek additional services as long as they judge that the benefits of those services equal or exceed their out-of-pocket cost, which is only a fraction of the true cost. That is, the amount consumers would be willing to pay for the new medical products and services they purchase may fall far short of the total cost of producing them.

needy and elderly patients from obtaining the same quality of care as the privately insured patient. The social equity issues inherent in such differential effects of the purchase of high cost medical care on disadvantaged and nondisadvantaged populations are substantial.

In addition, if (as some claim) a shortage of nurses exists in the Cleveland area, expansion of inpatient facilities without some simultaneous action to increase the supply of nurses might place even greater pressure on the existing supply. The issue of whether there is a shortage of nurses in Cleveland is quite controversial, however, and a careful and objective analysis of this (which was beyond the scope of this case study) should be undertaken.

The tertiary-care activities of the major Cleveland hospitals are probably not the segment of the local health care industry that will require the most attention from the community over the next few years. As Medicare and Medicaid benefits are reduced, all communities in the United States will be faced with the choice of finding new ways to help pay the cost of care for the disadvantaged or seeing the quality of care received by these populations decline. Cleveland, however, may well face a current shortage of facilities to provide care to the aged. Cleveland had 47.3 nursing home beds per 1,000 persons 65 years of age or older in 1976. The equivalent figures were 59.7 for Baltimore, 75.1 for Boston, 67.3 for Detroit, and 23.9 for Pittsburgh. At the same time the national average was 61.7 and the Ohio average was 59.5. These figures alone do not prove that Cleveland has a shortage of nursing home beds, but they do suggest that the adequacy of local facilities in this segment of the health care industry should be investigated carefully. Among the issues facing the local health care industry, this one is especially important because the demand for such facilities is certain to increase with the aging of the population.

A strong health services industry can be built only on the base of an active medical research and training community. Federal government support for medical research and training is not likely to grow and may decline over the next few years. Even in the past 10 years, medical research has been declining as a proportion of GNP. The next few years may see large reductions in federal funding for medical and health services research and for education on the undergraduate, graduate, and postgraduate levels. Therefore, a substantial proportion of the financial support that medical research and development has enjoyed in the past may be withdrawn. Furthermore, to continue to serve the poor and near-poor in the face of considerable cuts in Medicare and Medicaid, some institutions may have to dip into endowments and other resources that they might otherwise have had available to support research and training. Communities that wish to maintain a preeminent position in these fields will be called upon to provide even more local financial support for medical research and training than they have in the past.

It might be possible to remedy whatever shortages of nursing home beds Cleveland faces *and* provide high quality medical services for the poor, the near-poor, and the elderly *and* maintain and enhance Cleveland's reputation as a center for certain advanced, tertiary medical services. If the community wishes to do all three simultaneously, however, it must be prepared to devote substantial local resources to the health care industry. If the resources to be devoted to that particular industry are limited, choices will have to be made among the problems to be tackled.

In sum, then, some advantages for economic development might be obtained if the export segment of the medical care industry were induced to grow. At the same time, growth of that segment could create a number of problems. Any decision to advance this sector should be carefully considered; if health services were targeted for development, steps should be taken to minimize the adverse side effects of the "health services export" strategy.

Building on Cleveland's Strengths as a Health Services Center

Our purpose here, as elsewhere in this report, is not to present fully developed action programs for local economic growth. In the remainder of this chapter, we simply note two general types of activities that might promote economic development and indicate what types of research and analysis would need to be undertaken before either or both of these general strategies were initiated.

First, if Cleveland is to build on its role as a center for certain types of advanced medical services, the community will have to continue to provide financial support to the major local institutions of medical research and training. Any community that wishes to "export" medical services must be a place where advanced medical research flourishes; it must be able to attract the most talented medical residents, clinicians, and academicians. As federal support for these activities decreases, the communities that remain in the forefront of the industry will be those areas most willing to support medical research and training internally. In fact, Cleveland may have a comparative advantage in this respect. Medical research and training in Cleveland appears to be supported by a smaller proportion of federal funds and a higher proportion of local, state, or private funds than in most other health service centers. If this is true, it may mean that Cleveland could emerge from this and coming rounds of federal budget cuts in a relatively better position than some other cities. In any case, if Cleveland is to retain or enhance its competitive position, local financial support will have to continue and increase.

Just what allocation of resources among segments of the health care industry would be best for Cleveland is unclear. Factors that should be taken into account in allocating financial support include the following: the local community's health care requirements now and in the future; the need to protect the disadvantaged against declines in the quantity or quality of the medical care they receive; the relative financial needs of different groups of institutions (e.g., the downtown research and teaching hospitals, community clinics, nursing homes, smaller suburban hospitals); the supply of and demand for different types of health care personnel; changes in the regional and national market for medical services; the cost of health care in Cleveland 'and the effect of rising costs on wages; and changes in the level and composition of federal support for the health services industry. Analysis of all of these issues would plainly be a major research undertaking. Given the rapid changes taking place in the national health care industry and the many and complex needs of the medical services sector in Cleveland, all should be given some consideration as the community decides just what role this industry should play in the region's economic development strategy.

The second general type of activity would be some form of community support for interactions between the local medical services industry and the medical technology industry. Because another study of medical technology in Cleveland was under way when this case study was undertaken, this chapter has been confined to health services per se. The other study (Midwest Research Institute, 1981) identified, in addition to the local centers of purely medical research, a number of strengths in the field of medical technology. These included Case Western Reserve University's program in biomedical engineering, Lewis Research Center's program in ion beam technology, and such firms as Technicare and the Picker Corporation. With some stimulus from the community, these assets might merge into an important part of an economic growth strategy. One proposal that has been discussed in Cleveland is the possible development of a unified medical technology marketing center. Because of the high cost of setting up complex medical instruments for display to prospective purchasers, a single center where equipment would be on permanent display might attract buyers, suppliers, and medical conventions to the Cleveland area. We have not analyzed any specific "medical mart" plan in enough detail to determine whether it is at all a viable enterprise. We can agree, however, that proposals such as this, which build on existing strengths in the metropolitan area, deserve serious attention.

PERSPECTIVES FROM THE THREE CASE STUDIES

In this chapter and the two that precede it, we have sought to answer some key questions about three sectors that are important to metropolitan Cleveland's economic future. In each, we have found that Cleveland has many sources of current strength as well as potentials for growth in the future. However, the sources of strength are threatened by a rapidly changing economic environment and the outcome of each potential is uncertain. There are actions that Cleveland should consider that could assist each of these sectors, but only a few well formulated proposals are on the table.

The Cleveland machine tool industry, a traditional source of metropolitan export earnings, is threatened by rapid technological change, an aging stock of human and physical capital and, possibly, an obsolescent skill mix. Initial community actions should focus on a more precise diagnosis of the industry's problems, particularly whatever difficulties it has in finding a productive labor force with the right mix of skills. That diagnosis should lead to a choice among the proposed training and retraining programs that community groups have generated. One aspect of the machine tool industry that must be considered in any growth program is the small size of the typical firm. Programs that would assist firms with sales up to, say, $3 million per year survive in a changing environment would help preserve Cleveland's position in this market.

A great many changes for the better are taking place in downtown Cleveland. Plans for Tower City and Playhouse Square, to mention just two, could lead to a basic prerequisite for hotel development—life and activity in the streets. However, current levels of activity and current occupancy rates in downtown hotels have not yet been sufficient to attract a major chain hotel to downtown Cleveland. Community support for the timely implementation of existing downtown development plans may be the best avenue to generating conditions that will attract the right kind of hotel in the future.

The medical and health services industry grew very rapidly over the last two decades, and Cleveland shared a part of that growth. However, analysis of available data does not indicate that Cleveland stands out as a national, or even necessarily as a regional, center for all medical services. Nevertheless, certain Cleveland institutions maintain leading positions in a number of medical specialties, and these strengths might be built upon as part of an economic growth strategy.

Even though growth of the "export" segment of the health care industry could contribute to economic development, the community should think very carefully before it embarks on any large, new program of supporting the advanced tertiary care institutions in Cleveland. Development of this segment could have a number of undesirable side effects, and other segments of the local health care sector have serious and complex problems that are also worthy of community attention.

If Cleveland leaders decide to build upon the area's existing strengths in advanced medical services, activities should include financial support for medical research and training in Cleveland and projects aimed at developing linkages between the medical care and medical technology institutions in the region.

PART E

CONCLUSIONS

This last part presents the conclusions of our research to date. Because the main purpose of this effort was to start a process of continual monitoring of the Cleveland economy, many of our conclusions refer to the monitoring process and the initial work agenda of a monitoring group. However, the work we have completed over the last year also leads to conclusions about a number of aspects of economic development strategy. We present no fully developed "action plans," because that was not our task, but we do present the general conclusion growing out of our first year's research.

X. ECONOMIC MONITORING AND ECONOMIC DEVELOPMENT

THE NEED FOR ECONOMIC MONITORING

Three overall conclusions of our work on the Cleveland economy stand out most clearly:

- The Cleveland economy is quite complex and diverse,
- It has been changing rapidly in response to changes in its economic environment,
- As one's understanding of the economy becomes deeper and more detailed one's perceptions and the policy implications one draws can change radically.

Numerous specific findings reported in previous chapters support each of these points. The best evidence, however, is the fact that any single, broad statement about the Cleveland economy is either not entirely true or not likely to remain true for very long. Consider even the commonly held view that the Cleveland economy is "declining." This contention has been repeated so often as to become a cliche, but it is only partly true. As noted in Chapter II, employment in Cleveland actually increased annually on average between 1967 and 1977. Conventional wisdom about the role of the automotive industry may be changing rapidly. The automotive industry is important to Cleveland but not as important as to a number of other cities. Furthermore, we have indirect evidence that some Cleveland industries, traditionally suppliers of the automotive industry, have managed to diversify their clientele over the past decade. So Cleveland is dependent on the automotive industry only to some extent and stands a better chance of surviving a major decline of that industry than many other cities in the region.

If perceptions of and statements about the Cleveland economy were of only academic interest to economists, economic monitoring would not have a high priority in the community. Perceptions are more important than that. They influence decisions made and policies adopted by the area's leaders. Crash programs to train skilled machinists, based on an unexamined perception of a looming shortage, might fail as firms locate elsewhere in search of the electronic technicians that were really needed. Complacency about an infinite supply of fresh water might prove foolhardy, if municipal water systems cannot provide enough pressure to meet manufacturers' needs. A false perception that local efforts alone can "turn Cleveland around" might lead to inadequate local preparation for the social consequences of national recessions. At the same time, an equally misguided perception that "nothing can be done locally" might lead to missed opportunities.

As some of the items in the previous two paragraphs indicate, the research effort reported here improves our perceptions of the Cleveland economy in a number of ways. Now we have a more complete understanding of Cleveland's role in the national economy (Chapter III), of Cleveland's advantages and disadvantages as a place to live and do business (Chapter IV), of changes in the size, performance, and industrial composition of the regional economy over the past decade (Chapters II, V, and VI), and of the prospects of three important Cleveland industries (Chapters VII, VIII, and IX). However, the ideas and facts presented in this report are just the beginning of what could be known about the Cleveland metropolitan economy. The contents of the previous chapters leave a great many questions unanswered. An example from each chapter will indicate what more needs to be learned.

Chapter II indicates that the City of Cleveland has been declining very rapidly in population and employment and that its population has been becoming relatively more poor and elderly. However, other central cities in the United States that had appeared to be on similar downward paths have experienced something of an "urban revival," with middle class residents returning, renovating central city housing stocks, and filling city government coffers with tax revenues. This report does not deal with the question of whether or by how much this sort of "gentrification" is in the cards for Cleveland. An assessment of the prospects of middle class return to the central city would help answer a number of questions about municipal finance, downtown commercial and hotel development, and potential relocation problems for current central city residents.

Chapter III concludes with a discussion of the proportions of blacks and youth employed by different industries. The data indicate substantial industrial segregation in 1970. A number of our doubts about the equal distribution of benefits of different patterns of economic development depend on the assumption that the 1980 Census data will reveal continued segregation across similar lines. Analysis of those data as soon as they become available will indicate whether the problem discussed in this report is as substantial as it was in 1970.

Chapter IV begins an exploration of the issue of Cleveland's manufacturing wages. We are able to conclude that, on an industry-by-industry basis, average wages are higher in the Cleveland area. However, a simple statistical analysis shows no correlation between local industry employment growth and wage differentials (ratios of local to

U.S. average wages for the same industries). We are not able to discover, on the basis of this initial work, the extent to which high wages are a cause of Cleveland's relatively slow economic growth rate over the last decade, and this is certainly one of the key questions to be answered.

Chapter V presents key indicators of the recent performance of Cleveland's detailed manufacturing industries. Just collecting and organizing that information suggested a number of conclusions, but work with this data should not stop with the tabulations and comparisons presented. The analysis leaves us with a list of industries that have performed well or poorly on a number of criteria, but without further analysis we do not know what factors determine just which industries did well and which did not. Further statistical analysis and in-depth case studies should provide an understanding of those factors and this information would be most useful to those charged with developing local growth policies. Also, the basic analysis we performed should be updated as soon as more recent data become available to identify any changes in the rates or directions of change for the detailed industries.

Chapter VI reports fast absolute but slow relative growth in a number of nonmanufacturing industries. Again, we did not take the analysis far enough to determine why the industries that did relatively well over the decade were successful while others were less so. Furthermore, without careful case studies, we do not really understand the performance of such diverse industrial categories as "business related services."

Chapter VII suggests a number of programs or projects that might assist the local machine tool industry. However, we were not able to determine exactly which types of labor were in the shortest supply or how the community might best go about helping small firms adjust to new circumstances.

Chapter VIII probably leaves us with the fewest unanswered questions. However, it does suggest that community efforts in support of currently planned downtown development projects would be important in making the area more attractive to hotel developers. This particular study did not indicate what types of help those projects needed or which of the projects were most likely to be cost beneficial.

Chapter IX points to a number of problems in the medical services sector that could be subject to more careful analysis including a possible shortage of nurses in Cleveland, the availability of nursing home beds, and the relative financial circumstances of various health care institutions. The chapter also suggests a careful evaluation of the "medical mart" concept.

This is only a partial list of the questions raised, but not answered, by our work. Sound responses to each of these questions would expand and deepen the insights developed in this study.

THE PROCESS OF ECONOMIC MONITORING

To understand how economic monitoring would work, one must first have some conception of how economic development policy is made in a community like metropolitan Cleveland and how information and analysis fit into that policymaking process. In as large a metropolitan area as Cleveland, ideas for economic development strategies, programs, and projects are continually being proposed. Right now the community's attention has been called to the action agenda proposed by the Cleveland Tomorrow campaign, by the city's proposal for an urban development zone, by various plans to improve vocational education in the city and the region, by the Playhouse Square project, by the medical mart proposal, and so on. These ideas are presented to the area's leaders who consider them, sometimes formally and sometimes informally. Proposals are considered in the context of a climate of opinion about the problems and prospects of the regional economy. Ideas that are in accord with the current climate of opinion are more likely to be accepted and implemented than those that are not.

Of the projects that are implemented, some are relatively successful—they solve or avert an identifiable regional problem. Others are not. The concept of economic monitoring is based on the belief that the more the current "conventional wisdom" is in accord with the reality of the Cleveland metropolitan economy, the better the chances that development proposals accepted by the community will be successful. The more knowledge is available to permit comparisons of costs and benefits among different kinds of projects, the more strategic thinking will be facilitated.

What Would the Monitoring Group Do?

A monitoring group would consist of a group of professional analysts—economists, policy analysts, and others—who would devote full-time effort to analyzing the Cleveland economy. The group could be either a free-standing institution or attached to a university or other existing body. The group's main formal products would be regular briefings to community leaders, regular publication of findings, and use of an up-to-date and systematic regional economic data base. The briefings and the publications would report three kinds of research work. First, regular updates of recurrent statistics on the regional economy's recent performance would be reported and discussed. These statistics would include unemployment rates, retail sales, and a number of other indicators of current and future general economic conditions. Second, projections of near-future national economic trends derived from a consensus of government and commercial macro-economic models of the U.S. economy should be translated into implications for the Cleveland economy. Projections of employment by industry, regional unemployment, and, possibly, local government tax revenues, should be presented along with clear indications of the degree of uncertainty behind those figures. Finally, briefings and reports should contain a number of clear and concise analyses of local economic issues or of the condition and prospects of important local industries. For example, as the detailed 1980 Census figures become available, the monitoring group should be expected to report on any potential problems of labor availability by skill category in the area. To take another example, fairly frequent updates on the competitive position of the United States, and, therefore, the Cleveland, machine tool industry would be useful.

By maintaining a complete, easily accessible, and up-to-date data base on the local economy, the monitoring group would be able to provide a direct service to local governments and to the planning or sales departments of a number of locally based firms. It is likely that the local utilities, major retailers, and local media would want to subscribe to the group's data base services, as might national marketing consultation firms.

In addition to working on these formal products, the group staff would be expected to participate in discussions of the region's economy in a number of forums. Staff analysts would speak before community groups, serve on or advise the community task forces that are formed from time to time to work on specific issues or problems, provide fast turnaround information and analyses to community leaders when the latter are called upon to testify in Washington or Columbus, and generally serve as a dedicated, informed, and clear-thinking resource to the metropolitan community.

After such a group reported research findings and interacted with the community for a few years, it is likely that the conventional wisdom about the regional economy would be much more realistic and deeper than it is now.

Conclusion

Our work to date has generated a number of insights and interpretations that were not available before. However, the process of developing a better understanding of the Cleveland economy should not stop with this report. Instead, we recommend that the Cleveland community establish an ongoing economic monitoring capability—a group of professional researchers who will devote full-time effort to analysis of the local economy. By providing Clevelanders with an ever expanding and deepening understanding of their own regional economy, an economic monitoring capability could improve the effectiveness of community resources devoted to economic development.

The results of economic analysis should be disseminated and discussed broadly within the community. It must be remembered that Cleveland's sociopolitical diversity has implications for development policymaking. As a major metropolitan area, Cleveland is the home of a diverse set of ethnic groups and a wide variety of economic and political interests. Here, public policy, if it is to achieve acceptance, must receive at least the acquiescence of a wide variety of interest groups. No single group should consult only its own interests and expect, on that basis alone, to promulgate development policy for the whole metropolitan area.

LESSONS FOR POLICY

What we have learned about the Cleveland economy can be translated into a number of general lessons about the kinds of development strategies and programs that are likely to work in this area. This final section of the report draws a number of such conclusions. We suspect, however, that as the material presented here is disseminated around the Cleveland community, many other inferences about policy will be drawn. In other words, our ultimate objective was not to draw these conclusions, although we think that they are useful. Instead, we aim at providing a realistic conception of the Cleveland economy against which suggestions for economic development can be judged.

Economic Development Proposals Must Be Viewed in the Context of Cleveland's Role in the U.S. Economy

Cleveland's economic fate is partly in its own hands, but is also partly determined by outside events. It is certain that external events, from the passage of the Northwest Ordinance that effectively opened Ohio's Western Reserve to settlement to recent changes in the world market for machine tools, play the dominant role. Nevertheless, actions by Clevelanders can have a relatively small but important effect on the region's future.

In a sense, it does not matter exactly how much impact local actions can have on local growth, because the community should try to do the best it can with the resources at its command. The important point is that local actions are more likely to succeed if they work with, not against, trends in the national economy as they affect Cleveland. Furthermore, to the extent that Clevelanders can influence trends in the U.S. economy, through their representations to Congress, for example, they should support actions that will do best by the region.

In Chapter III we identified Cleveland's role in the U.S. economy by estimating the composition of the region's exports. That same methodology can be used to analyze the differential impacts of different national trends on various aspects of the Cleveland economy. The results of such a simulation are presented in Table 10.1, which presents the results of the following series of experiments: In each case we assumed that Cleveland's "export" earnings (see Chapter III) grew by $1 million as the result of some change in the national economy. We simulated the effects of increases in consumption (stimulated, perhaps, by a cut in personal income taxes), increases in business investment, increases in defense procurements, and increases in nondefense federal procurements. These scenarios are meant to illustrate how information on Cleveland's economic structure can be used to evaluate different national trends from a local perspective.

The numbers in Table 10.1 do not represent, in any sense, a prediction of what is likely to happen in the regional economy given any specific tax cut or federal budget. The results of the computations do indicate quite clearly, however, that the best possible trend in the national economy for the Cleveland economy as a whole would be an increase in business investment. The table suggests that this eventuality would produce the most total income, the highest average wages, and the most total jobs of all four scenarios. The worst of the four trends considered here from the point of view of the Cleveland economy as a whole would be relative growth in household consumption nationwide. Presumably a consumption growth would be better for Cleveland than continued recession, but the overall performance of the regional economy as a whole would be much better if national growth were driven by investment.

The clearest policy implication to be derived from these findings is that Cleveland's representatives in Congress should enthusiastically support policies that would stimulate business investment, but the implications for local policy are also important. The sensitivity of the region's economy to business investment suggests that local economic development strategies should be geared to expectations about the performance of this national economic variable over the near future. If Clevelanders expect a national investment boom, then they should

Table 10.1

EFFECTS OF $1 MILLION INCREASES IN CLEVELAND SMSA EXPORT EARNINGS
GENERATED BY NATIONAL INCREASES IN CONSUMPTION, INVESTMENT,
GOVERNMENT DEFENSE PROCUREMENT, AND GOVERNMENT
NONDEFENSE PROCUREMENT

Trend	Total New Earnings Generated ($ million)	Total New Jobs Created	Percent of New Jobs Going to:			Average Annual Wages per New Job
			Blacks	Youth	Central City	
Consumption	1.41	39	10	29	48	$ 9,127
Investment	2.55	47	8	24	42	13,145
Defense Procurement	2.20	44	8	24	44	12,404
Nondefense Procurement	2.23	45	8	25	45	12,313

SOURCE: Rand analysis of Cleveland SMSA input–output relationships based
on data from U.S. Department of Commerce, Bureau of Economic Analysis (see
Appendix C).

devote community resources to maintaining their current strengths in
the producers' durables industries. Progress aimed at maintaining
this strength might include emphasis on technical education, subsi-
dized industrial R&D, infrastructure development, etc.

If, however, current efforts by the federal government to stimulate
business investment are likely to fail, then the community should
prepare for a period of relative local economic stagnation and should
adopt policies that will minimize the pain of adjustment to a smaller
regional economy. Policies aimed at "graceful decline" might include
consolidating infrastructure (e.g., closing some bridges and repairing
only a few others), and building up public financial reserves for infrastructure maintenance and for caring for a more-or-less perma-
nently dependent population.

The figures in Table 10.1 also indicate that investment growth
would not solve all of Cleveland's economic problems. Specifically we
see that $1 million dollars of export demand generated by business
investment would create the most total jobs, but, in 1970, at least, it
would have created fewer jobs for blacks than a similar total value of

exports stimulated by national consumption demand. The community should be aware that as beneficial as an investment boom might be, policies may have to be designed to insure that all segments of the local community benefit appropriately from the local growth that is stimulated. Programs aimed at assisting Cleveland's minority communities might have three elements: immediate job creation in industries that lure proportions of disadvantaged workers, improved education and training, and affirmative action in Cleveland's mainstream durable goods industries.

This discussion has illustrated how information about trends in the national economy can be translated into implications about the course of the Cleveland economy and how those implications can lead to guidance about local development policy. The exercise reported here has two further implications. First, it supports our suggestion that an economic monitoring group devote considerable effort to tracing out the effects of national macro-economic and industry-specific trends on the regional economy. Second, the importance of national trends suggests that any evaluation of an economic development strategy or program for Cleveland should explicitly consider expectations about the national economy and perceptions of Cleveland's role in the national economy.

Toward an Industrial Strategy

Much of the material presented in this report is most useful in helping Cleveland determine which general industrial development strategies are most suited to the region's particular advantages and needs. An industrial strategy is not a formal plan and it is not an exclusive list of industries that deserve community assistance. Instead, it is a general guide that can help leaders decide which problems and projects deserve immediate attention and which proposals might be assigned a somewhat lower priority.

In general, three factors should be taken into account in determining the priority that should be assigned to an industry's regional development:

- The degree to which the industry contributes to overall regional growth,
- The degree to which the industry contributes to the solution of the region's economic problems,
- The difficulty involved in inducing an industry to grow in the region.

It is not our purpose here to list the specific projects or programs that would be influenced by an industrial strategy. However, a few illustrations will help make the following discussion more concrete. One major area of community policy that would be influenced by an industrial strategy would be the vocational education curricula of public and private institutions. Of course the city and schools and the region's community colleges should provide training in both mechanical, technical, and clerical skills. However, an industrial strategy favoring nonmanufacturing would call for relatively greater emphasis on the latter. Likewise, a regional emphasis within manufacturing on fabricated metals or machine tools might influence the relative growth rates of different departments within the Case Institute of Technology.

Likewise consider the choices that must be made by the City of Cleveland with respect to its own economic development. Certainly both Playhouse Square *and* the "industrial" blocks of the Euclid Corridor should be developed, but an overall regional development strategy might suggest which projects should be advanced most quickly. To take one final example, current plans to renovate the region's public infrastructure—the roads, bridges, water mains, etc.—should take economic development strategy into account. Certain elements of the infrastructure may be more important to some industries than others, and the elements that are most important to the industries being emphasized may deserve higher priority. With the three principles and a set of illustrative policy issues in mind, we will review and summarize the material in the body of this report to identify the industries that appear to satisfy the requirements.

Industry Contributions to Economic Development

The first two factors that should be taken into account in determining an industry's role in Cleveland's economic development strategy might be loosely termed the "benefits" of industrial growth. Growth of different industries stimulates different amounts of total local income and employment growth for the variety of reasons discussed in Chapter III. The first column of Table 10.2 presents the results of computations similar to those presented in that chapter and indicates how much total regional income would be generated by an increase in export revenues (or decrease in import expenditures) of $1 million for each industry. The results follow the discussion of industry multipliers in Chapter III. With a few exceptions among the service industries, some of the durable goods manufacturing industries generate the greatest local stimulus.

The remaining columns of Table 10.2 evaluate different industries

Table 10.2

EFFECTS OF $1 MILLION INCREASES IN EXPORT EARNINGS IN CLEVELAND SMSA INDUSTRIES

Industry	Total New Earnings Created ($ million)	Total New Jobs Created	Average Annual Wages per Job ($)	Percent of new jobs going to:		
				Blacks	Youth	Central City
Durable Goods Manufacturing						
Primary Metals	2.55	43	13,217	10	19	47
Fabricated Metals	2.74	48	13,217	8	20	41
Nonelectrical Machinery	2.70	51	17,980	8	23	43
Electrical Equipment	2.49	45	12,549	7	20	40
Motor Vehicles	2.71	40	14,403	12	21	45
Other Transport Equipment	2.88	55	13,372	6	26	41
Instrument	2.55	69	9,802	4	11	41
Miscellaneous Manufactures	2.61	58	10,669	12	27	52
Nondurable Goods Manufacturing						
Stone Products	2.13	42	11,840	5	18	38
Textiles	2.07	63	7,055	3	7	61
Apparel	1.94	40	10,825	4	28	79
Paper Products	2.11	41	11,627	31	12	23
Printing	2.51	52	12,124	5	17	52
Chemicals	2.41	39	11,897	10	20	47
Rubber Products	2.46	50	10,887	8	23	54
Lumber Products	2.60	54	10,821	5	27	56
Food Processing	2.42	104	5,541	11	41	48
Sales						
Retail	2.33	76	8,634	8	31	40
Eating and Drinking	2.42	104	5,541	11	41	48
Wholesale	2.43	63	10,476	8	21	47

Table 10.2 (Continued)

Industry	Total New Earnings Created ($ million)	Total New Jobs Created	Average Annual Wages per Job ($)	Percent of new jobs going to:		
				Blacks	Youth	Central City
Services						
Finance	2.61	56	10,244	10	33	55
Insurance	2.89	81	10,329	9	22	53
Real Estate	1.50	19	7,534	12	13	45
Hotels	2.40	82	6,923	19	45	62
Personal Services	2.76	104	7,506	26	35	35
Business Services	2.44	69	9,799	10	23	59
Health Services	2.31	56	10,578	11	18	51
Other						
Transportation	2.51	40	16,692	8	26	46
Communications	2.01	36[a]	13,368[a]	16	35	63
Utilities	1.92	109[a]	2,656[a]	10	19	70
New Construction	2.69	47	13,717	8	25	41
Maint. Construction	2.74	53	14,110	10	29	42
Agriculture	2.18	50	10,095	4	36	77

SOURCE: Rand analysis of Cleveland SMSA input-output relationships based on data from U.S. Department of Commerce, Bureau of Economic Analysis. (See Appendix C.)

[a] These figures probably represent errors in the data.

with respect to the degrees to which they help solve a variety of community problems. Because structural unemployment, especially among minority group members and young workers, is a major problem of the Cleveland metropolitan area, the table presents rough estimates, based on 1970 data, of the proportion of jobs generated by export growth for each industry that would go to members of these groups. As noted, it will be important to see whether the problem of industrial segregation suggested by these figures is still reflected in the 1980 Census data.

Another major problem of the metropolitan area is the financial condition of the central city government. Although the crisis of a few years ago has passed, no one would suggest that Cleveland's fiscal future is sure to be untroubled. We have no direct measure of an industry's contribution to central city finances, but the proportion of employment in that industry located in the central city and, given increased reliance on payroll taxes in Cleveland, the industry's average wages are good indirect indicators of that contribution. As noted in Chapter III, the industrial composition of the city's economy is similar to that of the metropolitan area, so, with few exceptions, growth of any industry is as likely as any other's to contribute to central city growth. Of course, the anchor industries pay higher average wages, in general, and to that extent they contribute more to city fiscal health.

Which Industries Will Be Easiest To Stimulate?

The benefits generated by growth of different industries, some of which are measured by the data in Table 10.2, must be compared with the costs associated with inducing growth in each industry. It would, to take an outlandish example, be much more difficult to generate $1 million worth of forestry exports than to market an additional $1 million worth of fabricated metal products. Even though we cannot calculate exactly what it would cost to induce any given amount of export growth in each of these industries, we do have a great deal of circumstantial evidence that indicates which industries are the easiest to stimulate. This evidence includes information on the current composition of Cleveland's exports (Chapter III) and the recent performance of each of Cleveland's industries. The composition of exports identifies the established markets for Cleveland's products. The relevance of this information is that it indicates whether inducing growth in an industry would involve creating new markets, which may be more difficult than expanding or maintaining existing markets. Information on recent industry performance is useful in two ways. It indicates whether inducing industry growth would involve working with or against recent trends.

When we relate the information in Table 10.2 to the analysis of Cleveland's current exports presented in Chapter III the importance of the durable goods manufacturing industries—particularly fabricated metals and nonelectrical machinery—to the Cleveland economy as a whole becomes much more apparent. Not only are these two industries relatively highly stimulative, but they pay relatively high wages. Furthermore, they produce things for which Cleveland is well known. Stimulating growth of exports by these industries would not involve creating a new regional strength from scratch but would build on existing strength and an established regional reputation.

The Relative Performance of Manufacturing and Nonmanufacturing Industries

Information on recent industry performance can be summarized in two ways. First, we compare the manufacturing (Chapter V) and nonmanufacturing (Chapter VI) sectors. Then we look at a list of manufacturing industries that have performed well over the 1967-77 decade to see if any common patterns can be discerned.

A comparison of the performances of Cleveland's manufacturing and nonmanufacturing industries is summarized in Table 10.3. Even though nonmanufacturing employment as a whole grew much more rapidly in Cleveland than manufacturing employment over the decade, it does not appear that Cleveland was becoming a "service center." In fact, the bulk of regional nonmanufacturing employment was in industries that were growing much more slowly than their national counterparts. This was not true of manufacturing, as Table 10.3 indicates. In other words, even though Cleveland was following the general national trend in employment toward the nonmanufacturing sector, the industries in which Cleveland appears to have a competitive edge are still concentrated in the manufacturing sector.

The policy implications of this finding are neither simple nor entirely clear. The fact that Cleveland's specialty is still manufacturing certainly does not mean that efforts to make the area attractive to nonmanufacturing industries should be abandoned. In fact, Cleveland does offer a number of strengths that should make it attractive to nonmanufacturing firms, especially in the business-related services sectors. As Chapters II and VI indicated, Cleveland has and retains substantial advantages as a headquarters city, and it would be foolish to allow these advantages to erode. Nevertheless, a number of individual items of evidence—the export composition, the recent industrial

Table 10.3

PROPORTION OF SECTORAL EMPLOYMENT IN INDUSTRIES
BY CHANGE IN CLEVELAND SHARE OF U.S.
INDUSTRY EMPLOYMENT

Percent Change in Cleveland Share of U.S. Employment	Percent of Sectoral Employment in Industries	
	Manufacturing	Nonmanufacturing
+5 or more	27.8	7.2
-4 to +4 (i.e., no change)	13.1	9.3
-5 or less	59.1	83.5
Total	100.0	100.0

performance figures, the case studies we conducted—all support the assertion that Cleveland's economic specialty and greatest strengths still lie in the durable goods manufacturing industries. Community attention should be paid to the nonmanufacturing industries, especially those service and administrative sectors most closely linked to the manufacturing industries, but, in general, the highest priority and greatest care should be devoted to preserving and enhancing Cleveland's fundamental strength.

The Best Performances Among Manufacturing Industries

Within the manufacturing sector a diverse set of industries has been performing relatively well over the recent past. However, inspection of a list of recent "winners" does suggest a number of common factors that may characterize the types of industries that can do well in Cleveland. Table 10.4 lists the 20 (out of 84 discussed in Chapter V) manufacturing industries for which Cleveland increased both employment and market share or concentration ratio[1] between 1967 and

---

[1]An increase in market share indicates that the proportion of total U.S. employment in an industry located in Cleveland had increased between 1967 and 1977. Such an industry would have been performing *extremely* well because Cleveland's share of total

Table 10.4

CLEVELAND INDUSTRIES INCREASING EMPLOYMENT AND MARKET SHARE, GROWTH RATE RANKINGS, 1967-77

SIC	Industry	Growth Rate Rank in U.S.
Industries Increasing Market Share		
332	Iron and Steel Foundries	79
343	Plumbing and Heating Exc. Elec.	75
34X	Other Fabricated Metal Products	11
3444	Sheet Metal Work	67
3564	Blowers and Fans	9
3559	Special Industrial Machinery	49
362X	Other Electrical Industrial Apparatus	36
39X	Other Misc. Manufacturing Industries	39
29	Petroleum and Coal Products	45
203	Canned Cured and Frozen Food	65
26X	Other Paper and Allied Products	47
38X	Other Instruments and Rel. Products	12
23X	Other Apparel and Textile Products	56
2653	Corrugated and Solid Fiber Boxes	41
30	Rubber and Misc. Plastic Products	7
Industries Increasing Concentration Ratio		
3341	Secondary Nonferrous Metals	29
369	Misc. Electrical Equip. Supplies	6
3273	Ready Mix Concrete	18
233	Women's and Misses' Outerwear	31
382	Measuring and Controlling Devices	1

SOURCE: Rand analysis of data file compiled from Census of Manufactures records (see Appendix B).

1977. The table also lists each industry's ranking with respect to national growth rate among all 84 industries. In other words industries with rankings above 42 grew faster than the median industry and those with rankings below 42 grew slower.

U.S. employment and population was, of course, decreasing. An industry that increased its Cleveland concentration ratio, i.e., was losing market share more slowly than Cleveland was losing population, had also been performing better than the metropolitan economy's average performance. Such industries must also be considered to be doing well locally and have, therefore, been included in the discussion.

As Table 10.4 indicates, the Cleveland area did well in several of the industries that had good records nationally; e.g., 382, measuring and controlling devices which ranked first in U.S. growth; 369, miscellaneous electrical equipment supplies ranking sixth; and 30, rubber and miscellaneous plastic products ranking seventh. It is striking, however, that many of Cleveland's strongest industries were those that did not exhibit outstanding growth rates in the United States as a whole.

This suggests that Cleveland's manufacturing industries are responding to changes in the environment along two general paths. The first is typical of the U.S. economy as a whole. Some of the high technology industries manufacturing electrical control devices and new types of machinery have been performing better than the local economy as a whole. The second path of evolution may represent an even more important opportunity in the aggregate. Cleveland manufacturing firms appear increasingly to engage in what might be termed "market niche" manufacturing: highly adaptive production that fills some need that has fallen between the cracks in conventional large manufacturing operations. Note on the listing above that many of the successful industries in the Cleveland metropolitan area in the 1970s were the "miscellaneous" groups: e.g., 34X, other fabricated metal products; 3559, special industrial machinery not elsewhere classified; 362X, other electrical industrial apparatus. In other words, Cleveland has done well in manufacturing industries that are not easily classifiable in relation to conventional standards. These may or may not be industries with high growth rates nationally.

The specific list of industries in Table 10.4 should *not* be taken as a prediction of the "winners" of the next decade. Instead, the list suggests that Cleveland should support the local development of industries likely to grow rapidly nationwide, but should not rely solely on projected national "winners." At the same time as Cleveland works on building strength in the newer high technology industries, local manufacturers who are flexible and able, therefore, to fit into whatever market niches appear should receive a generous, effective measure of community encouragement and support.

A SUMMARY OF CONCLUSIONS

The conclusions presented in this chapter fall into two categories. First we recommend that systematic analysis of the Cleveland metropolitan economy not cease with this project, but that the Cleveland community establish and support an ongoing economic monitoring capability.

Second, we draw the following conclusions with respect to economic development policy for the Cleveland metropolitan area:

- Economic development programs should be consistent with sound views of Cleveland's role in the U.S. economy and with reasonable projections of what is likely to happen in the U.S. economy.
- Clevelanders should take every potentially effective opportunity to support national policies that will lead to an increase in the proportion of GNP devoted to business investment.
- Specific development-related projects should be evaluated in light of their differential impacts on different industries and of the industries' potential local contribution.
- Project proposals should be sought that will assist a variety of industries that advance a variety of community interests. Care should be taken to insure that the package of development programs, taken as a whole, addresses the problem of structural unemployment of minority group members and youth.
- Projects aimed at maintaining and enhancing the competitive position of Cleveland's durable goods manufacturing industries—especially semi-finished goods and industrial equipment manufacturing—should be given serious consideration.
- Projects aimed at development of the region's nonmanufacturing industries should exploit linkages with manufacturing and should also be aimed at maintaining Cleveland's role as a corporate headquarters city.
- Well-designed efforts to maintain the region's competitiveness in technologically advanced industries experiencing rapid national growth should be accompanied by programs that support firms with a great deal of market flexibility in traditional, lower technology fields.

Perhaps the most notable characteristic of metropolitan Cleveland's economy is its diversity. The fact of this diversity has a fairly clear-cut implication for local development policy. Because local efforts to stimulate economic growth require focus and simplification, development plans in a number of cities have relied on some unifying "grand concept" of the city's future—for example, the city should become predominantly a "center for international trade" or a "center for high technology manufacturing" or a "center for advanced business services." From what we have learned, this approach would be a mistake for metropolitan Cleveland, at least if it involved selecting a single economic sector as the focus for support. Cleveland's grand concept, if one is necessary, should be, as it has been, as a "center for diversified business activity." The region is a congenial environment for almost every type of economic activity, and the mix can be mutually reinforcing.

Appendix A

ADVISORY COMMITTEE, CLEVELAND FOUNDATION RAND PROJECT

Richard W. Pogue
Advisory Panel Chairman
Partner, Jones, Day, Reavis & Pogue

Stanley C. Pace (ex-officio)
President
TRW Inc.

Thomas V. H. Vail
Publisher and Editor
The Plain Dealer

M. Brock Weir
Chairman of the Board
AmeriTrust of Cleveland

Theodore M. Alfred
Dean, Weatherhead School of
  Management
Case Western Reserve University

Brian A. Bowser
Director, Department of Economic
  Development
City of Cleveland

Frank B. Carr
Partner in charge of Corporate
  Finance
McDonald & Company

John J. Dwyer
President
Oglebay Norton Company

James M. Dawson
Senior Vice President and Economist
National City Bank

Mary Jane Fabish
Vice President
CWC Industries

Allen C. Holmes
Managing Partner
Jones, Day, Reavis & Pogue

Martin J. Hughes
Vice President
Communication Workers of America

E. Bradley Jones
President and Chief Operating Officer
Republic Steel Corporation

Joseph H. Keller
Partner
Ernst & Whinney

Dr. William S. Kiser
Chairman of the Board
The Cleveland Clinic Foundation

Morton L. Mandel
Chairman of the Board
Premier Industrial Corporation

David K. McClurkin
Financial Administrator
Cleveland Public Schools

Charles R. McDonald
President
McDonald Equipment Company

David T. Morgenthaler
Senior Partner
Morgenthaler Associates

James R. Stover
President
Eaton Corporation

Dr. Robert Teater
Director
Ohio Department of Natural
  Resources

Alton W. Whitehouse
Chairman and Chief Executive
  Officer
The Standard Oil Company (Ohio)

James M. Whitley
President
Whitley-Whitley Incorporated

Willis J. Winn
President
Federal Reserve Bank of Cleveland

Appendix B

COMPONENTS OF THE METROPOLITAN CLEVELAND DATA BASE

Below we identify the components of the computer data base that supported the analysis in this report and that was designed as a foundation for further monitoring of the Cleveland area economy. Under each component we identify the agency responsible for data collection and the areas of coverage time period observations, and variables in the present version of the data file. We then note the frequency with which new data are regularly collected by the source agency.

A. *CENSUS OF MANUFACTURES* (U.S. Department of Commerce, Bureau of the Census).

Area of Coverage: U.S. totals, Cleveland SMSA and City of Cleveland, northeastern central states (Ohio, Indiana, Illinois, Michigan, and Wisconsin), selected southern states (Alabama, Arkansas, Florida, Georgia, Mississippi, North Carolina, South Carolina, Tennessee, and Virginia).

Time Periods: 1977, 1972, and 1967 (except for southern states).

Observations: Four-digit SICs.

Variables Included: Employment, payroll, number of production workers, plant hours, wages, value added, capital expenditures, number of establishments, establishments with 20 employees or more.

Frequency of Collection: Every five years.

B. *COUNTY BUSINESS PATTERNS* (U.S. Department of Commerce, Bureau of the Census).

Area of Coverage: All counties in Cleveland SCSA, all United States.

Time Periods and Observations: Four-digit SICs for 1975-1978, two-digit SICs for 1964, 1965, 1967, and 1969 through 1974.

Variables Included: Employment by firm size, wages.

Frequency of Collection: Annually.

C. *EMPLOYMENT AND EARNINGS, STATES AND AREAS* (U.S. Department of Labor, Bureau of Labor Statistics).

Area of Coverage: All states and selected SMSAs.

Time Periods: 1945 through 1980.

Observations: Selected two-digit SICs.

Variables Included: Total employees, production or non-supervisory workers—average weekly earnings and average hourly earnings.

Frequency of Collection: Annually.

D. *EMPLOYMENT, PAYROLL AND EARNINGS UNDER THE OHIO UNEMPLOYMENT COMPENSATION LAW* (Ohio Bureau of Employment Services).

Area of Coverage: Counties of Cuyahoga, Geauga, Lake, Lorain, Medina, Portage, and Summit.

Time Periods: 1943 through 1979.

Observations: Seven major industry categories.

Variables Included: Employment, payroll, average weekly earnings.

Frequency of Collection: Monthly.

E. *REGIONAL INPUT-OUTPUT MODELING SYSTEM* (U.S. Department of Commerce, Bureau of Economic Analysis).

Area of Coverage: Cleveland SMSA.

Time Period: Based on 1972 U.S. Input-Output Table.

Observations: 39 broad industries; 495 four-digit industries.

Variables Included: Direct requirements, total multipliers, earnings multipliers.

Frequency of Collection: Occasionally.

F. *ANNUAL SURVEY OF MANUFACTURERS 1975-1976, PART 7, ORIGIN OF EXPORTS OF MANUFACTURING ESTABLISHMENTS* (U.S. Department of Commerce, Bureau of the Census).

Area of Coverage: Selected SMSAs, Atlanta, GA; Baltimore, MD; Boston, MA; Cleveland, OH; Detroit, MI; Houston, TX; Minneapolis-St. Paul, MN-WI; Pittsburgh, PA; St. Louis, MO.

Time Periods: 1976.

Observations: Three-digit SICs.

Variables Included: Value of shipments (total, for export, exports as percent of total), manufacturing employment (total, export-related, export employment as percent of total), relative standard error or estimate for total value of shipments and total manufacturing employment.

Frequency of Collection: Occasionally.

Appendix C

TECHNICAL SPECIFICATION OF THE INPUT-OUTPUT MODEL

This appendix describes the methods used to derive the figures presented in Tables 3.1, 3.2, 3.3, 10.1, and 10.2. The documentation presented here should indicate that these are very rough estimates, so that only very large differences across sectors or scenarios should be taken as indicative.

We begin with a 39 sector input-output matrix for Cleveland developed by the Bureau of Economic Analysis of the Department of Commerce. The methods used to recognize the 1972 U.S. Input-Output (I-O) Table are described in Cartwright, Biemiller, and Gustely (1981). That document also presents evidence that the regionalized coefficients are usually very close to coefficients for specific regions estimated by survey methods. The regionalized I-O matrix is used in a standard input-output framework, viz.

$$X_t = AX_t + F_t \qquad (C.1)$$

where

X is a 39×1 vector of output levels by industry at time t,[1]

A is an input-output matrix with typical element A_{ij} representing the proportion of the value of output of the jth sector used to purchase, as inputs, the products of the ith sector, and

F is a vector of final demands by sector at time t.

The earnings multipliers reported in Table 3.1 are the result of computing the effects of a one dollar increase in final demand for each sector:

$$M_j = (I - A)^{-1}U_j \qquad (C.2)$$

where

M_j is the sector j earnings multiplier, and

U_j is a vector with a 1 in the jth row and zeros elsewhere.

---

[1]Tables in the text do not include entries for all 39 sectors: results for a few smaller sectors were excluded because of data problems.

Because in this application the A matrix includes a row representing the value of labor inputs to each industry and a column representing the purchase made by industry out of local wage income, the sum of the elements of the F vector does not represent Gross Regional Product. Instead, the F vector represents the (vector) sum of:

- Purchases made in Cleveland using net transfer income,
- State and local government purchases, and
- Exports to the rest of the world.

Because the first two of these items are likely to be small relative to the last, we assume that the F vector essentially represents the magnitude and composition of Cleveland's exports to the rest of the world.

We have no direct observations of the F vector for Cleveland. All we have, in fact, across all industries on a regular basis, are observations of employment and wages. Because we also "know" the proportion of wages in the value of output of each industry (this is a row of matrix A), we can compute the value of each industry's output, viz.

$$X_t = W_t \#/A_{39.} \qquad (C.3)$$

where

W_t is a vector of aggregate wages by sector at time t,

$A_{39.}$ is the 39th row of A, the row representing the proportional value of labor inputs by industry, and

$\#/$ represents the operation of elementwise division.

With this estimate of total product, we can estimate export output by computing:

$$F_t = (I - A)X_t \qquad (C.4)$$

$$= (I - A)(W_t \#/A_{39.}) \qquad (C.5)$$

For reasons of comparability with readily available data and for computational convenience, we wish to report export activity in terms of employment. To translate F_t as estimated in Eq. (C.5) into employment levels by sector we would multiply F_t in terms of total earnings by the wage share for each industry and then divide by average wages per job by industry.

$$F_t^E = (I - A)(W_t \#/A_{39.}) \# A_{39.} \# (E_t \#/W_t) \qquad (C.6)$$

where

E_t is a vector of employment by industry at t, and

$\#$ represents elementwise multiplication.

Equation (C.6) reduces to

$$F_t^E = (I - A)E_t$$

and these are the figures reported as export employment levels in Tables 3.2 and 3.3.

The figures in Table 10.1 were computed as follows. We aggregated the final demand vectors for consumption (F^c), business fixed investment (F^i), federal defense procurements (F^d), and federal nondefense procurements (F^n) from the 1972 U.S. I-O Table into the 39 sectors used in this analysis. We then normalized these vectors—multiplied them by \$1 million and then deleted the elements associated with sectors that are very small in Cleveland (e.g., coal mining) and sectors for which Cleveland is a net importer. This process led to a series of experimental final demand vector F^c, F^i, F^d, and F^n. We then computed

$$X^c = (I - A)^{-1}F^c$$

where

X^c is a vector of industrial revenue levels induced in Cleveland by \$1 million of potential export business generated by an increase in U.S. household consumption levels.

The first column of Table 10.1 is computed by taking the sum of the elements of X^c. Then we computed

$$E^c = X^c\#[A_{39.}\#(E_t\#/W_t)]$$

giving an estimate of total employment generated by F^c. The second column of Table 10.1 is the sum of the elements of E^c. The third, fourth, and fifth columns are computed, for example, by taking

$$P^B = E^c \cdot B$$

where

P^B is the number of jobs for blacks generated by F^c, and

B is a vector of proportions of industrial workforces who are black (see Table 3.4).

The final column was computed by dividing total wages generated by, say, F^c

$$X^c \cdot A_{39.}$$

by total employment generated by F^c

$$X^c[A_{39.}\#(E_t\#/W_t)]$$

Appendix D

IS CLEVELAND AN AUTO TOWN?

Because the automotive industry is such an important component of U.S. manufacturing, it must be very important to an economy like Cleveland's. There are many who argue, though, that Cleveland's dependence on this industry is much greater than that of most U.S. manufacturing centers and that Cleveland, very nearly as much as Detroit, is an auto town. It might be the case that the primary metals, fabricated metals, and nonelectrical machinery industries in Cleveland are, almost to a firm, suppliers of the automotive industry. This type of specialization would not be detected by a methodology based on a regionalized input-output table because available data do not indicate whether, say, Cleveland manufacturers of "bolts and fasteners" supply a greater proportion of their output to the automobile industry than do firms with the same SIC in other locations. Because the belief that Cleveland is an "auto town" is fairly widespread, we devised a rough test for the hypothesis that Cleveland is atypically dependent on the health of the U.S. automobile industry.

Specifically, we developed a statistical representation of the relationships depicted in Fig. D.1. Our test estimated the effects depicted by arrows A and B in Fig. D.1.

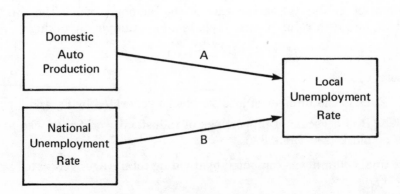

Fig. D.1—Metropolitan unemployment, U.S.
unemployment, and domestic car and
truck production

We estimated a series of equations of the following form:

$$U_{it} = \alpha_0 + \alpha_1 U_{t-n} + \alpha_2 A_{t-m} + \alpha_3 D_1 + \alpha_4 D_2 + \alpha_5 D_3 + v_{it}$$

where

U_{it} is the unemployment in city i during month t,

U_{t-n} is the national unemployment rate during month $t-n$,

A_{t-m} is U.S. domestic automobile and truck production in month $t-m$,

D_1 is a dummy variable taking the value of 1 for March, April, and May,

D_2 is a dummy variable taking the value of 1 for June, July, and August,

D_3 is a dummy variable taking the value of 1 for September, October, and November, and

v_{it} is a random variable with zero mean and variance exhibiting first-order serial correlation.

The results are shown in Table D.1. To measure Cleveland's relative sensitivity to the auto industry, we compared measures of the relative strengths of arrows A and B in Cleveland and in eight other cities. The other cities were selected to compare Cleveland with some places that are definitely "auto towns" (Detroit), some that are definitely not (New Orleans), and some that are of ambiguous status with respect to the automobile industry (Pittsburgh, Indianapolis). The results of the test can be summarized as follows:

- In Seattle and Phoenix there is no significant relationship between domestic auto and truck production and metropolitan unemployment.
- In Philadelphia and New Orleans there is a counterintuitive relationship between U.S. auto and truck production and regional unemployment in the regressions that maximize r-squared.[1] Explaining this anomaly would require more analysis than we can undertake here.
- Our measure of the relationship between auto and truck production and metropolitan unemployment took the following values in the five other cities. (These numbers indicate by how many points unemployment goes up when U.S. domestic auto and truck production decreases by one million units per month).

---

[1]Other specifications of the lag structure yielded results that were insignificant or of the right sign.

Table D.1

REGRESSION RESULTS: REGIONAL UNEMPLOYMENT, U.S. UNEMPLOYMENT, AND U.S. DOMESTIC AUTO AND TRUCK PRODUCTION

City	Constant	U.S. Unemp.	U.S. Auto & Truck Production	Spring	Summer	Autumn	Unemp. Lagged Months[a]	Prod. Lagged Months[a]	R-sq.
Cleveland	1.86	1.00[b]	-2.6	-0.11	0.27	-0.68	1	2	0.80
Columbus	0.23	0.99[b]	-1.3[b]	-0.08	0.27	-0.58	3	2	0.67
Detroit	4.82[b]	1.30[b]	-5.3[b]	1.13	0.06	0.25[b]	-1	-1	0.60
Indianapolis	6.93[b]	0.29[b]	-2.8[b]	-0.32	0.17[b]	-1.14[b]	1	2	0.55
New Orleans	1.49[b]	0.58[b]	1.1[b]	-0.24	0.53[b]	0.30	6	0	0.65
Philadelphia	-1.15	0.99[b]	2.0[b]	0.37	0.67	0.49	1	3	0.53
Phoenix	-4.47[b]	1.75[b]	-8.8[b]	-0.04	0.65	0.22	3	6	0.55
Pittsburgh	7.89[b]	0.26[b]	-3.1[b]	-0.39	0.03	-0.97	6	2	0.57
Seattle	-2.68	1.44[b]	0.1	-0.18	-0.11	-0.25	3	6	0.72

[a] These happen to be the lag structures that maximize the R-squared statistic for each city. The rankings of the cities are similar regardless of which lag structure is adopted.

[b] Significant at the one percent level.

Cleveland	2.6
Columbus	1.3
Detroit	5.3
Indianapolis	2.8
Pittsburgh	3.1

Our test indicates that the automobile industry is clearly important to Cleveland, which ranks among the cities whose unemployment rates are sensitive to domestic auto and truck production. Among these cities, however, Cleveland does not stand out as being particularly sensitive to the automobile industry. Cleveland is much less sensitive to the auto industry than Detroit, of course, but other cities, that are not ordinarily thought of as "auto towns," like Pittsburgh and Indianapolis, are, in fact, more sensitive to that industry than Cleveland is. We conclude that, while the auto industry plays an important role in the economic structure of the Cleveland metropolitan area, our original characterization of Cleveland's specialty—general durable goods manufacturing—should not be narrowed to focus solely on automotive production.

BIBLIOGRAPHY

Abend, Jules, "Statistics Can't Tell You Where To Do Business," *Inc.,* October 1981, p. 23.

Advisory Commission on Intergovernmental Relations, *Regional Growth: Flows of Federal Funds, 1952-76,* Washington, D.C., June 1980.

Alexander Grant and Co., *Business Climate Study,* Chicago, Illinois, March 1979.

Allman, Peter M., and David L. Birch, "Components of Employment Change for Metropolitan and Rural Areas in the United States by Industry Group, 1970-1972," Working Paper No. 8, Inter-area Migration Project, Joint Center for Urban Studies of Massachusetts Institute of Technology and Harvard University, Cambridge, Massachusetts, September 1975.

Altman, S. H., and Robert Blendon (eds.), *Medical Technology: The Culprit Behind Health Care Costs?,* Proceedings of the 1977 Sun Valley Forum on National Health, U.S. Department of Health, Education, and Welfare, National Center for Health Services Research, DHEW Publication No. (PHS) 79-3216, Washington, D.C., 1979.

Altman, S. H., and H. M. Sapolsky (eds.), *Federal Health Programs,* University Health Policy Consortium, Lexington Books, D. C. Heath and Company, Lexington, Massachusetts, 1981.

"America's Restructured Economy," *Business Week,* June 1, 1981, pp. 55-100.

American Hospital Association, *Guide to the Health Care Field,* 1980 Edition, Chicago, Illinois, 1980.

American Hotel and Motel Association, *Labor Turnover in the Lodging Industry,* New York, New York, July 1973.

American Medical Association, *Physician Distribution and Medical Licensure in the United States, 1979,* Chicago, Illinois, 1980.

Aronson, Leanne, and Carol Shapiro, *The State's Role in Urban Economic Development: An Urban Government Perspective,* U.S. Department of Commerce, Economic Development Administration, September 1980.

Ashburn, Anderson, "The 1980 Machine-Tool Standings," *American Machinist,* February 1981.

Barro, Stephen M., *The Urban Impacts of Federal Policies: Vol. 3, Fiscal Conditions,* The Rand Corporation, R-2114-KF/HEW, April 1978.

Berry, R. E., "On Grouping Hospitals for Economic Analysis," *Inquiry*, Vol. 10, December 1973, pp. 5-12.

Bice, T. W., "Health Planning and Regulation Effects on Hospital Costs," *Annual Review of Public Health*, Vol. 1, 1980, pp. 137-161.

Birch, David L., *The Job Generation Process*, Massachusetts Institute of Technology Program on Neighborhood and Regional Change, Cambridge, Massachusetts, 1979.

Birch, David L., "Who Creates Jobs," *The Public Interest*, Fall 1981, pp. 3-14.

Bloom, Gordon, and Herbert Northrup, *Economics of Labor Relations*, Eighth Edition, Richard D. Irwin, Inc., Homewood, Illinois, 1976.

Bombelles, Joseph T., *Energy in Cleveland, A Report Prepared for the New Cleveland Campaign*, John Carroll University, Cleveland, Ohio, 1979.

Bornino, Bruno, "Full Faith Plus $60 Million, Will Build Downtown Hotel," *Cleveland Press*, October 30, 1981.

Boyer, Richard, and David Savageau, *Places Rated Almanac*, Rand McNally, 1982.

Bradbury, Katharine L., Anthony Downs, and Kenneth A. Small, *Futures for a Declining City: Simulations for the Cleveland Area*, Academic Press, Inc., New York, 1981.

Carroll, Stephen J., Anthony H. Pascal, and Michael N. Caggiano, *The Relevance to HUD of Recent Scholarly Research in Urban Economics*, The Rand Corporation, N-1298-HUD, September 1979.

Cartwright, Joseph V., Richard M. Biemiller, and Richard D. Gustely, *RIMS II: Regional Input-Output Modelling System*, Bureau of Economic Analysis, U.S. Department of Commerce, April 1981.

Choate, Pat, and Susan Walter, *America in Ruins: Beyond the Public Works Pork Barrel*, The Council of State Planning Agencies, Washington, D.C., 1981.

Cleveland Planning Commission, *Cleveland Policy Planning Report*, Vol. 1, Cleveland, Ohio, 1975.

Cleveland Planning Commission, *Jobs and Income, Vol. 1*, Cleveland, Ohio, February 1978.

Coffman, C. Dewitt, *Marketing for a Full House*, School of Hotel Administration, Cornell University, Ithaca, New York, 1975, pp. 46-52.

College of Urban Affairs, Cleveland State University, *A Survey of Greater Cleveland Data Sources, Analyses, Reports: Handbook for Community Research*, Cleveland, Ohio, November 1980.

Denison, Edward F., *Accounting for Slower Economic Growth: The United States in the 1970s*, The Brookings Institution, Washington, D.C., 1979.

Denne, Steve, Keith Harris, and Kathy Misichko, *A Survey of Economic Development Related Reports, Plans and Studies for the City of Cleveland,* Cleveland Department of Economic Development, Cleveland, Ohio, October 9, 1981.

Enthoven, A., "Consumer Choice Health Plan" (Parts I and II), *New England Journal of Medicine,* Vol. 298, March 23 and March 30, 1978, pp. 650-653 and 709-920.

Epps, Richard W., "Suburban Jobs and Black Workers," *Business Review,* Federal Reserve Bank of Philadelphia, October 1969, pp. 3-13.

Fawcett, Clifford, "Factors and Issues in the Survival and Growth of the U.S. Machine Tool Industry," Ph.D. Dissertation, The George Washington University, Washington, D.C., February 1976.

Federal Reserve Bank of Cleveland, Research Department, *1978 Annual Report/Economic Review,* Cleveland, Ohio, 1978.

Fellner, David, Timothy H. Hannan, Mary M. Hinz, Robert E. Hopkins, Nonna A. Noto, and Anthony M. Rufolo, "Jobs in Philadelphia: Experience and Prospects," *Business Review,* Federal Reserve Bank of Philadelphia, December 1975, pp. 3-51.

"Foreign Competition Stirs U.S. Toolmakers," *Business Week,* September 1, 1980, pp. 68-70.

Freeland, M. S., and C. E. Schendler, "Short-Term Outlook and Long-Term Projections," *Health Care Financing Review,* Vol. 2, No. 3, December 1981, pp. 97-138.

Fuchs, V. R., *Who Shall Live? Health Economics, and Social Choice,* Basic Books, Inc., New York, New York, 1974.

Garn, Harvey A., Thomas Muller, John Tilney, and John Kordalewski, *Vol. 1: Final Report, A Framework for National Urban Policy: Urban Distress; Decline and Growth, A Summary,* The Urban Institute, Washington, D.C., December 15, 1977.

Garn, Harvey A., Thomas Muller, John Tilney, John Kordalewski, and Jacqueline Swingle, *Vol. II: A Framework for National Urban Policy: Urban Distress, Decline and Growth,* The Urban Institute, Washington, D.C., December 15, 1977.

Glickman, Norman, *International Trade, Capital Mobility, and Economic Growth: Some Implications for American Cities and Regions in the 1980s,* Department of City and Regional Planning and Regional Science, University of Pennsylvania, Philadelphia, June 1980. (Also presented as a paper at the Symposium on Policies and Prospects for Metropolitan and Nonmetropolitan America in the Eighties, Washington, D.C., June 3-4, 1980.)

Government of the District of Columbia, *Tax Burdens in Washington, D.C., Compared with the Nation's Thirty Largest Cities, 1979,* Washington, D.C., June 1981.

Gray, William S., and Salvatore C. Liguori, *Hotel and Motel Management and Operations*, Prentice-Hall, Englewood Cliffs, 1980.

Greater Cleveland Growth Association, *Basic Data on the Cleveland Area*, Cleveland, January 1979.

Greater Cleveland Growth Association, *Greater Cleveland Facts*, Cleveland, Ohio, n.d.

Green, Eric F., "New Requirements of the Hotel Feasibility Study," *Lodging*, March 1979.

Greenwood, Michael J., "Research on Internal Migration in the United States: A Survey," *Journal of Economic Literature*, Vol. XIII, No. 2, June 1975, pp. 397-433.

Gruenstein, John, "A New Job Map for the Philadelphia Region," *Business Review*, Federal Reserve Bank of Philadelphia, Philadelphia, Pennsylvania, January/February 1979, pp. 13-22.

Gruenstein, John, "Jobs in the City: Can Philadelphia Afford To Raise Taxes?," *Business Review*, Federal Reserve Bank of Philadelphia, Philadelphia, Pennsylvania, May/June 1980, pp. 3-11.

Gruenstein, John, and Sally Guerra, "Can Services Sustain a Regional Economy?," *Business Review*, Federal Reserve Bank of Philadelphia, Philadelphia, Pennsylvania, July/August 1981, pp. 5-19.

Gurwitz, Aaron S., *The Service Sector in Urban Revitalization: Sectoral Composition, Employment Density Gradients, and Central City Fiscal Capacity*, The Rand Corporation, R-2817-HUD, June 1982.

Gurwitz, Aaron S., and Sheila Nataraj-Kirby, *The Service Sector in Urban Revitalization: Quantity and Quality of Jobs*, The Rand Corporation, N-1847-HUD, forthcoming.

Harris, Leon, "Cleveland's Come-Around," *Town and Country*, October 1981, p. 288.

Health Care Financing Administration (HCFA), *Health Care Financing Review*, Department of Health and Human Services, Baltimore, Maryland, Quarterly, 1979.

Health Care Financing Administration (HCFA), *Health Care Financing Trends*, Department of Health and Human Services, Baltimore, Maryland, Quarterly, 1979.

Henderson, J. Vernon, "Evaluating Consumer Amenities and Interregional Welfare Differences," *Journal of Urban Economics*, Vol. II, No. 1, January 1982, pp. 32-59.

Horwath, Ernest B., et al., *Hotel Accounting*, Ronald Press, New York, New York, 1970, pp. 7-8.

Humphrey, Nancy, George E. Peterson, and Peter Wilson, *The Future of Cleveland's Capital Plant*, The Urban Institute, Washington, D.C., 1979.

Isard, Walter, et al., *Methods of Regional Analysis: An Introduction to Regional Science,* John Wiley and Sons, Inc., New York, 1960.

James A. Hamilton Associates, Inc., *The Northeast Ohio Health Service Area and Its Hospital Needs,* Minneapolis, Minnesota, August 1976.

"Japan's 20-Firm Joint FMS Plan," *American Machinist,* February 1981, pp. 98-100.

"Japan: FANUC Edges Closer to a Robot Run Plant," *Business Week,* November 24, 1980, p. 56.

Keeler, Emmett, and William Rogers, *A Classification of Large American Urban Areas,* The Rand Corporation, R-1246-NSF, May 1973.

Knight, Richard V., *The Cleveland Economy in Transition—Implications for the Future,* College of Urban Affairs, Cleveland State University, Cleveland, Ohio, July 1977.

Knight, Richard V., "The Region's Economy: Transition to What?," prepared for the Second Annual Fall Seminar of the College of Urban Affairs, Cleveland State University, Cleveland, Ohio, 1980.

Kordalewski, John, *An Initial Exploration of the Relationship Between Industrial Composition and Urban Economic Distress,* The Urban Institute, Washington, D.C., February 1981.

Laventhol and Horwath, *U.S. Lodging Industry,* Philadelphia, Pennsylvania, 1980.

Lawson, Fred, *Hotels, Motels, and Condominiums: Design, Planning, and Maintenance,* Cahners Books International, Boston, Massachusetts, 1976 (especially pp. 216ff).

Levin, A. (ed.), "Regulating Health Care: The Struggle for Control," *Proceedings of The Academy of Political Science,* Vol. 33, No. 4, The Academy of Political Science, New York, New York, 1980.

Lohr, Kathleen N., John D. Winkler, and Robert H. Brook, *Peer Review and Technology Assessment in Medicine,* The Rand Corporation, R-2820-OTA, August 1981.

Mayfield, Jerry, "Delivery Times Lengthening for Machine Tool Industry," *Aviation Week and Space Technology,* April 9, 1979, p. 50.

McCall, J. J., and Anthony Pascal, *Agglomeration Economies, Search Costs and Industrial Location,* The Rand Corporation, P-6348, June 1979.

McCarthy, Michael D., and Colin Loxley, "An Econometric Forecasting Model of the Cleveland Metropolitan Area," Case Western Reserve University, Working Paper No. 71, Cleveland, Ohio, January 1976.

Midwest Research Institute, "Economic Development from Biomedical

Research and Technology in Cleveland" (final report), MRI Project No. 7048-D for the Greater Cleveland Growth Association, Cleveland, Ohio, June 1981.

Mieszkowski, Peter, "Recent Trends in Urban and Regional Development," in Peter Mieszkowski and Mahlon Straszheim (eds.), *Current Issues in Urban Economics,* The Johns Hopkins University Press, Baltimore, Maryland, 1979, pp. 3-39.

Milbank Memorial Fund Quarterly, "Special Issue: Competition and Regulation in Health Care Markets, *Health and Society,* Vol. 59, No. 2, Spring 1981, pp. 107-296.

Moloney, T. W., and D. E. Rogers, "Medical Technology—A Different View of the Contentious Debate over Costs," *New England Journal of Medicine,* Vol. 301, December 27, 1979, pp. 1413-1419.

Moore, John L., Richard W. Buxvaum, William A. Testa, David A. Berger, and Marnie Shaul, *Cleveland Regional Economic Issues: An Overview,* Academy for Contemporary Problems, Columbus, Ohio, September 18, 1979.

Morrison, Peter A., *The Current Demographic Context of National Growth and Development,* The Rand Corporation, P-5514, September 1975.

Morrison, Peter A., *Current Demographic Change in Regions of the United States,* The Rand Corporation, P-6000, November 1977. (Condensed version appears in *American Demographics,* May 1979.)

Morrison, Peter A., Roger J. Vaughan, Georges Vernez, and Barbara R. Williams, *Recent Contributions to the Urban Policy Debate,* The Rand Corporation, R-2394-RC, March 1979.

Mulhern, John J., "The Defense Sector: A Source of Strength for Philadelphia's Economy," *Business Review,* Federal Reserve Bank of Philadelphia, Philadelphia, Pennsylvania, July/August 1981.

"A Multi-Tiered Economy," *Business Week,* January 12, 1981, pp. 51-85.

Nathanson, Josef, *Early Warning Information Systems for Business Retention,* U.S. Department of Commerce, Economic Development Administration, Washington, D.C., September 1980.

National Machine Tool Builders Association (NMTBA), *Economic Handbook of the Machine Tool Industry,* McLean, Virginia, 1980-81, pp. 67-68.

Newhouse, Joseph P., *The Erosion of the Medical Marketplace,* The Rand Corporation, R-2141-HEW, August 1977.

Newhouse, Joseph P., *The Economics of Medical Care: A Policy Perspective,* Addison-Wesley, Reading, Massachusetts, 1978.

Newhouse, Joseph P., Charles E. Phelps, and William B. Schwartz,

Policy Options and the Impact of National Health Insurance, The Rand Corporation, R-1528-HEW/OEO, June 1974. Also published in *New England Journal of Medicine,* Vol. 290, June 13, 1974, pp. 1345-1359.

Newspaper Enterprise Association, Inc., *The World Almanac and Book of Facts, 1980,* New York, 1980.

"No Vacancy Means Big Profit for U.S. Hotels," *Business Week,* July 17, 1978, pp. 70-71.

Northern Ohio Urban System Research Project, *A Concept Plan for Future Development, Final Report,* Doxiadis Associates, Inc., Washington, D.C., January 1973.

Norton, James A. (Dolph), "Suggestions and Recommendations," in *The Greybelt versus the Sunbelt, Implications for Northeast Ohio, Proceedings of a Public Conference, November 8, 1979,* John Carroll University, University Heights, Ohio, 1979.

Office of Management and Budget, *Standard Industrial Classification Manual,* Washington, D.C., 1972.

Ohio Bureau of Employment Services, *Employment, Payroll, and Earnings Under the Ohio Unemployment Compensation Law by County, 1943 Through 1971,* Division of Research and Statistics, Columbus, Ohio, n.d.

Ohio Bureau of Employment Services, *Employment, Payroll, and Earnings Under the Ohio Unemployment Compensation Law by County, 1972 Through 1979,* Division of Research and Statistics, Columbus, Ohio, n.d.

Ohio Bureau of Employment Services, *Average Employment and Earnings in Manufacturing Industries Producing Durable and Nondurable Goods, 1970 Through 1979,* Division of Research and Statistics, Columbus, Ohio, n.d.

Olson, Susan, *An Evaluation of Tax Incentives as a Means To Encourage Redevelopment,* Cleveland City Planning Commission, Cleveland, Ohio, April 1978.

Padda, Kuldarshan, "Report Card on the States," *Inc.,* October 1981.

Pascal, Anthony H., and Aaron S. Gurwitz, *Systematic Planning for Local Economic Development,* The Rand Corporation, R-2932-HUD, forthcoming.

Peltzman, S., "An Evaluation of Consumer Protection Legislation: The 1962 Drug Amendment," *Journal of Political Economy,* September-October 1973, pp. 1049-1091.

Peters, Clarence H., "Pre-Opening Marketing Analysis for Hotels," *Cornell Hotel and Restaurant Administration Quarterly,* May 1978.

Peterson, George E., "Federal Tax Policy and the Shaping of Urban Development," in Arthur P. Solomon (ed.), *Prospective City Eco-*

nomic, Population, Energy, and Environmental Developments,
M.I.T. Press, Cambridge, Massachusetts, 1980, pp. 399-425.

Phelps, Charles E., and Joseph P. Newhouse, *The Effects of Coinsurance on Demand for Physician Services,* The Rand Corporation,
R-976-OEO, June 1972.

Pittsburgh Regional Planning Association, *Economic Study of the
Pittsburgh Region: Volume I. Region in Transition,* University of
Pittsburgh Press, Pittsburgh, 1963a.

Pittsburgh Regional Planning Association, *Economic Study of the
Pittsburgh Region: Volume II. Portrait of a Region,* University of
Pittsburgh Press, Pittsburgh, 1963b.

Pittsburgh Regional Planning Association, *Economic Study of the
Pittsburgh Region: Volume III. Region with a Future,* University
of Pittsburgh Press, Pittsburgh, 1963c.

Rand Computation Center, *Rand's Data Facility: A Guide to Resources and Services,* The Rand Corporation, R-1555/18, April
1980.

Regional Economic Development Division, *1978 Business Climate
Survey,* Greater Cleveland Growth Association, Cleveland, Ohio,
January 1979.

Ross, Robert, and Don M. Shakow, "Local Planners—Global Constraints," *Policy Sciences,* Vol. 12, 1980, pp. 1-25.

Rufolo, Anthony M., "Philadelphia's Economy in the National Setting," *Business Review,* Federal Reserve Bank of Philadelphia,
September/October 1978, pp. 13-20.

Russell, L. B., *Technology in Hospitals: Medical Advances and Their
Diffusion,* The Brookings Institution, Washington, D.C., 1978.

Russell, L. B., "An Aging Population and the Use of Medical Care,"
Medical Care, Vol. 19, 1981, pp. 633-643.

Salkever, D. S., and T. W. Bice, "The Impact of Certificate-of-Need
Controls on Hospital Investment," *Milbank Memorial Fund
Quarterly—Health and Society,* Vol. 54, No. 2, Spring 1976, pp.
178-193.

Schmenner, Roger W., *The Manufacturing Location Decision: Evidence from Cincinnati and New England,* Harvard-M.I.T Joint
Center for Urban Studies, Cambridge, Massachusetts, March
1978.

Schmenner, Roger W., *Location Decisions of Large Multiplant Companies,* Harvard-M.I.T. Joint Center for Urban Studies, Cambridge,
Massachusetts, September 1980.

Schnorbus, Robert H., John J. Erceg, and Roger H. Hilderliter, *Cleveland and Northeast Ohio: An Economic Perspective,* Federal Reserve Bank of Cleveland, Cleveland, Ohio, August 28, 1981.

Schnorbus, Robert H., John J. Erceg, and Roger H. Hinderliter, *The*

Pittsburgh Economy—A Sketch, Federal Reserve Bank of Cleveland, Cleveland, Ohio, September 25, 1981.

Schwartz, William B., Joseph P. Newhouse, Bruce W. Bennett, and Albert P. Williams, "The Changing Geographic Distribution of Board-Certified Physicians," *New England Journal of Medicine,* Vol. 303, October 30, 1980, pp. 1032-1038.

Seidman, David, "Protection or Overprotection in Drug Regulation? The Politics of Policy Analysis," *AEI Journal of Government and Society,* July/August 1977, pp. 22-37.

Stein, Bob, *Marketing in Action for Hotels, Motels, Restaurants,* Hayden Book Co., Rochelle Park, New Jersey, 1971, pp. 31-34.

Subcommittee on the City, Committee on Banking, Finance and Urban Affairs, *Urban Revitalization and Industrial Policy,* 96th Congress, 2nd Session, Washington, D.C., September 16-17, 1980.

Summers, Anita A., "Which Industries Should Be Targeted for DFP Assistance? A Case Study of Philadelphia SMSA and City," paper prepared for a conference convened by The Rockefeller Brothers Fund and the Economic Development Administration, Washington, D.C., January 18-19, 1980.

Sutton, George, "Technology of Machine Tools," *A Survey of the State of the Art by the Machine Tool Task Force,* Vol. 1, University of California Research Laboratory, 52960-1, Livermore, California, October 1980.

Temin, P., *Taking Your Medicine—Drug Regulation in the United States,* Harvard University Press, Cambridge, Massachusetts, 1980.

"Toolmakers Rush into the U.S.," *Business Week,* June 16, 1980, p. 98.

"Trades Association Fund Aids East Tech Machine Shop," *Cleveland Press,* October 29, 1980, p. 2.

Trutko, James M., *An Analysis of Manufacturing Composition and Change in Greater Cleveland (1964-1978),* Greater Cleveland Growth Association, February 1981.

Trutko, James M., "Testimony on Industrial Revitalization Before the Subcommittee on Economic Stabilization of the Committee on Banking, Finance and Urban Affairs," U.S. House of Representatives, Greater Cleveland Growth Association, Cleveland, Ohio, August 28, 1981.

Trutko, James, and Fran Feiner, *Small Business in the Greater Cleveland Area,* Greater Cleveland Growth Association, Cleveland, Ohio, August 15, 1980.

The Urban Institute, "America's Urban Capital Stock: An Interview with George Peterson," *Policy and Research Report,* Vol. 10, No. 1, Spring 1980.

The Urban Institute, "Cleveland and Cincinnati: A Tale of Two Cities," *Policy and Research Report*, Vol. 10, No. 1, Spring 1980.

The Urban Institute, "Cities and Economic Development: An Interview with Larry C. Ledebur," *Policy and Research Report*, Vol. 11, No. 1, Spring 1981.

U.S. Department of Commerce, Bureau of the Census, 1970 Census of Population, Subject Reports PC(2)-2C, *Mobility for Metropolitan Areas*, Washington, D.C., March 1973.

U.S. Department of Commerce, Bureau of the Census, Social and Economic Statistics Administration, *County and City Data Book 1972*, 1973.

U.S. Department of Commerce, Bureau of the Census, *County and City Data Book 1977*, 1978.

U.S. Department of Commerce, Bureau of the Census, *Illustrative Projections of State Populations by Age, Race, and Sex: 1975 to 2000*, Series P-25, No. 796, Washington, D.C., March 1979.

U.S. Department of Commerce, Bureau of the Census, *County Business Patterns*, CBP-78-53, U.S. Government Printing Office, Washington, D.C., 1980a.

U.S. Department of Commerce, Bureau of the Census, "Estimates of the Population of Counties and Metropolitan Areas: July 1, 1977 and 1978," *Current Population Reports*, P-25, No. 873, U.S. Government Printing Office, Washington, D.C., 1980b.

U.S. Department of Commerce, Bureau of the Census, *State and Metropolitan Area Data Book 1979*, 1980c.

U.S. Department of Commerce, Bureau of the Census, *Provisional Estimates of Social, Economic, and Housing Characteristics*, 1982.

U.S. Department of Commerce, Bureau of the Census, *Statistical Abstracts*, U.S. Government Printing Office, Washington, D.C., selected years.

U.S. Department of Commerce, *1980 U.S. Industrial Outlook for 200 Industries with Projections for 1984*, U.S. Government Printing Office, Washington, D.C., January 1980.

U.S. Department of Commerce, *1981 U.S. Industrial Outlook for 200 Industries with Projections for 1985*, U.S. Government Printing Office, Washington, D.C., January 1981.

U.S. Department of Health, Education, and Welfare, *Health in the United States, 1979*, National Center for Health Statistics and National Center for Health Services Research, Hyattsville, Maryland, DHEW Publication No. (PHS) 80-1232, 1980.

U.S. Department of Housing and Urban Development, *Changing Conditions in Large Metropolitan Areas*, Office of Policy Development and Research, HUD-PDR-637, Washington, D.C., November 1980.

U.S. Department of Housing and Urban Development and U.S. Department of Commerce, *Local Economic Development Tools and Techniques, A Guidebook for Local Government*, HUD-PDR-483(2), Washington, D.C., July 1980.

U.S. Department of Housing and Urban Development and U.S. Department of Commerce, *The Private Economic Development Process, A Guidebook for Local Government*, HUD-PDR-482(2), Washington, D.C., July 1980.

U.S. Department of Justice, Federal Bureau of Investigation, *Uniform Crime Reports for the United States*, Washington, D.C., 1980.

U.S. Department of Labor, Bureau of Labor Statistics, *Handbook of Labor Statistics, 1978*, 1979a.

U.S. Department of Labor, Bureau of Labor Statistics, *Work Stoppages*, 1979b.

U.S. Department of Labor, Bureau of Labor Statistics, *Employment and Earnings, States and Areas, 1939-78*, 1979c.

U.S. Department of Labor, Bureau of Labor Statistics, *Employment and Earnings, United States, 1909-78*, 1979d.

U.S. Department of Labor, Bureau of Labor Statistics, *Area Wage Survey, Cleveland, Ohio, Metropolitan Area, September 1980*, 1980.

U.S. Department of Labor, Bureau of Labor Statistics, *Occupational Earnings in all Metropolitan Areas, July 1980*, 1981.

U.S. Department of Labor, *Directory of National Unions and Employee Associations*, September 1980.

U.S. Department of Transportation, *The U.S. Automobile Industry, 1980*, Office of the Assistant Secretary for Policy and International Affairs, Washington, D.C., January 1981.

Vaughan, Roger J., *Public Works as a Countercyclical Device: A Review of the Issues*, The Rand Corporation, R-1990-EDA, July 1976.

Vaughan, Roger J., *The Urban Impacts of Federal Policies: Vol. 2, Economic Development*, The Rand Corporation, R-2028-KF/RC, June 1977.

Vaughan, Roger J., *Local Business and Employment Retention Strategies*, U.S. Department of Commerce, Economic Development Administration, September 1980.

Vernez, Georges, and Roger J. Vaughan, *Assessment of Countercyclical Public Works and Public Service Employment Programs*, The Rand Corporation, R-2214-EDA, September 1978.

Vernez, Georges, et al., *Regional Cycles and Employment Effects of Public Works Investments*, The Rand Corporation, R-2052-EDA, January 1977.

Vernez, Georges, et al., *Federal Activities in Urban Economic Development*, The Rand Corporation, R-2372-EDA, April 1979.

Vernon, Raymond, *Metropolis 1985: An Interpretation of the Findings of the New York Metropolitan Region Study,* Anchor Books, Doubleday and Co. Inc., Garden City, New York, 1963.

Victor, Richard B., and Georges Vernez, *Employment Cycles in Local Labor Markets,* The Rand Corporation, R-2647-EDA/RC, March 1981.

Wattenberg, Benjamin, *The Statistical History of the United States,* Basic Books, New York, 1976.

Weeks, L. E., and H. J. Berman (eds.), *Economics in Health Care,* Aspen Systems Corporation, Germantown, Maryland, 1977.

Zook, C. J., S. F. Savickis, and F. D. Moore, "Repeated Hospitalization for the Same Disease: A Multiplier of National Health Costs," *Milbank Memorial Fund Quarterly—Health and Society,* Vol. 58, No. 3, Summer 1980, pp. 454-471.